TOURIST DISTRACTIONS

TOURIST DISTRACTIONS

TRAVELING AND FEELING

IN TRANSNATIONAL HALLYU CINEMA

YOUNGMIN CHOE

DUKE UNIVERSITY PRESS DURHAM AND LONDON 2016

Library of Congress Cataloging-in-Publication Data
Choe, Youngmin, author.
Tourist distractions : traveling and feeling in transnational
hallyu cinema / Youngmin Choe.
pages cm
Includes bibliographical references and index.
ISBN 978-0-8223-6111-4 (hardcover : alk. paper)
ISBN 978-0-8223-6130-5 (pbk. : alk. paper)
ISBN 978-0-8223-7434-3 (e-book)
1. Motion pictures—Korea (South)—History—21st century.
2. Cultural industries—Korea (South)—History—21st century.
3. Popular culture—Economic aspects—Korea (South). 4. Tourism
in motion pictures. 5. Travel in motion pictures. I. Title.
PN1993.5.K6C4844 2016
791.43095195—dc23 2015036266

A different version of chapter 2 appeared as "Affective Sites: Hur
Jin-ho's Cinema and Film-Induced Tourism in Korea," in *Asia on
Tour: Exploring the Rise of Asian Tourism*, ed. Tim Winter, Peggy
Teo, and T. C. Chang, 109–26 (New York: Routledge, 2009). An earlier
version of chapter 5 was published as "Postmemory DMZ in South
Korean Cinema, 1999–2003," *Journal of Korean Studies* 18.2 (2013):
315–36. Reprinted by permission.

Cover art: Detail from a tour-site marker depicting an image
from the film *April Snow*. Photo by the author.

FOR MY MOTHER AND FATHER

CONTENTS

ACKNOWLEDGMENTS

The earliest drafts of this book were written as a dissertation at the University of California (UC) Berkeley. My time there was formative, and I owe much gratitude to my doctoral advisors. Chris Berry and Nelson Graburn have been models of the kind of scholar I aspire to be, and also of the kind of mentor I try to be. Without their guidance, my scholarship would not have been able to take on the forms that it eventually did, and I thank them for their continued encouragement, support, and friendship. My thanks also to Andrew Jones, for his advice over the years, and for being a wonderful teacher and friend. I am grateful to Lydia Liu, Jiwon Shin, Alan Tansman, and Bonnie Wade. Soyoung Kim, whom I first met when she was a visiting professor at UC Berkeley, continues to be a source of inspiration. The UC Berkeley Tourism Studies Working Group allowed me to participate in the exchange of scholarship through which I could vicariously travel to places in ways I might otherwise never have gone.

The year I spent at the University of Illinois, Urbana-Champaign (UIUC), as a Korea Foundation postdoctoral fellow was a tremendously productive one. I feel privileged to have been able to revise the book under the mentorship of Nancy Abelmann, whose insightful reading of my manuscript was vital to the shape of its final form. I am also thankful to Poshek Fu, Jungwon Kim, Robert Cagle, Jin-Heon Jung, and the Center for East Asian and Pacific Studies, who welcomed me into their midst that year. My chapter on "transient monuments" benefited from feedback I received at the UIUC Korea Workshop, and aspects of my introduction were formed at a roundtable discussion on pan-Asian cinema with Poshek Fu, Stephanie DeBoer, and Michael Raine.

I am most grateful to my colleagues in the East Asian languages and cultures department at the University of Southern California (USC). As chairs, Dominic Cheung, David Bialock, and Audrey Li have been generous in their support of junior faculty. I thank Brian Bernards, Geraldine Fiss, George Hayden, Namkil Kim, Satoko Shimazaki, and Andrew Simpson for a congenial environment to work in, and Christine Shaw for everything she does for our department. Special thanks to Bettine Birge, Sonya Lee, and Lori Meeks for their guidance. Above all, I have benefited enormously from the intellectual engagement, mentorship, and friendship of Akira Mizuta Lippit, Kyung Moon Hwang, and Sunyoung Park. I also thank David James, Stanley Rosen, Panivong Norindr, Aniko Imre, and Ruth Chung. David Kang and Elaine Kim at USC's Korean Studies Institute have fostered an inviting research community at the Dosan Ahn Chang Ho Family House, as has Grace Ryu at USC's East Asian Studies Institute. I thank Joy Kim, Sun-Yoon Lee, and Ken Klein at the Korean Heritage Library for ceaselessly drawing my attention to new additions to an already wonderful collection. I also want to acknowledge the former and current graduate students Crystal Mun-Hye Baik, N. Trace Cabot, Melissa Chan, Wooseok Kang, Kathryn Page-Lippsmeyer, Gladys Mac, Jinhee Park, Young Sun Park, Yunji Park, Myoung-Sun Kelly Song, Chad Walker, Shannon Zhao, and the visiting scholar Jinim Park.

Many friends and colleagues have shared their thoughts through collaborations and conversations that helped shape this book: Jinsoo An, Charles Armstrong, Chua Beng Huat, Michelle Cho, Steve Choe, Kyeong-hee Choi, Steven Chung, Stephen Epstein, Chris Hanscom, Todd Henry, Ted Hughes, Kelly Jeong, Alice Kim, Kyu-hyun Kim, Su-yun Kim, Youna Kim, Nayoung Aimee Kwon, Jin-kyung Lee, Nam Lee, Sohl Lee, Hyung Il Pai, Aaron Magnan-Park, Albert Park, Hyun Seon Park, Michael Robinson, Youngju Ryu, Andre Schmid, and Jun Yoo. I am grateful to Suk-Young Kim and Clark Sorensen for their critical comments on individual chapters, and to Christine Yano and David Desser for extensive comments on the entire manuscript. I am greatly indebted to Kyung Hyun Kim for his indispensable criticism and caring support. I thank him not only for the many opportunities he gave me to present chapters-in-progress at UC Irvine, but also for the chance to work together on something larger than my own monograph. The book's clarity and readability is thanks to the sage advice of Courtney Berger, my wonderful editor at Duke University Press, with whom I feel fortunate to be working. Christine Riggio, Amy Ruth Buchanan, and Danielle Szulczewski also deserve special thanks.

The writing of this book was made possible by generous financial support from the UC Berkeley Center for Korean Studies, the UC Berkeley Institute for East Asian Studies, the UC Berkeley Department of Asian Studies, the Korea Foundation Dissertation Fellowship, the 2008 Korea Foundation Postdoctoral Fellowship, a 2008 Northeast Asia Council Travel Grant, the Academy of Korean Studies Grant (AKS-2010-R-23), and at USC, the Korean Studies Institute Faculty Research Grant, the Sejong Society Research Grant, and the 2013 James H. Zumberge Individual Research Award. In its final stage, it was supported by the Yonsei University Future-leading Research Initiative of 2015. I thank Noh Suntag for his generous permission to reprint photographs from his "reallyGood, murder" series, and Lee Mun-woong, professor emeritus in the department of anthropology at Seoul National University, for sharing photos from his fabulous archive of exhibition photos.

I reserve my deepest gratitude for my family, Sehyo Choe, Youngjae Choe, and my parents, Jun-seok Choe and Soon-nyu Choe. My parents have shared their love of travel with me for as long as I can remember, and I thank them for their sustained interest in the places and forms of travel I have found on my own. My father especially has been my greatest intellectual supporter, and it is thanks to my mother that I have never questioned the possibility of having both family and work. I also thank my parents-in-law, Sang Joong Jeon and Chung Ja Jeon, for their kind support. My life with Joseph Jeon is inscribed in various ways throughout the book. His boundless intellectual generosity and unstoppable quick wit enlivens and grounds our every day together. And Izzi—I know you can read this now—I am most thankful for you.

INTRODUCTION

Distracted Attractions

There is a moment in Park Chan-wook's *Joint Security Area* (*Kongtong kyŏngpi kuyŏk*, 2000) when the routine duties of choreographed conflict are disrupted. Soldiers stand guard at the heavily guarded Panmunjŏm, a cluster of buildings that form the demilitarized zone (DMZ) between North and South Korea. A group of foreigners on a guided tour of the southern side are surveying the Military Demarcation Line that runs through the middle of the DMZ, separating the two sides, when a sudden gust of wind blows a baseball cap off one of the tourist's heads, and over the 38th parallel into North Korea. A North Korean soldier picks the red cap up and stretches his hand out to return it, while the American military tour guide reaches over the demarcation, takes the cap, and thanks the soldier. The film's perspective switches at this moment, from a close-up shot taken from the point of view of the cap's owner to an aerial view hovering directly above the demarcation line (see fig. I.1). Just as the U.S. military guide retreats, leaving the frame, a tourist abruptly rushes up to the line, taking photographs, which are prohibited. We see a South Korean

I.1 A tourist gazes through his camera across the border
between North and South Korea. *Joint Security Area.*

soldier leave his post at the left of the frame and move toward the center to block the tourist's gaze by holding his hand in front of the camera. The tourist keeps clicking in spite of the warning until the soldier finally pushes him back toward his group, who are outside of the frame, and then returns to his position. Witnessed aerially, with only the sound of a camera shutter audible, the scene then ends with a return to a long shot as the tourists leave the site.

The significance of this scene, in which the gaze of the tourist and the perspective of the film camera overlap in a site of conflict and surveillance, is not apparent until the end of the film. The film's end is signaled by a return to the shot of the North Korean soldier returning the cap and the sound of the camera shutter. The film freezes at this point on one of the tourist's photographs, and proceeds to zoom in to various elements of the image, panning from figure to figure within the otherwise still shot (see figs. I.2–I.7). The photograph fades gradually from color to black-and-white, and in the panning we see a condensed version of the story that the film has just narrated. *Joint Security Area (J.S.A.)* as a whole chronicles a murder investigation in the demilitarized zone in which both North and South Korean soldiers are implicated. In the repeated close-up shot over the U.S. military tour guide's shoulder, the North Korean soldier who has just handed over the cap is recognizable as Sergeant Oh Kyŏng-p'il (Song Kang-ho), the older of the two North Korean soldiers who befriend two South Korean soldiers throughout the course of the film; behind him to the right, captured in mid-march and mid-smile, is his junior comrade, Chŏng U-jin (Sin Ha-gyun), one of the men who gets killed when their fraternization with South Korean soldiers is discovered by a North Korean commanding officer. The camera continues to pull back south of the demarcation line and out to the left, where we see Private Nam Sŏng-sik (Kim T'ae-u), the soldier who instigates the bloodshed in the film's climax by firing at the visiting commanding officer. The shot pulls further back to the hand that had blocked the tourist's camera, which belongs, we now see, to Sergeant Yi Su-hyŏk (Lee Byung-hun), the South Korean soldier who had originally initiated the border-crossing friendship. Finally, the shot ends with a full view of the entire picture taken by the tourist, an alternate version of the scene that we had witnessed earlier from an aerial angle. This photograph seen at the end of the film displaces our limited view of the North as mediated by the U.S. military presence with a more revealing view remediated by the tourist gaze.

Prompted by an accident (the gust of wind blowing the hat) that distracts the tourist from the regulated course of the tour, the tourist's picture becomes a privileged object, having unknowingly captured the reconciliation underway between the four soldiers stationed at this embodiment of cold war tension. It offers a transformative view of an otherwise familiar political environment: what had seemed a photo of hostility reveals itself as one of friendship. Through the tourist's photograph, we see how easily hostility and friendship can be mistaken for each other, a point of the film that becomes clear not in the photograph itself, but in the film's narration of what has occurred in the forbidden exchanges between the four soldiers. The tourist's photo, as it is remediated within the film, comes to frame the film's larger narrative of inter-Korean reconciliation and hints at the problematic relationship between visibility, truth, and reconciliation.

In addition, the intervention of tourist photography follows the literally transnational exchange of an object, namely the red cap, which, blown by the sudden gust of wind across the border and then returned, reifies in commodity form the border crossings undertaken by the two South Korean soldiers earlier in the narrative. By the end of the film, however, we know that the civil exchange of the cap is markedly different from the exchange between the soldiers, which erupts in fatal violence. The trope of cross-border exchange recurs throughout the film: in the playful exchange of spit by the soldiers as they try to maintain their serious poses; in the letters that they attach to rocks and hurl at each other across the 38th parallel; and also in the mass-produced sweets and magazine cutouts that the South Korean soldiers bring as gifts to the North. Like the soldiers themselves, these literal and figurative commodities circulate across this national boundary, stand-ins for the perpetual movement of human bodies across all different kinds of boundaries.

From the perspective of those tourists at the 38th parallel, this crossing of boundaries is what we more commonly call travel. And it is the experience (and many ramifications) of this movement across boundaries that brings us to the heart of this book. Much of our understanding of South Korea today emerges from the much-discussed phenomenon of *hallyu*, referred to in English as "the Korean Wave." The term commonly refers to the widespread consumption of Korean popular culture overseas starting in the late 1990s. Here I attempt to find some clarity within this overused and increasingly overdetermined term, and within its abundant meanings, by focusing on one particular slice of hallyu creations (film) and one particular theme that abounds in hallyu (travel). In hinting at the links between travel and commodity exchange, all under the rubric of tourism, *J.S.A.* embodies a crucial characteristic of what I will term *hallyu cinema*. I use *hallyu cinema* to differentiate a specific group of films that is informed by the dominant characteristics of the

I.2–I.7 (*above and opposite*) A closer look at a tourist's photograph taken at the border. *Joint Security Area*.

larger hallyu, or Korean Wave, phenomenon. These films are distinct from the broad, undifferentiated category of new Korean cinema that has been subsumed under hallyu. Within these films, we will see the repeated ways in which human travel speaks to the flows of capital, material goods, and cultural products that epitomize the hallyu phenomenon, and vice versa. Just as close examination of a tourist's intervening gaze and snapshot reveals a more complicated story, travel in hallyu cinema becomes an optic through which to understand the beguiling possibilities and anxious perils of regionalism and transnationalism, two trends essential to the structures of soft power that characterize millennial Korea in an era of more flexible, border-crossing citizenship. By underscoring negotiations with the colonial and Cold War past on one hand and the neoliberal East Asian present on the other, hallyu cinema will thus help us understand key shifts in the South Korean culture industry, emerging approaches by South Koreans to Cold War history (especially their history of national division), and rapidly changing reimaginings of the East Asian geopolitical scene.

Perhaps not coincidentally then, *J.S.A.* embodies a larger trend surrounding Korean cinema, starting in the late 1990s, in which the creation (and consumption) of film was intrinsically linked to travel, not only in its representation of the tourism, but also in the material legacy of its production. *J.S.A.*'s border scenes were not shot on location, as ongoing tensions at Panmunjŏm have made any such filming nearly impossible since the signing of the 1953 Korean Armistice Agreement brought three years of war to a truce. Rather, it was filmed on an outdoor set at the KOFIC Namyangju Studios in Yangsuri, South Korea. Furthermore, the producers left the fabricated "border" at the complex long after the film was completed, since it drew tourists interested both in the film and in the historical tension between North and South Korea; those tourists who gathered in Yangsuri thus uncannily doubled the aforementioned scene in the film itself. At Yangsuri, both film and history conspired to induce tourism, and the practices of tourists, who there (and only there) were free to walk back and forth across the 38th parallel, reenacting the transnational itinerancy of the red cap.

Tourism is thus doubly relevant, both as a critical thematic in *J.S.A.*, and also in the afterlife of the film, as its box-office success unexpectedly generated a good deal of travel, both to the actual DMZ and to the simulacrum as well. As the *J.S.A.* example demonstrates, the complicities between film and tourism— specifically in their relation to reconciliation efforts in Northeast Asia—are manifold. If the film suggests that the solution to historical antagonism is travel across boundaries, and thematizes this travel via the movement of commodities and other objects across the 38th parallel, then the tourist response has seemed to take up this combination of transnational political reconciliation and transnational commerce with great enthusiasm. Thus, since the late 1990s, the thematic of travel became a way to consider, beyond just broaching the problem of North-South Korea relations, broader shifts in an era of Asianization. By Asianization, I refer to the increased regional cooperation of often formerly antagonistic nations, particularly in East Asia, aimed at obtaining a competitive advantage in the global marketplace.[1] In various forms, tourism in this period speaks to the evolving transnational political relations that such a regional transformation entailed.

In *Tourist Distractions* I explore South Korea's venture into trans-Asian cinema production and distribution in the late 1990s, and its relation to the emergence of hallyu, the undifferentiated general term for the popular-culture phenomenon in which Korean entertainment and cultural products, including film, television drama, and music, found enthusiastic international reception. By focusing on the explicit representation of travel in these films in relation to the practices of travel that emerged in relation to film spectatorship, I examine the ways in which aspects of Korean popular cinema were slowly adapted according to the hallyu market, in which films became an integral part of the ancillary market generated by Korean television dramas, and in which consumption practices associated with hallyu, such as travel, came to reformulate aesthetic concepts and shared affects with deep roots in the nation's history. I narrow the field of inquiry by focusing on hallyu cinema and set aside other forms of cultural production because hallyu cinema offers a particularly useful, self-reflexive perspective for viewing the complexities—the anxieties, tensions, and celebratory gestures—of a new East Asian affective economy. Precisely due to the nebulous and inclusive boundaries of hallyu, we need to explore the particular relationship between popular Korean cinema and hallyu, in order to contemplate the production and consumption of films in a world where new media challenge film as the dominant mode of mass culture.[2] And thus, perhaps the largest ambition of my study is to transform *hallyu*, which has become first and foremost a marketing category, into a bona fide critical term.

To this end, I focus on the links between filmic form and transnational commerce. In this context, one of the most notable features of hallyu's rise, especially in East Asia, was a convergence of the film and tourism industries. In much the same way that Dean MacCannell saw in tourism a new way of theorizing the leisure class in the postindustrial age, I identify travel and tourism as an important critical lens through which to examine the affective capabilities of South Korean national cinema as part of a larger project of recalibrating the nation's position within the rapidly changing landscape of postcolonial East Asia.[3] As the region becomes increasingly disconnected from the painful histories, bitter conflicts, and political rivalries that shaped affective experiences along national lines for the better part of the twentieth century, tourist films and film tourism become part of a larger project of forming the transnational emotional bonds that contribute to the shaping of a newly imagined East Asia and that might presage more concrete transnational economic bonds between nations that were fairly recently antagonistic.

I therefore think of Asianization not primarily in the political and economic terms that are most frequently mobilized to speak about the phenomenon, though these concerns of course underlie my analysis. Rather, my aim is to enlarge our vision of what Asianization encompasses and how it shapes contemporary life in East Asia. More specifically, I hope to answer Lauren Berlant's question about historical sense for the present context: "How does a particular affective response come to be exemplary of a shared historical time, and in what terms?"[4] I am most interested in the formation of a shared *affective* experience that transnational cooperation requires in order to build its networks for the exchange of products and capital, a sense of what Giorgio Agamben refers to as the "con-sent" at the heart of friendship.[5] By emphasizing the etymological elements of consent, which in the original Latin infers "feeling together," this formulation in the context of contemporary Asianization suggests the need for a shared sense of affective experience in order to turn once rival nations into cooperative friends. To this end, I am not merely interested in the dissemination and flow of cultural products that Asianization entails, of which hallyu serves as an example, but more significantly in how these cultural flows are suffused with affective flows. Given the tumultuous modern history of northeast Asia, Asianization demands not only these political and economic forms of partnership, but also a newly emergent feeling of cooperation and the production of an affective economy to underlie the financial one.

Hallyu-lujah!

Hallyu did not come to the attention of South Korean cultural critics until early 2001, when dispatches from China on the "Korean Wave"—or "Korea mania," as it was also referred to—set off similar reports from Hong Kong, Taipei, and Vietnam.[6] The apparent spontaneity with which hallyu had emerged in China in 1997 was in stark contrast to the measured and carefully thought-out cultural liberalization policies South Korea had been implementing since 1998. In the wake of the devastating financial crisis, South Korea had started looking to its neighbors for interregional collaboration as a part of its recovery process, which had entailed much postcolonial negotiation and symbolic reparations. The intellectual labor of working toward an understanding of the hallyu phenomenon, taking place about four years after the wave's emergence, in its belated recuperation of the period essentially redefined a significant period in the initiation of interregional cultural cooperation and collaboration in film production as one marked by an unforeseen surge in Korean soft power, namely the rise of hallyu.[7]

The element of surprise, viewed in hindsight, has become a cornerstone in the study of hallyu, a central task that has entailed chronicling and investigating the underlying conditions and reasons that enabled the surprising phenomena to emerge. In fact, one theory of the etymology of the term *hallyu* suggests that it comes from the Taiwanese media, expressing surprise over the popularity of Korean dramas and K-pop (Korean popular music), and specifically their use of the phrase *hail hallyu*, a local expression that translates as "winter ice storm in summer" and refers to unexpected and unlikely events.[8] The serendipitous nature of the phenomenon's origins, however, is posed in hallyu discourses more as a windfall and less as a problem, the question being "Why did it happen?," rather than "Why didn't we notice?"[9]

Hallyu thus began not as a carefully orchestrated enterprise, but rather as a serendipitous cultural phenomenon in the late 1990s when the Korean culture industry realized that its products were beginning to have regional and international appeal. It continued in subsequent years, not only as an attempt to continue and replicate this success in cultural forms and media other than K-pop and dramas, but also in the self-conscious transformation of the trade and circulation logics that characterized the initial phenomenon into an explicit aesthetics, which attempted both to make sense of the early surprising success and to capitalize on it. Hence, I argue that tourism becomes a central trope in the films of this period because it literalizes the forms of circulation that inhere in its international success. Travel, in other words, serves to make sense of the more difficult to perceive networks of circulation that made hallyu's rise possible in the first place, and in this context, travel and tourism become interchangeable terms because the movement of bodies through unfamiliar spaces (what we call travel) is inseparable in these films from the commercialization of such behavior (what we call tourism).

Hallyu, the generic term that is usually rendered in English as "Korean Wave," has more recently been subdivided into a series of sequential waves. The general consensus is that the first wave started circa 1997 and lasted until 2003, with the unexpected impact of the television drama *Winter Sonata*.[10] Though the term *hallyu*, which was coined in the Chinese press (according to some accounts), was supposedly inspired by a compilation CD of Korean popular music, the first wave was actually defined by the popularity of Korean television dramas.[11] Beginning in 2003, the second Korean Wave (also referred to as *sin hallyu*, or the New Korean Wave) was led by K-pop, and bolstered by the continued popularity of television dramas and by the growing popularity of Korean films and video games. In addition to the growth in the types of products between these waves, the other major transition was in the types of distribution. In the first wave, these cultural creations were circulated via television and cable broadcasts, CDs, and DVDs; in the second wave, that distribution expanded to include social-network services. In this transition, the audience also expanded, from predominantly middle-aged women to both male and female children and teenagers.[12]

Whereas the first wave is considered to have occurred spontaneously, the second was created by private entrepreneurs, supported by government initiatives, who harnessed the perceived potential of Korean popular culture.[13] Sin hallyu included a conscious attempt by the Korean National Tourism Organization to bring the consumption of hallyu home to Korea, in the form of inbound tourism and shopping catered to tourists, fan attendance at Korean pop concerts, and travel to drama and film locations. Thus, in addition to diffusion through social-networking sites, the second wave witnessed an expansion in the nature of hallyu consumption. In 2012 Culture Minister Ch'oe Kwang-shik called for a "third hallyu" that would consist of "the Korean culture overall—the content, the core," which would include in particular the marketing of traditional Korean culture abroad.[14] Whether or not the distinction proves useful remains an open question; more pertinent to the present discussion is the way in which Ch'oe's initiative demonstrates the extent to which hallyu in recent years has become the name of an explicit enterprise. Now an even more unwieldy term, *hallyu* in this context not only refers to all manner of Korean consumables, but also to the production of a highly marketed and globally distributed culture that is quite deliberately conceived of as an export commodity.

Part of the reason for *hallyu*'s ambiguity as a term is the way in which the business model of these cultural creations increasingly encouraged hybridity.

Jinhee Choi has described how the demand for Korean dramas that characterized hallyu's first wave provided the Korean entertainment industry with significant crossover opportunities into other entertainment media.[15] Following success in television dramas, actors such as Jun Ji-hyun, Choi Ji-woo, Lee Byung-hun, Jang Dong-gun, and Kwon Sang-woo crossed over to the film industry, which benefited immensely from the popularity of these actors, as demonstrated by the demand in other countries for the rights to distribute and export Korean cinema. These trends were further buttressed by the ubiquity of film stars in music videos and advertisements as well as the rising presence of K-pop idols starring in films and dramas, for which they also often provided original music for the soundtrack. Tourism to drama and film locations followed, as did remakes of a few Korean films in Europe and the United States. Perhaps more than any other hallyu text, the drama *Winter Sonata* (2003) set the standard for the crossover and tourist potential of hallyu texts, motivating consumption that ranged from spectatorship to tourism, both of which foregrounded affective experiences such that the more mediated experience of watching a television drama cohered with the haptic experience of visiting the sites where it was filmed.

Such opportunities were not lost on tourism promoters: the "Dynamic Korea" advertisement released by the Korean National Tourism Organization in 2003—a difficult moment for the tourism industry due to the outbreak of SARS (Severe Acute Respiratory Syndrome), the Iraq War, and the North Korean nuclear controversy—featured then president Roh Moo-hyun and emphasized the senses: "Listen. Can you, can you hear them? Look. Can you, can you see them? Now feel. It feels wonderful! Come feel it. Korea."[16] From images of Korean traditional culture and food, it jumps to the roaring crowds of the Red Devils from the 2002 FIFA World Cup, gesturing to the affective energies it is attempting to generate. The dynamism of the advertisement is an example of the "Korea of *shinmyoung*" (*shinmyŏng*) concept that the government was promoting at the time as its national brand image, which along with *shin* and *shinbaram*, are affects that might translate as "exhilaration, delight, excitement, hilarity, joviality, and enthusiasm."[17] After 2002 and the fervor surrounding South Korea's success in the World Cup, it was used to describe the energy and enthusiasm of soccer fans, but here in the advertisement, it is associated specifically with travel.

The Korean National Tourism Organization started its explicit hallyu campaigns shortly after the World Cup, in its 2003 tourism campaign, going on to designate 2004 as the year of the Korean Wave, appointing stars as ambassadors, and maximizing the use of celebrity images everywhere from newspapers to electronic billboards.[18] Most significantly for the present study, it used drama and film footage to draw tourists, and encouraged the development of new tour programs that highlighted film locations. Extending from these strategies were concerts and fan meetings in Korea, and the organization of fan clubs into region-wide networks that could be utilized as an expansive marketing base. By 2005, tourism marketing campaigns focused on creating "a structure of consciousness and feeling through which South Korea could make itself known to the world."[19] The concept of "feeling Korea" encapsulated this effort, which attempted to mobilize the affective impact of the circulating cultural products by maximizing the ancillary nature of the hallyu market.[20] The association of feeling with affect induced by the postcinematic and touristic becomes directly palpable in the 2006 tourism ads for Southeast Asia, Japan, China, Hong Kong, and China, launched with the slogan "Korea, something more!"[21] In the advertisements, a female tourist arrives at Inch'on Airport, where she is met by the popular actor Ryu Si-won. She attends a Rain concert, where she is superimposed standing alongside Bae Yong-joon in a scene from the film *April Snow*, in which he plays a light technician for K-pop concerts. The female tourist takes in the serene urban nocturnal landscape of Seoul side-by-side with Jun Ji-hyun in a scene from the film *Windstruck* (*Nae yŏjach'in'gurŭl sogaehamnida*, 2004), and the wintry nights of rural Korea trailing behind Jeon Do-yeon and Hwang Jung-min in a scene from the film *You are My Sunshine* (*Nŏnŭn nae unmyŏng*, 2005). She walks the fields talking to Son Ye-jin in a scene from the television drama *Summer Scent* (*Yŏrŭm hyanggi*, 2003), and is a guest at a palatial ceremony in the drama *A Jewel in the Palace* (*Taejanggŭm*, 2003), as well as in a home in the drama *Wedding* (*We-ding*, 2005).

The prominence of tourism in these marketing efforts is symptomatic of a national desire to represent, in aesthetic terms, the mobility of hallyu commodities—an example of what Arjun Appadurai describes as the social life of commodities. The problem with the current critical discourse about hallyu is that it ignores what Appadurai describes as "the constant tension between the existing frameworks (of price, bargaining, and so forth) and the tendency of commodities to breach these frameworks" due to the fact that "not all parties share the same interests in any specific regime of value, nor are the interests of any two parties in a given exchange identical."[22] By characterizing and populating the networks of hallyu's transnational circulation with the actual movements of actual bodies, the films examined in this study make visible these frameworks as well as the points of their breaching. Such dynamics are especially important considering the various postcolonial or otherwise asymmetrical power relations of the region in which these products circulate. The social life of hallyu is inseparable from this regional history.

In this context, I attempt to historicize the phenomenon by focusing on the production and circulation of film from 1998 to 2006, a period toward the end of which the Korean film industry began to suffer from a downturn and tourist self-consciousness in its cinema begins to decline. Sketching the intersection during this busy period—defined by the surge of hallyu, a renaissance in Korean film, and Korea's interregional reconciliation efforts—I examine the way film both represents and negotiates this changing terrain along with what is at stake as hallyu rapidly morphs from a descriptor of a specific phenomenon into a generic term that applies to all things Korean. The films examined herein are situated in and speak to the development of the hallyu moment, as marketing begins to subsume history. Hallyu cinema both responds to and takes advantage of the hallyu phenomenon, but in so doing, it also tries to think about what hallyu is and its relationship to the new forms of inter-Asian communality emerging in the period.

Korean film has not been the progenitor of any of the subwaves within hallyu, and it is fair to say that, as a whole, Korean film's ascent is not directly indebted to hallyu. To indiscriminately incorporate directors associated with the socially conscious films of the Korean New Wave cinema emerging in the late 1980s, or the noncommercial auteurs connected to international film-festival circuits, and even some of the "high-quality" directors of the "Korean film renaissance" or "New Korean cinema" garnering renown abroad as commercially appealing mainstream filmmakers within hallyu is to suspend critical evaluation of the relevance of the term *hallyu* and to buy into the convenience with which it has become a catch-all phrase.[23] It is only later, and gradually, that these various starts from different corners of the cultural industry converge and begin to cohere under the category of hallyu. Paradoxically, to eschew or minimize mention of hallyu at all in analyses of contemporary Korean cinema now is also to risk treating the cinema industry as if it were insulated from the influences of hallyu that now reach beyond the cultural spheres into the social and historical.

I thus regard film as a microcosm of larger phenomena and argue that hallyu's aesthetics self-referentially reflects its own transnational distribution, constructing out of this reflection an affective sensorium that validates emerging transnational economic relations through the positive emotions one associates with travel. That tourism induced by television dramas, films, and music has become a defining hallyu characteristic is not coincidental or merely the outcome of successful marketing of destination images; rather, it is the manifestation of a tourist imaginary produced in the interregional discourses serving postcolonial reconciliation in East Asia following the 1997 financial crisis, specifically the films and dramas coproduced by different countries as part of larger efforts to promote friendship, intimacy, and increasing mobility across borders. In this context, the desire to travel becomes inseparable from an economic desire for increased transnational exchange of goods and services. In turn, the hallyu aesthetics of travel affect makes transnational consumption appealing, helping to fuel the demand for hallyu cultural products.

Film tourism is a particularly useful way to examine the transnational flows implicit in hallyu not only because it helps us think about the movement of bodies and cultural products across national boundaries, but also because it foregrounds the multivalent practices of consumption on which the hallyu phenomenon depends; such practices involve economic transactions, everything from the purchase of movie tickets, DVDs, airfare to film sites, and entry passes to film theme parks, as well as affective transactions, in which consumers cathect to once-foreign emotional states. In this context, film tourism becomes a way of figuring both the material transnational flows of hallyu as well as the equally significant immaterial flows that reconnect, realign, and reimagine the networks that connect Korea to the world in late capitalism. In addition, the films examined herein seem to anticipate the travel of their audiences, who would subsequently become tourists, often presented as if to a non-Korean audience. Although it is too much to say that hallyu is fundamentally about tourism, it is not too much to say that understanding the tourist imagination is crucial to understanding hallyu.

The emergence of hallyu is not the story of the emergence of a coherent style or content that subsequently finds audiences abroad, but rather the story of a developing style and content that emerges *because* of its surprising transnational appeal.[24] Its distribution and circulation outside of Korea is fundamental, not ancillary, to its very being, and we might say that it self-reflectively speaks to its own "commodity situation," which Arjun Appadurai has described as "the situation in which its exchangeability (past, present, or future) for some other thing is its socially relevant feature."[25] We know in retrospect that hallyu was a highly unplanned, consumer-centric phenomenon driven by the mass production of *commercial* culture.[26] Although they are often cited as an explanation for the rise of hallyu, the government's cultural liberalization policies starting in 1998—which officially lifted the (already porous) ban on the import of Japanese popular culture, in place since Korea's independence from Japanese colonialism in 1945—were inherently *political*, and were motivated by a need to resolve latent postcolonial issues as part of recuperation efforts following the region's financial crisis in 1997. So though they helped provide conditions for the increased exchange of cultural products and the forms of cooperation that made possible the 2002 FIFA World Cup, which was jointly hosted by Korea and Japan, they were far from a highly premeditated cultural policy intended to exert the global soft power of Korean popular culture.

The category of hallyu has become too vague. That hallyu's breadth is now being extended, for example, to the Asuka period (A.D. 538–710) in Japan, in order to acknowledge the influence of Korean art on Japan's art and architecture through cultural exchange during the Baekje period (18 B.C.–A.D. 660), suggests the degree to which it has become unmoored from its original context.[27] But as Michael Levenson suggests about his central term in the opening lines of *Genealogy of Modernism*, "Vague terms still signify."[28] Although the term often obscures more than it elaborates, *hallyu* remains useful for thinking about the Korean culture industry in a moment of unprecedented transformation precisely because its history reveals how a historical designation devolves into a state-sponsored marketing term, the usage of which has become so broad that it now seems to signify any Korean cultural export. I thus wish to historicize *hallyu*, separating it from its generic contemporary usage and returning it to its original logics, politics, and aesthetics, all of which emerged within particular circumstances. I will then attempt to locate film, and what I am calling *hallyu cinema*, within this more specific context.

In his account of *virtual hallyu* in relation to contemporary South Korean cinema, Kyung Hyun Kim invokes "cinema's modernist ambitions," which played a "subconscious" role in hallyu's otherwise more populist interests. Whereas Kim posits these modernist cinematic aesthetics in opposition to populist entertainment—arguing that popular films (as hallyu films tend to be) "failed to establish an aesthetic standard in the local film culture the way the films of Bong Joon-ho, Park Chan-wook, Hong Sang-soo, or Lee Chang-dong did throughout the 2000s"—my study attempts to articulate the aesthetics *of* these popular forms and the way in which they reflect the terms of their own popularity.[29] Kim's notion of "virtual hallyu" thus refers to "a reflection of both the modernist ambition to engage cinema as a technological tool that could challenge language and literature as the principal mode of creative expression and the postmodern failure to extend cinema's power beyond populist entertainment."[30] He is skeptical of Korean cinema in this era "where only ahistorical (that is, postmodern) films thrive" to "render an aesthetic that is still socially relevant."[31] Hallyu functions like the Deleuzian *virtual-actual* in Kim's formulation, positioned within the gap between modernism (associated with auteur aesthetics, political allegory, and the sublime) and postmodernism (associated with market forces and the ahistorical); hallyu's "virtuality" lies in its ability to collapse the two, blurring and crossing through "the boundary between 'the way things are remembered' and the 'way things really were'" through "the massive repository of images collected over the past decade."[32] Kim's recognition of the Deleuzian virtuality of Korean cinema is not a refusal of the past in its multiple rewritings and reconfiguration of the multiple conditions of the past, and in its coexistence with the present, an acknowledgment of its state in a condition of possibilities. But because his coordinates are more ontological and epistemological, Kim is less concerned with the material history of hallyu—the primary concern of *Tourist Distractions*—than he is with its possibilities as a theoretical figure of being and expression.

Like *Virtual Hallyu*, *Tourist Distractions* is interested in cinematic aesthetics, but my study is more primarily interested in the way in which these aesthetics inflect cultural and historical phenomena. In particular, the affect and aesthetics of tourism become important because of tourism's inherent concern for making local products available for global consumption. Reflecting on both the various locations of non-Korean consumers as well as the itinerancy of the cultural products themselves as they travel, I argue that the aesthetics of tourism and travel affect that characterizes hallyu cinema is an aesthetics of distribution.[33] That is, hallyu cinema not only thematizes the flows that characterize the circulation of hallyu products as narratives of travel, but also adopts a filmic aesthetics, as for example in the aforementioned ending of *J.S.A.*, that places the film's stylistic elements in service of producing a series of affective formations that accompany hallyu's material networks.

In particular, the characteristic of exportability figures centrally in hallyu cinema's distribution aesthetics.[34] In export-centric views, the success of a cultural product with foreign audiences is a prerequisite to its categorization as hallyu.[35] The basis of such categorizations relies, for example, on the drama *Winter Sonata*, which aired domestically to higher popularity in its rebroadcast in April 2005 following its success abroad in Japan than in its initial run in

2002, a process in which, as Jeongmee Kim describes, the program, the stars, and the director "became Hallyu."[36] Kim suggests that "perhaps it is more profitable to think about the term less as a generic definition that signifies the 'Korean-ness' of cultural products, but rather as a nationalistic sentiment that essentially means 'successful in Asia.' Korean cultural productions that attain genuine global success are seen as something else entirely and not labeled hallyu even though they may contain as much 'Korean-ness' as a hallyu product."[37] The slippage in these comments between "Korean-ness," "successful," and "profitable" all under the rubric of "hallyu" is striking; the slippage speaks to an uncanny desire to recode economic prosperity in aesthetic terms.

Because they are commodities, it is tempting to view cultural products in the same way that one views other exports. The sociologist John Lie, for example, in reference to the appeal of K-pop, suggests that "the appeal of K-pop to non-Korean audiences—both across Asia and beyond—is in a pattern with South Korean export products, such as Samsung or Hyundai, that have broad appeal precisely because of the combination of reasonable price and dependable quality."[38] But when we talk about cultural products, hallyu and otherwise, as commodities not unlike other exports, we must also acknowledge their unique capacity, not only to circulate, but also to function as carriers in a regime of *affective* value; hallyu is built on financial exchanges, of course, but, just as important, it is built on affective exchanges. This history of hallyu thus needs to be a history that maps not only the flow and distribution of Korean cultural products, but also one that shows how these flows and distributions become *inscribed* in the emerging aesthetics of hallyu's visual commodities.

Tourism in a State of Distraction

Returning for a moment to the tourist scene in *J.S.A.*, we recall that the crucial photograph that ends the film was taken at a moment of distraction, and the revelation of its true content, a picture of friendship not antagonism, depended on this divergence from the usual course of the guided tour. In theorizations of Western modernity, distraction has become understood in a similar vein, not as interruption of attention, but rather, as Walter Benjamin suggested, an alternate mode of attention that emerges within the context of the increasingly fragmented, disorienting experiences that define modern popular culture, what he terms "reception in a state of distraction."[39] With the distracted attention of the film viewer serving as a quintessential example, Benjamin implies that distraction is not the opposite of attention, but an alternate version. In a similar vein, Jonathan Crary suggests that in the technological environments that define contemporary life, "it's questionable whether it is even meaningful to distinguish between conscious attention to one's actions and mechanical autoregulated patterns."[40] And pulling Benjamin in a more radical direction, Paul North makes a case for what he calls *non-attentional distraction*, which is "released from its subordination to attention, to perception, and to the subject."[41] For North, the final value of distraction is not the synthesis to which a good deal of modern thought aspires, but dissolution, "an internal dissipation that, brought about through new media, will lead to an uncommon politicization. . . . Where philosophy, criticism, and art theory are traditionally concerned with principles for the formation of things, distraction is concerned with their de-formation, disintegration, and ceasing to be."[42]

At a moment in Korean history defined by dramatic change—the International Monetary Fund (IMF) crisis, the election of the former political dissident Kim Dae-jung, the rise of posthegemonic anti-American fervor, the renewed prospect of reunification in the form of the Sunshine Policy, and the possibility of new regional integration and reconciliation with former adversaries—the critical view of hallyu gathered from an analysis of hallyu cinema disturbs the nationalist pull toward a progressive narrative. Hallyu instead offers a moment of distraction that interrupts the story of development and forces a reflection on what has escaped attention.[43] It is in this sense that I use the term *distraction* in the title of this book, *Tourist Distractions*, a play on the term *tourist attraction*. As epitomized by the tourist in *J.S.A.* who loses her hat to an unanticipated gust of wind, the experience of the tourist in unfamiliar locales figures this model of productive distraction. In the logic of Culture Minister Ch'oe and others, the surprising success of hallyu validates Korea's rise from Third to First World, a trajectory that has dominated national discourse in the second half of the twentieth century; soft power reflects hard power. In the late 1990s, the position of South Korea's cultural industries, once regarded as secondary to postwar efforts to develop the industrial economy, radically changed as their products were placed on equal status with traditional exports like automobiles. But the serendipity of hallyu, the fact of its surprise emergence, while no one was paying attention, suggests that hallyu embodies not seamless continuity with the twentieth-century discourse of political and economic ascension, but rather a moment of readjustment, crisis, and rupture when, according to North, "politics needs to be repoliticized, that is, dissolved once again into a war of elements against wholes."[44]

By "tourist distractions," I refer to moments within a visual text or in its widespread consumption in which images and practices associated with travel or tourism abruptly intervene or interrupt, thereby disturbing the very "*image or the idea* of society" that is presumed to be generated by "the collective act" of sightseeing at tourist attractions.[45] Implied in Dean MacCannell's notion here is the idea that the "orderly representation of the social structure of modern society" is itself motivated by the act of sightseeing.[46] However, the proliferating, self-reflexive integration in hallyu cinema of the tourist imaginary into the very fabric of visual texts goes beyond the mere categorization of such images featuring attractions as destination images or reproductions.

I trace the unexpected ways in which the tourist imagination found form and practice, placing a particular emphasis on Korea's film collaborations with Japan, China, and Hong Kong going back to the period of 1998 to 2002. I argue that the trope of travel featured in this intercultural cinema, initially intended to promote cross-cultural understanding, also became a means to propagate a film's affective experience beyond the screen, and to provide ersatz historical experiences of political and historical negotiation, ones that paradoxically distract from the task of collective historical memory endorsed by the state, even in texts whose production and distribution were enthusiastically aided by the state. I seek to show then how the unanticipated distractions from the state-sponsored narrative can alert us to the ways in which new structures of feeling interrogate and redefine the new Asian order. If we take distraction as a starting point, it becomes possible to conceptualize hallyu as an affective aesthetic formed by the particularities of the conditions underlying its emergence, as opposed to articulating it using the terms prescribed in the process of marketing national culture. Driven by nationalist interests, the deployment of hallyu coincides with the coming-of-age of a generation with no direct memory of Japanese colonialism, Korean War trauma, the effects of postwar poverty, or democratic struggles against authoritarian regimes. Although these traumatic events and experiences remain lodged deep within the nation's psyche—and have instilled palpable, and collective, emotions like humiliation, anger, shame, and *han* (unresolved sorrow and regret due to suffering)—these once dominant emotions no longer dominate. If distraction is understood as an adjustment of the field of perception, then it also entails a new sensorium of affect, engendered by new structures of feeling. Within the context of crisis and change in the late 1990s, the ground shifts beneath Korean feet and thus shifts to what Sara Ahmed calls a "cultural politics of emotion," which acknowledges the "doing" of emotions as opposed to merely questioning what they are.[47] Circulating between bodies and working "through signs and on bodies to materialize the surfaces and boundaries that are lived as worlds," emotions are bound up in specific histories, and not only show but also open up new possibilities.[48]

Hallyu Cinema and Transnational Collaboration

The intercultural interest in hallyu cinema as demonstrated in Korea's collaborations with other countries has decades-old roots in the intercultural reconciliatory film collaborations initiated between Korea, Japan, Hong Kong, and China. From as early as 1957, with the Korean director Jeon Chang-geun's (Chŏn Ch'ang-gŭn) melodrama *Love with an Alien* (*Ikukchŏngwŏn*), made in collaboration with Hong Kong's Shaw Brothers and Japan's Mitsuo Wakasugi, the Korean film industry, flailing in the aftermath of the Korean War, had looked to other Asian nations as a way of promoting cultural exchange while maximizing resources and market potential across Asia.[49] The Japanese hand in Korean film production, forcibly implemented under Japanese colonialism in the early twentieth century, had continued to make its mark in such coproductions even after Korea's national independence following the Second World War, but went publicly unrecognized in compliance with Korea's ban on Japanese popular culture. Furthermore, in the relationship between Korea's Shin Films and Hong Kong's Shaw Brothers, for example, which yielded a number of successful epics, including *The Last Woman of Shang* (1962), *The Goddess of Mercy* (1966), *The King with My Face* (1967), and *That Man in Chang-an* (1967), the reliance on Chinese historical material tended to render Korea's participation invisible. This problem of a "denationalized" cinema resulting from coproductions persisted in their cooperation with Hong Kong's Golden Harvest, a film production, distribution, and exhibition company, on martial arts films in the 1970s.[50] With the problem of how a burgeoning Korean cinema could reconcile the contradictory desires of pursuing the transnational without relinquishing nationalist pride left unresolved, coproductions gradually ceased.

More recently, however, the rigid barriers of regional politics—such as the postcolonial past that turned the Korean film industry away from Japan and toward Hong Kong, or the Cold War that closed mainland China to Hong Kong's filmmakers, forcing them to search for China in Korea—have largely become a thing of the past. (The relatively defiant isolation of North Korea from its neighbors is, of course, the one notable exception to this historical shift.) The late 1990s saw a resurgence of intraregional film collaborations, capitalizing on South Korea's "China Fever," China's "Korea Wave," and Taiwan's "Japan Fever." Current East Asian cultural regionalism, however, distinguishes itself from the ventures into intra-Asian collaboration in the 1960s and 1970s, reflecting the shifting regional dynamics of cultural trade after the 1997 Asian financial crisis. From 1980 to 1998, intraregional trade in cultural goods in East Asia grew exponentially, concurrent with the integration of Asian national economies, as China emerged globally as one of the "Big Five" cultural importers and exporters alongside Japan, the United States, the United Kingdom, and Germany. Region-wide cultural liberalization policies officially lifted the last of the trade restrictions on Japanese pop culture imposed at the end of the Second World War. In Korea, globalization, localization and the new media technology wrought major changes in the perceptions and value of the culture industry across the 1990s. Popular culture was no longer marginal but now a dominant industry, bolstered by the boom in the Asian multimedia and audiovisual industries, such as film and television, which gave a major boost to interregional cultural flows.[51]

Bilateral film coproductions between Korea and Japan, Korea and China, and Korea and Hong Kong began to gather momentum after 1998. In April 2000, the Hong Kong director Peter Chan launched Applause Pictures with the director Teddy Chen and the distributor Allan Fung, in the hopes of attracting Asian talent to produce pan-Asian films. The film Chan produced under Applause Pictures in 2001, *One Fine Spring Day* (*Pomnalŭn kanda*, 2001), became a model of trilateral collaboration, involving the cooperation of three film industries—Korea, Japan, and Hong Kong—in the form of joint financing to maximize impact on the Asian market. *Three* (*Saam gaang*, 2002), a horror film collaboration featuring several short, thematically linked segments by the directors from each participating country (Kim Jee-woon from Korea, Peter Chan from Hong Kong, and Nonzee Nimibutr from Thailand), was also produced around this time, presenting a different model for collaboration. By 2006, multiple trilateral pan-Asian productions on a much larger scale, such as Tsui Hark's *Seven Swords* (*Qī Jiàn*, 2005) and Chen Kaige's *The Promise* (*Wú Jí*, 2005), were de rigueur, and the concept of an "East Asian cinema" seemed to exist before it had adequately been conceptualized. The tourist imagination that emerges in this period, especially in Korea's jointly produced pan-Asian films, reflects the rapidly changing terrain of regional cultural production and exchange in Northeast Asia and the unprecedented, relatively free movement across political and cultural barriers that nurtured such possibilities.

In addition, the emphasis on touristic motifs provided these films with a way of working around the denationalizing tendency of collaborations, a way to perform cultural nationalism and appreciation while simultaneously advocating the transcendence of boundaries. Through an ideology of tourism, these films thus offered a non-antagonistic way of negotiating between competing national interests, a cinematic means to reconcile a complex past.

Although the connection between film and travel is far from new—the metaphorics of virtual transportation to unfamiliar locales and different times is as old as the medium itself—the use of travel in these recent Korean, pan-Asian coproductions departs radically from its predecessors in Korean cinema. In the 1980s travel in Korea charted a path toward social and historical consciousness; yet starting around 1998, travel became complicated by the logic of commodities as cinema began to address the emerging conditions of transnational commerce. Nationalist discourse may underscore the work ethic and corporate structures that enable a highly efficient and rewarding production process, but in the end, it is its reach in distribution and fluid circulation that gives hallyu and its products value as an export. Travel in the hallyu realm imagines what it is like to be a commodity in regional and global circulation.

One prominent location, for example, that is deeply connected to the figure of the tourist—"the road" in Korean national cinema—is described by Kyung Hyun Kim as the site of "heartbreaking emotional chords because of the violent modern history that forcibly separated family members for more than a generation after the war."[52] A figure of loss and homelessness, "a permanent site for many thousands of refugees who have lost their homes and families," the road shatters hopes of any possibility of finding a route toward freedom or escape.[53] Prior to hallyu, that was certainly the case. Park Kwang-su's 1988 *Chilsu and Mansu* captures this kind of immobility in its depiction of Mansu's home, where the pool lounge and blown-up plastic palm tree signal how displaced dreams of leisurely travel are part of the grim social reality of Seoul. As in the video game Chilsu plays in the arcade, imagining himself in a convertible driving down a palm-tree-lined U.S. coastal highway until he crashes and burns, or as with the billboard of the suntanned blond woman in sunglasses drinking a cocktail that Chilsu and Mansu must paint, travel imagery indexes the displacement of the characters, ironically indicating the unavailability of actual travel. Jang Sun-woo's (Chang Sŏn-u) documentary *Cinema on the Road* (*Kilwiŭi yŏnghwa*, 1995) similarly encapsulates the function of the travel trope in the socially conscious films of Korean New Wave cinema, especially the association of travel with a quest mired in national history. Finding Seoul void of inspiration and unable to find anything worth filming, Jang, on a "quest for the core of Korean cinema," heads to the foothills of Mount Baek, the site of the 1894 Tonghak Peasant Revolt, then proceeds to Kwangju, the site of the May 1980 uprising. Travel here is nostalgic historical consciousness, a way to re-immerse oneself in a violent past.

More recently, with increased mobility and emerging cultures of leisure among younger generations, travel comes to connote the freedom and escape reminiscent of the familiar holiday or travel film genre, in which travel and leisure stand in opposition to work and social life, rather than for political freedom and historical oppression. Travel ceases to be directly related to national suffering, and comes to be more about the self and one's access to a happier and freer state of life. In the decade between *Cinema on the Road* (1995) and *April Snow* (2005), a film that famously yielded significant film-inspired tourism, travel in its relation to Korean cinema was drastically transformed. The trope of travel in late 1990s Korean film, as it turns to interregional production and distribution, is critical in the recalibration and reformulation of Korean cinema in its ascent alongside and, later, as part of hallyu, as the frame shifts from national to transnational and the concerns from the historical traumas of the past toward the new economies of the future.

Sightseeing, Site-Seeing

My methodology reflects the intertextual nature of my subject matter, bringing together tourism studies, visual and cultural anthropology, cultural studies, and film studies. In order to account for the way in which hallyu cinema makes Korean popular culture an actor in the larger world system, this method builds on the anthropologist George E. Marcus's brand of mobile, comparative ethnography, "multi-sited ethnography," which "takes unexpected trajectories in tracing a cultural formation across and within multiple sites of activity."[54] I thus examine tour sites as extensions of logics rooted in film texts and vice versa.

In addition to tracking the transnational cultural exchanges implicit in tourism, my framework also attends to the transnational affective sensorium that results from such exchanges. My attention to the overlapping logics of touristic and cinematic space thus finds inspiration in Giuliana Bruno's critical reformulation of the voyeur figure into that of the voyageur, or "a passenger who traverses a haptic, emotive terrain."[55] In *Atlas of Emotion* Bruno conceptualizes in cinema a "haptic space of 'site-seeing,'" a shift from the ocularcentric act of "sight-seeing" that has been the long-standing focus of film theory. As Bruno explains, the haptic, implying contact with the skin and therefore the sense of touch, "constitutes the reciprocal con*tact* between us and the environment, both housing and extending communicative interface. But the haptic is also related to kinesthesis, the ability of our bodies to sense their own movement in space," and thus the haptic, ultimately, helps map "our ways of being in touch with the environment."[56] As a challenge to ocularcentrism and the assumption that film is solely a visual medium, Bruno suggests a shift from the "old cinematic voyeur" to a "film voyageuse," in which travel through motion pictures constituting "a spatial form of sensuous cognition" becomes possible.[57] Crucially for the present context, Bruno argues that these "psychogeographic journeys," or "site-seeing," allow for "mapping a geography of intimate space itself."[58]

But though I borrow from anthropological ideas and methods, I employ no interviews with tourists (or film viewers) or empirical observations about the practices of specific tourists and moviegoers. My study sidesteps the quantitative methodology and analysis that has been predominant in studies of hallyu screen tourism (primarily the television dramas *Winter Sonata* and *Taejanggŭm*); those studies have sufficiently established through questionnaires and interviews with television program producers, viewers, and tourists that, in the instances of hallyu television-drama tourism, "personal attachment with the filmed locations as a metaphor of sense of place represents an emotional or affective and positive bond between viewers and certain places/locations in the process of consuming television drama. Similarly . . . when viewers visited filmed locations this kind of personal attachment with the locations would be partially understood as 'symbolic memory' or 'nostalgia' which is a longing for the locations' meanings for them and a fondness for possessions and activities associated with the days of experiencing the programme which has been over."[59] These findings echo those of Leshu Torchin, which are based on TV tours in Manhattan, namely that firsthand familiarity with the program referenced at the filming location is crucial to accessing the multiple symbolic layers being referenced there.[60] Film as a category in hallyu studies is all too readily and uncritically subsumed into larger, undifferentiated general categories of popular texts; while such studies, for instance, acknowledge the presence of unspecified visual "attractive elements" and "production values" in popular texts that construct, contextualize, and guide consumption influencing touristic experience in diverse ways, the text's specific capacity for any self-reflexivity on the cultural and social impact of these values do not get acknowledged or explored, and the questions that have driven screen-tourism studies in the West (traced back to literary tourism) are not brought to bear specifically on hallyu cinema (or hallyu texts) within the context of Korean cultural history.[61]

Why the film *April Snow*? And can the touristic phenomenon surrounding *April Snow* be presumed to be the same as was generated by the television drama *Winter Sonata*? I believe that it is not. While I do look at affects associated with travel, they are affects inscribed into the textuality and spatiality of and in between sights and sites, not people. In my effort to make sights and sites the subject of our exploration, I am following the daring example of John Dorst. Against what he perceives as Levi-Strauss's overly quantitative sensibility—"There is just too much stuff—forces, institutions, social relations and roles, and so on"—Dorst proceeds to reformulate ethnography's limitations instead in qualitative terms.[62] The problem postmodernity poses to ethnography, as Dorst sees it, is the problem of objectivity: "To put it in a formula, the culture of advanced consumer capitalism or, less acceptable but more fashionable, postmodernity, consists largely in the processes of self-inscription, indigenous self-documentation and endlessly reflexive simulation."[63] The practices of ethnography become, in short, absorbed into the very practices of culture: mass marketing, to take one example, engages in ethnographic research and generates ethnographic texts as part of its primary function.[64] The consequence for ethnographic practice is severe, rendering the professional ethnographer superfluous. As a "post-ethnographic" response to this dilemma, Dorst proceeds with a methodology in which there are no subjects.[65] Reading instead the "place" of Chadds Ford, a suburb and tourist site in Pennsylvania, which he signifies with the capitalized word "Site," Dorst's Chadds Ford is thus "an assemblage of texts" that produces its own "auto-ethnographies," which represent and interpret the Site's own cultural production.[66] Accordingly, tourism is not just a phenomenon for ethnography to decode, but is also itself a mode of ethnography. Dorst's ethnographic method eschews the task of describing "the culture, values or world view of a certain set of people."[67] Instead, his study attempts to document the way in which the Site generates its own ethnography.

By tracking the spatial and affective contours of such psychogeographic journeys through physical and filmic sites, I attempt to conceptualize an approach to hallyu cinematic texts that incorporates hallyu's intermedial and intercultural breadth, manifested in sites and practices *beyond* the screen, while paying close attention to the intricacies of narrative and aesthetics in each film, as well as the sociopolitical conditions underlying each film's production and consumption. Methodologically, I combine spatial ethnographies of relevant film locations with close readings of films, placing particular emphasis in both cases on the production of affective networks and distribution aesthetics that reflect and facilitate these emergent networks of exchange. Fundamental to hallyu cinema is an aesthetic that collapses the task of the voyeur and voyageur. As a result, viewing a film and traveling (particularly of the film-inspired variety), become synthesized under the broader effort to map not only the increasingly complex circuits of exchange that characterize the new East Asia, but also the affective sensorium that both validates and underlies those circuits.

The organization of *Tourists Distractions* reflects the connections I am making between hallyu cinema and the intercultural roots of its tourist imaginary, which I trace back to the intercultural collaborations of the 1998 to 2002 period. The book consists of three parts; each part juxtaposes two chapters organized around an emotion that begins to stir and attract attention in the late 1990s intercultural coproductions, then later gets rearticulated and fully fleshed out through various manifestations of tourist distractions in the 2000s under the influence of hallyu. The three parts and their ascribed emotion are also organized by Korea's relationship to its neighbors: *intimacy* between Korea and Japan, *amity* between Korea and China, and *remembrance* in relations between South and North Korea. The trajectory of these affects moves, first, from the backward-looking questions of intimacy in the context of Korea's vexed historical relationship with Japan to the forward-looking issues faced by Korea-China collaborators, with the possibility of a new Asian economy centered around China's economic emergence hanging in the balance; and second, to South Korea's relationship with North Korea, which in much contemporary discourse has been reified into the spatial and seemingly atemporal coordinates of the DMZ. The films I examine in the first chapter of each part of this volume is thus from the period 1998 to 2002, made during a time when hallyu was not yet self-reflexively reflected in the film creation process, since the hallyu discourse does not emerge in Korea until 2001. In the second chapter of each part of this volume, I look at films and their extended enterprises, including supplementary DVDs and tour sites, from the period 2003 to 2006. These second chapters are meant to respond to the limitations the collaboration films exhibited in centralizing certain emotions, and to reveal how hallyu and travel recontextualizes these emotions.

By 2008, with the release of *Romantic Island* by Kang Chul-woo, Korean hallyu cinema as I have described it—characterized by its critical, self-reflexive registering of the touristic impulses inspired by the circulation of hallyu commodities—ceases to reflect on the phenomenon and instead fully embodies this form of global circulation and commodification. The film stars the actor Lee Min-ki and the singer Eugene, a former member of Korean girl band S.E.S., which lasted from 1997 to 2002, in the role of a K-pop singer fed up with the demands of her hallyu stardom. It chronicles six Korean tourists, including the singer, who travel to the resort island of Boracay in the Philippines. The K-pop star's hallyu work does not cease with her escape to Boracay; in fact, her discontent and withdrawal from the demands of her job merely serve to reinforce her initiation into a form of affective labor (which constitutes the main plot) that involves her traveling to a place where she is relatively unknown and returning home to Korea as a better, upgraded version of herself, namely one in which her perceived, robotic public persona is capable of conveying genuine emotion. Instead of intervening in disjunctive, unanticipated ways, the touristic images from the Boracay trip get absorbed into the very fabric of hallyu production, either via social media or projected onto electronic billboards. *Romantic Island* gives full representation to the hallyu commodity as embodied by the tourist. In contrast, the figure of the traveler, as explored in hallyu cinema, in search of distractions against the mundane repetitions of the familiar and everyday, maps the affective routes that will serve as the emotional infrastructure for future transnational relations.

PART I

INTIMACY

1. FEELING TOGETHER

Pornography and Travel in *Kazoku Cinema* and *Asako in Ruby Shoes*

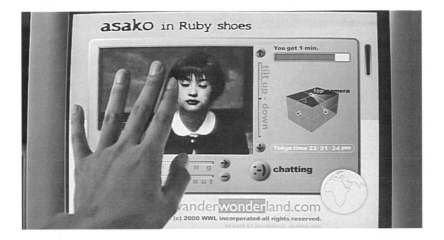

Park Chul-soo's *Kazoku Cinema* (Family Cinema), released in November 1998, was the first film collaboration between Japan and South Korea sanctioned by the cultural liberalization policies implemented by South Korea in October that year, following President Kim Dae-jung's historic visit to Japan.[1] As stated in Kim and the Japanese prime minister Keizo Obuchi's 1998 "joint declaration," the first of these new policies initiated a series of liberalizing measures permitting the import of Japanese popular culture, essentially lifting a ban created after the liberation of Korea from Japanese colonial rule in 1945.[2] Following on the heels of this historic event and coinciding with the early moments of hallyu's emergence, *Kazoku Cinema* was released as the first Korean film to be shot entirely in Japan and in Japanese.[3] Adapted from a novel by the Korean-Japanese author Yu Miri that had won the Akutagawa Literary Award in Japan, the film marked the first time Japanese actors were allowed to star in a Korean film directed by a Korean. The casting reflects the occasion: the Korean-Japanese actor and theatrical director Kim Su-jin plays the director,

1.1 Desiring touch. *Asako in Ruby Shoes.*

Katayama; Yang Sŏk-il, a Korean-Japanese bestselling writer, plays the father (Soji Hayashi), alongside the veteran Japanese actress Hiroko Isayama; and Yu Eri, the younger sister of the novelist Yu Miri, plays the eldest daughter.

Appropriately, *Kazoku Cinema* is a self-reflexive film about the making of a film, which focuses on the struggles of a Korean-Japanese family (though the fact of their ethnicity is only briefly mentioned) as they attempt to overcome an abusive past during a painful reunion after twenty years of separation.[4] The instigator of the plot is Katayama, a director who claims to be making a film concerned with atonement and familial reconciliation. But as he begins to shoot, the film within the film becomes farce, revealing his deeper desire: to make the private struggles of a family available for public entertainment. The film that the family agrees to create is an odd blend of improvised cinema verité, which often includes unheeded requests by the actors to turn off the camera, and scripted scenes based on the family's history, aspiring, in the words of one character, to go "beyond the boundary of documentary or fiction." Framed roughly around the reunion of a fractured family, the film within the film attempts to document both the family's attempt to make sense of their shared experiences and to explore together the prospect of reconciliation, which in turn serves as metaphor for the broader effort of cultural liberalization between Korea and Japan.

Though Katayama envisions the film, it is Yoko, the younger sister who is frustrated with her career as a pornography actor, who orchestrates the family's participation in it. Indeed, the film is her attempt to repair her degrading career with what she regards to be a more legitimate form of filmmaking. But Katayama, we soon realize, is more familiar with the pornographic than the documentary form, and the filming grows increasingly chaotic; it becomes unclear whether we are witnessing a fictionalized representation of the family's dissolution or, more pornographically, the thing itself. So despite the fact that the film Katayama directs is devoid of the explicitly pornographic scenes that have defined his career, the camera used to film the family's story retains a specific kind of prurience—one that takes a voyeuristic pleasure in witnessing physical exploitation and the imbalance of power between people. The intrusive prurience of the pornographic camera—witnessed in the opening scene of the film, with an unflattering depiction of the shooting of a pornography film—seems, in short, to abide in the family narrative that the film within the film takes as its subject.

The centrality of the pornographic camera in *Kazoku Cinema* parallels the more explicit prevalence of the trope in E J-yong's *Asako in Ruby Shoes* (*Suna-*

ebo, 2000), another of the earliest sanctioned Korea-Japan coproductions, and one carefully produced in accordance with cultural liberalization policies. The working title of the film was a provocative pun: *Uri-nation*, which plays both on the translation of *uri* from Korean to English as "our" (thus, "our nation") and on the English word *urination* and, in addition, evokes the male protagonist's name, U-in. This working title was eventually discarded, but the film nevertheless features a number of scenes that focus unblinkingly on urination and that foreground public toilets as a site of sexual voyeurism. This strange connection between fetish and nationalism, however, becomes most fully realized in the film's depiction of online pornography and, more specifically, in the unlikely relationship that flowers at the end of the film, in a scene of either coincidence or fate, between Aya, a young Japanese woman who performs for a pornography website, and U-in, a lonely young male Korean civil servant who becomes fascinated with her.

But as in *Kazoku Cinema*, sexual voyeurism becomes displaced into what becomes an intercultural preoccupation with the everyday lives of people separated by the various divisions and injunctions that have characterized Korea-Japan relations in the twentieth century. The pornography itself seems less about sexual stimulation and more about obtaining alternate views of daily life. And furthermore, what distracts characters from the banalities of daily life are ironically the same features of someone else's life across a national and cultural divide. So a common feature shared by these films is the way in which the pornographic, as a mode of tourist distraction, gets lodged into these new intercultural efforts, which function to interrupt a history of nationalist narratives that would contradict the new imperatives for transnational cooperation; pornography becomes an allegorical mode of historical reconciliation that foregrounds everyday banality. Intercultural appreciation of these prosaic scenes of ordinary life becomes recoded as a kind of muted pornographic titillation. Given all the careful policy making and government efforts to keep the process of postcolonial reconciliation on respectable terms, it is striking that collaborative filmmaking between Korea and Japan was resumed in such blatantly erotic terms. Though all pornographic images and intentions are rendered innocuous in the films, we still must ask why pornography is a central feature in these first coproductions. Why does pornography have an appeal in the context of reconciliation between two nations formerly in a colonial relationship? How does the pornographic intervene in postcolonial reconciliatory discourse?

Postcolonial Reconciliation and the Everyday

In the half-decade of postcolonial cultural reconciliation between South Korea and Japan—starting in 1998 and culminating with the 2002 FIFA World Cup—these first filmic coproductions, *Kazoku Cinema* and *Asako in Ruby Shoes*, focused on the display of quotidian culture (*saenghwal munhwa*) and family life. In its preoccupation with personal living environments and the interaction between people and objects within these spaces, for example, *Asako in Ruby Shoes* adopts a pseudoethnographic approach, juxtaposing the everyday feelings of isolation and loneliness in a pair of otherwise unremarkable characters. This interest in the quotidian reflects one of the goals of Korea's cultural liberalization policies: to familiarize young Koreans and Japanese with each other's private lives. As close neighbors, both governments believed, Koreans and Japanese should be able to relate to each other's daily existence; and the ability to visualize and observe how the other lived, government officials insisted and cultural critics believed, would lead to cross-cultural identification. Despite the fact that hallyu was not yet an explicit discourse when these films were produced, we see in them prototypes for the kind of affective work that the later films more explicitly perform.

The perception that Japan has impeded "genuine Asian reconciliation and regional communion" has long persisted in Korea, along with deep-rooted resentment over Japan's colonization of Korea and its reluctance to sufficiently redress the past.[5] After the 1997 Asian financial crisis, however, Korea adopted a detailed program based on a legislative proposal, drafted in 1994 by the Ministry of Culture and Sports, entitled "Three-Stage Liberalization Policy on Japanese Popular Culture" ("Ilbon Taejung Munhwa 3 Tan'gye Kaebang Taech'aek"), with the purpose of overcoming long-standing obstacles to its bilateral relationship with Japan (such as the ban on the import of Japanese popular culture) as a part of larger Asianization ambitions.[6] Although planned out in the early 1990s under the Kim Young-sam regime's discourse of globalization (or *segyehwa*, in Korean), under which Asianization was subsumed, Korea's "Japan Cultural Liberalization Program" really began to take shape and generate momentum amid the regional shift inward only after the Asian financial crisis of 1997–98 under newly elected President Kim Dae-jung (1997/8–2003). The 1998 joint declaration of cooperation was infused with a deep awareness of the connection between historical reconciliation and cultural commerce. The carefully worded statement contained Japan's "heartfelt apology" to Korea for its colonial past and included an endorsement of popular culture, among others, as a vehicle for reconciliatory efforts based in popular consensus.[7] As much of the world seemed to embrace a global, competitive economy in order to promote mutual prosperity, the Korean government realized that the ban on cultural exchanges with one country, while allowing other countries free access, ran counter to the international forces of market liberalization and failed to meet global standards.[8] The Korean government also sensed that economic security and progress in the Asia-Pacific region depended on cooperation between it and Japan. Thus, the deregulation of Japanese pop-culture imports was grounded in principles of caution and reciprocity, as part of a larger mutually beneficial cultural-exchange program between nations being advanced in northeast Asia.[9]

These policies reshaped cultural and economic exchange according to new transnational urgencies rather than to old historical resentments; as a result, they prepared a new generation for a cosmopolitanism that would draw from the material conditions of globalization, the kind of cosmopolitanism, described by Scott Lash and John Urry, that would presuppose "extensive patterns of mobility, a stance of openness to others and a willingness to take risks, and an ability to reflect upon and judge aesthetically between different natures, places and societies, both now and in the past."[10] The coproduced films I examine in this chapter indeed reflect what Kwame Anthony Appiah from a postcolonial stance has called a "rooted cosmopolitanism," which acknowledges the possibility of "cosmopolitan patriotism," in which people, both those who stay in their local culture and those who move away, "would accept the citizens' responsibility to nurture the culture and politics of their homes," while "taking pleasure from the presence of other, different, places that are home to other, different, people."[11]

As Korea engaged Japan, the government also began to see the potential in the relationship between culture and tourism, previously thought of as unrelated. Seeking to promote openness through culture, the period of cultural liberalization coincided with a "New Culture and Tourism Policy," implemented from 1998 to 2002, and a campaign called "Contents Korea Vision 21: The Promotion of Cultural Content Industries Development," which emphasized the significance of content-based cultural industries, along with a slew of white papers pushing policies such as the "Basic Plan for Tourism Development in 2001." Reflecting this change in ethos, the government arm of the tourism industry was moved in 1994 from the Ministry of Transportation to the Ministry of Culture and Sports, which shifted emphasis from building infrastructure to promoting cultural content. All of these efforts worked in concert

1.2 "Smile Campaign": "Fall 1998, at Kyŏngbok Palace with some Korean guy."
Asako in Ruby Shoes.

with similar initiatives elsewhere in Asia, including Japan's "Welcome Plan 21," Singapore's "Tourism 21: Vision of a Tourism Capital," and Hong Kong's "Hong Kong Tourism: Expanding the Horizons." The Japanese government also promoted tourism to South Korea in addition to cultural exchanges as part of upholding its commitment to the agreement of cooperation.[12]

Not surprisingly, the films that emerged in these years reflect this new interest in culture, tourism, and the transnational. In *Asako in Ruby Shoes*, Aya looks at an old photograph in which she is standing in front of Kyŏngbok Palace, in Seoul, next to U-in, the stranger with whom she begins a relationship at the very end of the film (fig. 1.2). U-in is wearing a sash that marks him as part of what was known as the "Smile Campaign," in which civil servants were instructed to smile in public places around Seoul in order to make foreign tourists feel more welcome. In the film, the first chance meeting between Aya and U-in, as documented by these tourist snapshots, anticipates their second, face-to-face encounter, in Alaska, where both happen to travel to in the final moments of the film.

While we can indeed read both *Kazoku Cinema* and *Asako in Ruby Shoes* as allegories of reconciliation and positive cultural exchange, our emphasis on tourism links this heady new era of cooperation to the darker history of postcolonial tourism between Japan and Korea.[13] In this respect, the incipient relationship between Aya and U-in at the end of *Asako in Ruby Shoes* uncannily reproduces the forms of tourism after Japan's liberalization of overseas travel in 1964, the normalization of Korea-Japan relations in 1965, and Korea's liberalization of overseas travel in 1989.[14] Japanese tourism to Korea from the mid-1960s until the late 1970s was predominantly male and centered around sex tourism, often combined with business meetings, enabled not just by the Japanese but also by their Korean hosts, in spite of opposition both by women's groups and the Korean government.[15] Known also as *kisaeng* (comparable to the Japanese *geisha*) tourism, this kind of sex tourism harkened back to colonial practices in *yojŏng* (establishments where kisaengs entertain; *ryotei* in Japanese) and epitomized the imperial consumption of the colony itself "as an object of desire."[16]

The reconciliatory films I will examine extricate tourism between Korea and Japan from the colonial and postcolonial legacy that defined the relationship between the two nations in the twentieth century.[17] But the persistence of the pornographic camera in these films, as they thematize travel within the context of changing attitudes about reconciliation, bind the contemporary flow of culture, capital, and tourists themselves precisely to the troubled history that these collaborations attempted to supersede. The abiding pornographic camera in popular cultural forms at this moment of political reconciliation preserves a strange element of exploitation in what professes to be a mutually beneficial relationship of collaboration and cooperation. Though these exploitative impulses are held in abeyance in these films, it is striking that the new modes of intercultural intimacy reproduce the scripts of colonial and postcolonial consumption in the very act of trying to move past them.

Open House

While Korea and Japan jointly hosted the 2002 World Cup, a pair of exhibitions were held simultaneously in Seoul and Osaka, aimed to foster Korean-Japanese intercultural identification by displaying the prosaic details of everyday life. The Seoul exhibition, entitled "Japan: Our Close Neighbor" and held at the National Folk Museum of Korea, was designed to make Japan understandable in intimate terms. The exhibition invited identification and empathy by emphasizing the most basic, everyday conditions of life in Japan, from the clothes people wore to the food they put on their tables to the houses in which they lived and slept (the exhibit was framed as a display of *uishikchu*, which roughly translates into "food, clothing, and housing"). Organizers hoped that such an exhibit would help lay to rest "old feelings" (*mukŭn kamchŏng*) regarding Japan, diminish a sense of "emotional remove" (*kŏrikam*), as well as encourage mutual understanding of each other's "interior depths of the mind to the very bottom of the lifestyle."[18]

The rhetoric of establishing newfound affective communality between the two nations, though posited as a radical departure from the past—here, "old feelings" are associated with "emotional remove" to imply that the old feelings were not positively intimate toward Japan—elides the critical role the cultural production of intimacy and amity played in consolidating colonial Japanese colonial power and in managing and shaping relations between the colonizer and colonized during Japanese rule; this was increasingly the case in the late 1930s under wartime mobilization. Though the particular nature of the intimacy being produced in the 1990s may differ, the tropes and forms utilized to culturally produce intimacy bear resemblances to the rhetoric of the colonial 1920s and 1930s. If we look at films from this period, such as Sŏ Kwang-je's *Military Train* (*Kunyongyŏlch'a*, 1938) or Hŏ Yŏng's (Japanese name Hinatsu Eitarō) *You and I* (*Kŭtaewa na/Kimi to boku*, 1941), visual elements legitimate and infer imperial assertions of corporeal, racial, and spiritual affinity as a way of controlling Korean colonial subjects under the rubric of the *naesŏn ilch'e* ("Japan and Korea as One Body," *naisen ittai* in Japanese) assimilation policy.[19] For instance, the "technointimacy" of *Military Train*, as Theodore Hughes argues, manipulates filmic montage and multiple temporalities, bringing together "the rationalized time of the train schedule and the machine and the affective, contingent temporality of love and attraction," in such a way that "the rational becomes immediate and intimate" in the film's narrativization of the desire to "volunteer" for the Imperial Japanese Army.[20] Later films also categorized as being in visual service to the rhetoric of "Japan and Korea as One Body," such as *You and I*, establish this "technointimacy" more literally as "colonial intimacy," in the sense demonstrated by Ann Laura Stoler, extending into the intimate formation of family and marriage as critical sites of imperial control.[21] In *You and I*, coproduced by the Chosŏn Army Press Section and Shōchiku Company with the support of the Chosŏn government-general, the focus on the interracial marriage between a Japanese woman and a Korean man is framed within a parallel narrative on "volunteer" military enlistment.[22] The narrative excess and sentimentality of melodrama narratives incorporated into political propaganda was later perceived as detrimental due to the "multiple codings, identifications, and interpretations" that the combination enabled, and it was gradually eliminated in the 1940s.[23] Thus, though the 2002 Seoul exhibition on Japan's intimate spaces and its emphasis on affective communality differed from post-1945 South Korean relations to Japan, it retread, in a way, pre-1945

1.3 *Grandmother's Kitchen.* The kitchen of a seventy-two-year-old citizen's home in Kyoto. Exhibited at the National Folk Museum of Korea in 2002.
Photo courtesy of Lee Mun-woong.

imaginings of the relationship between intimacy and familial spaces in fashioning Korea-Japan relations.

The Seoul-Osaka show included a wooden house, on loan from the National Museum of Ethnology in Osaka, Japan, of an "average" seventy-two-year-old woman living in Kyoto (fig. 1.3). Born in 1918 to a catering family in Kyoto, she had moved into the house in 1935 while attending a nearby girl's school and lived there for over sixty years. For a time, the house had also been a shop where she sold handmade crafts and ethnic arts. Significantly, any reference to the colonial period or postwar Korea-Japan relations was removed from this narrative. Instead, the Japanese curators in Osaka suggested that the house exuded an aura of the past, evoking the nostalgia of holiday visits to their own grandparents. They saw the meticulous collection, from personal furniture, toiletries, and bedding to kitchenware, as embodying the "frugality" (*alttŭlham* in Korean) traditionally imbued into Kyoto women from a young age.

To provide a more current complement to this older woman's home, the National Folk Museum of Korea also displayed the life and material possessions of

1.4 *Room.* A young female college student's one-room studio in Osaka.
Exhibited at the National Folk Museum of Korea in 2002.
Photo courtesy of Lee Mun-woong.

a Japanese female college student (fig. 1.4). Their choice emphasized a lifestyle that broke from traditional communal notions and hinted at contemporary isolation within a growing urban network. The college senior lived alone in a one-room studio rental in Osaka, exhibited in Seoul as *Room* in the section dedicated to *A Young Person's Life*. She attended classes in the morning and worked part-time in the afternoons and on weekends, spending a total of about twelve hours a day in the room, mostly watching TV or surfing the Internet. Around these two transported homes were a number of dioramas, contextualizing these lives by displaying various stages in life and representative features of those stages—everything from the figure of an average salary man to social sites like the wedding hall and the pachinko parlor, from youth trends and fashions to animation.

At the same time in Osaka, the National Museum of Ethnology transported the household contents of one entire multigenerational Korean family for the exhibit *Seoul Style 2002: Life As It Is with the Lee Family*. Every object in the Lee household was collected for the museum's permanent collection; a total of more than three thousand items like pay stubs, photos, toys, letters, and even underwear were put on display. From 2000 until the end of 2003, the museum also compiled an exhaustive written database and gathered video data of the Lee family at home. The exhibition and accompanying data started as a way for Japanese to a look at the home in contemporary Korean society, and evolved to become the subject of a long-term study of the ways humans navigate and interact with their objects at home.

Staged in the context of postcolonial reconciliation, both exhibitions prioritized the home, as well as the objects that one might find there, as a way to generate what Kathleen Stewart calls "ordinary affects," or "the varied, surging capacities to affect and to be affected that give everyday life the quality of a continual motion of relations, scenes, contingencies, and emergencies."[24] The observation of people's most banal activities within this most familiar space serves a popular ethnological purpose: challenging the audience's preconceived notions and then refamiliarizing us with the crucially mundane details of life (in these cases, a life that was devoid of any direct colonial references). Interestingly, these exhibitions, which were intended for locals and not tourists, were conceived of as acts of virtual tourism, a means of traveling without venturing too far from home. The museum brochure in Osaka asked, "Would you like to experience the ordinary life of our neighboring country, *something that we have never seen on our sightseeing trips?*"[25] And significantly, the objects of the potential tourist's interest are coded as intimate and personal, the intensely authentic artifacts of daily life that usually fall outside the tourist's view. Reminiscent of the cinema verité camera in *Kazoku Cinema*, this absorption of everyday life into a museum display exemplifies what Dean MacCannell calls "staged authenticity."[26] What the sightseer really wishes to see and believes to be more culturally authentic is that which is "backstage" or in the "back region," which in turn can be "set up," that is, also staged in anticipation of the tourist's desire to see beyond the tourist trappings. The kind of cultural exchange represented here in these exhibitions is premised on processes of museum display that show what is usually hidden from sight.

Both *Kazoku Cinema* and *Asako in Ruby Shoes* mirror this kind of ethnographic ethos, particularly as manifested in the museum's strategy of intimacy production.[27] But whereas the exhibitions posit intimacy as something interior, material, and spatially contained, these two films treat it as circulating through global networks. Like the museum exhibits, the films foreground homes, but in contrast to the exhibitions, which preserve the home as site of the intimate, and perhaps evidence of the new economic partnerships made possible by cultural liberalization, homes are dealt with in these films as property that can be inherited, sold, or refinanced, transactions which are presided over by the mother figures in each film, both of whom take a professional interest in real estate. Hayashi, the father in *Kazoku Cinema*, is bankrupt but holds the deed to the family home, which the mother conspires to sell to start a combination of real-estate office and coffee shop. Hayashi is secretly in debt and risks the bank seizing the house by refusing to sign over the deed, all the while pressing the family to come live with him as if there were no problems. In *Asako in Ruby Shoes*, Aya's mother is a realtor, and puts on the market the vacant house of her deceased grandmother (a former geisha), despite Aya's fondness for it; filled with photographs that document the world travels of her grandfather, the otherwise unoccupied home is Aya's retreat from the difficulties of her life. Similarly, in Korea, U-in lives alone in a largish apartment that he has inherited from his parents.

Both films, in short, worry over the question of what to do with old houses, and in so doing implicitly invoke a similar lingering question in an era of political reconciliation: what to do with old postcolonial discourse? The answer, in both cases, is a market solution. Freed at least temporarily from the baggage of historical resentment, these characters are invited, through the touristic imagination, to reengage each other's worlds and to seek new cultural encounters that leave the past behind. But even as films like *Kazoku Cinema* and *Asako in Ruby Shoes* seem to suggest new possibilities for cross-cultural engagement, they threaten to confuse political reconciliation with market liberalization. In these worlds, reconciliation becomes a kind of new mutual consumption, and the intimacy of these engagements constitutes a new commercial relationship built on the foundation of affective exchange.

Pornographic Travel

Like the 2002 exhibitions in Seoul and Osaka, both films hint that they are all-access ethnographies, but unlike the exhibits, the documentation in both films becomes tied to pornography. Just as with the standard template of a pornographic film, these films attempt to offer the viewer a privileged form of surveillance and to collapse the distinction between observer and observed such that we can imagine ourselves as present in the scene. Along with horror and melodrama, pornography is what Linda Williams describes as a "body genre," in which "the spectacle of a body caught in the grip of intense sensation or emotion" becomes the object of focus; in the process, these bodies-as-spectacle constitute both "the *moved* and the *moving*."[28] Foregrounding physical *movement* emphasizes the relationship between the pornographic choreography of bodies—in which they are moved around and repositioned according to the sex acts they perform—and the affective effect on the viewer, whose titillation or arousal constitute what is emotionally *moving* about these scenes. But in the films I discuss here, an additional element of movement emerges: the literal movement of travel. To be moved by the pornographic here involves less sexual stimulation, and more a kind of virtual tourism, in which the voyeur experiences through the pornographic body the sensations of a faraway place: no longer a voyeur, but, to use Giuliana Bruno's term, a voyageur.[29]

In *Kazoku Cinema* the direction of the diegetic director Katayama, a former pornographer, and the film's actual director, Park Chul-soo, become indistinguishable, exploiting the conventions of a film-within-a-film. We are first made aware of the split between the fictive director, who utilizes a self-proclaimed *matsuri*-style (which translates as "festival") of documentary film, and the actual director in the scene where the entire crew and family gather to start filming in Motomi's studio. The eldest daughter, Motomi, is not happy to find Katayama standing outside with his unhappy cast: Kiyoko, her mother, who now lives with a younger lover; Soji Hayashi, her father, who has just been fired after working for thirty years at a pachinko parlor; Yoko, her sister, the pornography actress and aspiring film producer; and Kazuki, her brother. They are all waiting for her to get home from work for a surprise birthday party. Ordering them to stay outside, she slips inside to clean up, hiding exactly the kind of personal effects that the 2002 museum exhibitions would make public. While the film crew waits, Park's camera is already positioned inside Motomi's place, and we see her scurrying around, cleaning up, removing traces of her boyfriend, throwing clothes and objects toward the camera, picking up her telephone messages. This camera is stationary and positioned low, as if hidden; later, from the same position, we see Katayama's camera crew set up their equipment and start filming.

It quickly becomes apparent that Katayama is being equally observed, not least for his increasing involvement with his actors. We see as many shots from Park's camera, filming Katayama while he films the family, as we see from Katayama's camera. Feeling restrained by the heavy camera, Katayama opts instead for a handheld model, which allows him to intrude more closely on the family. His interaction with them is reinforced when Kiyoko starts addressing the director behind the camera, including him in the family discussion in the scene while the camera continues to roll. Addressing the camera directly soon becomes routine, as if the director and his camera were members of the family. In one scene, Katayama captures the family in a shot taken through the bars of Motomi's window. By now, the mother has interiorized the director's gaze; she has given up on acting the role of perfect mother and instead has clear ideas about how she can create a spectacle and stage fights like the ones Katayama seems to like. Later, in a scene taken by Park, we see the director and his crew through the same barred window, doing the things families do when idling time away together. This self-reflexive doubling of the act of filmmaking thus constantly calls attention to the voyeuristic position of the audience, which is figured most prominently by Katayama himself, who as a habit inserts himself into the action in the scene without turning away the camera. And played by a Korean-Japanese actor, Katayama becomes a vehicle through which Korean audiences can immerse themselves within scenes that seem to typify Japanese everyday life, particularly in these scenes that take place within Japanese homes.

Rather than focusing on already hybrid Korean-Japanese figures, like the Hayashis, *Asako in Ruby Shoes* cuts back and forth between the mundane life of U-in, the civil servant in Seoul, and Aya, the depressed woman in Tokyo who works in the cyberporn business in order to fund a trip across the International Date Line, specifically to Alaska, where she hopes to commit suicide. Reflecting the reconciliatory spirit in which the film was made, it jostles object and subject positions in an act of repositioning, complicating the observed-observer relationship inherent in tourism's host-guest relationship; instead, both observer and observed are eventually conjoined and empowered, made capable of mutual observation.

U-in's life as a civil servant in Seoul is mundane, with days spent going door-to-door to inform people about proper garbage disposal and other neighborly acts, and then filing reports on these visits. His vocation is intimately tied with the most unbearably prosaic practices of everyday life. We follow him through the entirety of his mundane days, from when he wakes up in the morning until he goes to sleep at night. We watch him masturbating, eating, urinating, exercising, bathing, and taking the local bus to work (figs. 1.5–1.8). Essential to his routine are the hours before sleep, sitting at his desk in his apartment in Seoul logged onto a pornography site, which connects him to Aya, who listlessly performs as "Asako in Ruby Shoes" before a camera in the blue room of a studio in Tokyo. Aya insists on working only in the morning (which translates as *asako* in Japanese) and on always wearing her ruby-colored slippers (on which she spent all her savings so that she can wear them when she commits

1.5–1.8 U-in's mundane life in Seoul. *Asako in Ruby Shoes.*

suicide), prompting the director to name her "Asako in Ruby Shoes." U-in purchases twenty-four-hour access to Asako's "room," a blue screen set in a shabby studio, a dressed-up version of which he can see via webcam. Unlike the other women on the website, Aya's appeal lies in the fact that she is "boring," as the cyperporn director describes her, a characteristic that makes her seem very real. For much of her online life, it seems, she is scarcely doing anything. And though it lies outside the scope of the pornographic webcam, the film's account of her life is equally prosaic: she, her parents, and brother leave the house together every morning after breakfast, dutifully remembering to take their vitamins, and go their separate ways at the intersection, resigned to slog through their repetitive existences. For a while, she attends a cram school for students preparing for college entrance exams, but she eventually drops out. The live pornography site, in other words, is an extension of, rather than an exception to, the mundane essence of daily life.

U-in watches Asako through a Web interface that allows him the kind of controls generally reserved for a director; he can control the webcam in Asako's room, to zoom or to pan, to watch her from alternating angles. U-in's "cinematic" watching inflects our engagement with the film's actual director, E J-yong: his camera insists on giving us access not just to a narration about each character's stories, but more important, to a view of their daily routines, patterns, and preoccupations, the very minutiae which other films might deem unworthy of filming. These views of ordinary life, divided between Seoul and Tokyo, are the heart of the film, so that the very banality of life in these long-divided nations is seen through a pornographic voyeurism.

Significantly, the decidedly touristic sensibility of the cyberporn directors at the Tokyo studio, where fantasies are superimposed onto a blue room, magnify the connection here. Their website (www.winterwanderland.com) offers a number of famous tourist sites from around the world that the viewer can pick as backgrounds for the women and their performances. The viewer can thus be titillated while gazing at the Taj Mahal, the Arc de Triomphe, the Colosseum, or "serene and pure Alaska," which is the place that Aya picks for herself. The pornographic interface here thus becomes a means not of virtually experiencing another's body, but rather of experiencing another's place. Furthermore, these scenes of U-in endlessly watching Asako recast pornographic voyeurism as reciprocal. When U-in watches her, his gaze is captured in a full shot, his eyes darting back and forth as if he were reading the screen as he stares out at us. Then we see the screen, and then Asako on the screen, also in full shots, gazing back at us. The filmic viewer, who can see U-in, stands in for Aya, who cannot, in a kind of mediated shot/reverse-shot that both establishes a virtual relationship between cultural others and anticipates their eventual meeting in the final moments of the film.

In these sequences between U-in and Asako, mediated by the computer screen and the pornographic camera, the two eventually begin to connect. U-in begins to think of instructions that he would give Asako: "Stand up, come closer." We hear these unspoken instructions in a voiceover in Korean, but then they are uttered moments later in Japanese by the director in Tokyo, who is filming Asako as he looks through a flip-top video camera. The fact of mediation is imagined not as the dilution of U-in's voice, but as the fantasy of its successful transmission. The Japanese voiceover tells Asako to "stand up, walk . . . no, this way . . . this way . . ." The director thus becomes the conduit through which U-in moves beyond the computer screen and closer to Asako. Later in the film, when U-in goes online, he suddenly imagines that he, instead of she, is in the blue room, sitting on the couch under the window, temporarily inhabiting her space in her absence. That same night, Aya returns home and dreams that she is sleeping in the studio's blue room. In the dream she wakes up in the blue room and jumps out the window, later waking for real to realize she has fallen out of bed. The space of virtual and pornographic representation in these scenes thus becomes a separate, inhabitable space, removed and reappearing in the characters' minds and not just on screens, a space which they occupy outside of their otherwise fixed roles as observed and observer. To use Linda Williams's terms, they become moving sites through which they aim to move themselves, or alternately, inhabitable spaces of virtual intercultural intimacy.

Mediated Reconciliation

The tourist gaze, according to John Urry, is like the Foucauldian panoptic gaze, in the sense that the nature of the tourist gaze is also "systematic and regularized," socially organized and authorized by certain discourses, socialities, and practices; such a gaze is presumed to "implicate both the *gazer* and the *gazee* in an ongoing and systematic set of social and physical relations."[30] The tourist, like Foucault's medic who gazes upon the patient from a position of power, imposes certain ideological understandings onto the places and people that he sees; the culture of the destination is, by definition, the Other, and the tourist purposefully gazes from a totalizing and appropriating position of power that the tourist perceives as granted by the destination's place or people.[31] In Foucault's panopticon, the inmates interiorize the gaze to the point of becoming their own overseer, both surveyor and surveyed exercising surveillance "over, and against" oneself.[32] Carol Crawshaw and Urry have shown that tourism provokes similar regimes of panoptic surveillance. Implied surveillance intrudes on the tourist area, resulting in the processes of panoptic interiorization of the tourist's gaze.[33] Jonathan Crary has argued, however, against Foucault's opposition of surveillance and spectacle, suggesting that Foucault overlooks how the effects of the two regimes of power can coincide because he "neglects the new forms by which vision itself became a kind of discipline or mode of work."[34] More specifically, in his revaluation of vision, Crary shows how the special place occupied by the sense of touch in classical theories of vision in the seventeenth and eighteenth centuries is usurped by the sense of sight in the nineteenth century.

> The loss of touch as a conceptual component of vision meant the unloosening of the eye from the network of referentiality incarnated in tactility and its subjective relation to perceived space. This autonomization of sight, occurring in many different domains, was a historical condition for the rebuilding of an observer fitted for the tasks of "spectacular" consumption. Not only did the empirical isolation of vision allow its quantification and homogenization but it also enabled the new objects of vision (whether commodities, photographs, or the act of perception itself) to assume a mystified and abstract identity, sundered from any relation to the observer's position within a cognitively unified field.[35]

So, for Crary, the later sense of sight supplants an earlier sense of touch within the frame of a more commoditized market context, both usurping its function and rendering archaic the cognitive operations that tactility as an aspect of vision implies.

Urry's notion of the tourist gaze and Jonathan Crary's revaluation of the distinction between physical touch and abstracted sight within questions of surveillance and spectacle hold particularly important implications for cinemas of reconciliation. The use of the pornographic camera in *Kazoku Cinema* and *Asako in Ruby Shoes* calls attention precisely to the way in which spectacular voyeurism subsumes desires and fantasies that would otherwise foreground tactility. Both films use the mediation of pornography as a way to align the tourist gaze, an appropriating gaze that depends on power and surveillance, with the perspective of the pornographic audience, which seeks an intimacy modeled on physical contact. But at the same time, this rather idealistic and somewhat fantastical pairing belies an awareness of its own shortcomings that mitigate the larger utopian aspirations of these collaborative films. Though modeled on touch, the forms of intimacy that follow from spectatorship are limited.

Kazoku Cinema explicitly links tourism and pornography. The opening scene of the film, in which we watch a rough pornography film being shot, resolves into a kind of refrain toward the end of the film, which consists of a sequence of scenes about the act of watching; in the final scene we see the family in a darkened theater, viewing the film that they have made together. These later scenes draw a parallel between the pornographic image and ordinary travel images (from their camping trip to Beppu), and displace affects associated with the former onto the latter. The blue-toned images of Yoko's breasts in the pornographic film, pressed against a pane of glass as she is penetrated from behind, are echoed in the first of these later scenes in the similarly blue-toned images of the family's camping trip in Beppu, a hot springs (*onsen* in Japanese) destination. More specifically, it begins with a close-up of Motomi and her brother Kazuki in the rain, holding still under an umbrella, facing away from their anguished mother as she criticizes the father for his stubborn refusal to sign over the deed to the house, in spite of his impending bankruptcy. Hearing the mother collapse, we see Yoko run to her, followed by Kazuki, but not Motomi, who remains stoic underneath the umbrella, her back turned to the scene behind her. Her mother urges the director to turn off the camera and reasons, "Making this movie is useless. Stop it." Of course the director ignores the request because the pain of this family is precisely that which he wishes to capture on film. Not unlike Yoko's expression of pain in the film's opening pornographic scene, the shared pain of the Hayashis here becomes the affective payoff for the proximity toward which the film aspires. Katayama's desire for affect pushes toward melodrama—another of Williams's "body genres"—in scenes like this, provoking a visceral emotional identification analogous to the sexual titillation invited by explicit pornography. The similarity in positioning of Motomi, with her back toward the rest of her family, and Yoko, with her back toward her sexual partner, enforces this connection and reminds us that the intimacy provoked in both the pornographic film and the family film is inextricable from exploitation.

A few scenes later, we see the same exact scene, this time projected in the theater where the family has gathered to view the film—without the father, who has abandoned them. If the opening scene of *Kazoku Cinema* interpellates the film audience into a disconcerting position of voyeurism, then this closing mise en abyme literalizes this voyeuristic discomfort by installing the members of the filmed family in the audience, watching the film just as we do. The family members are uneasy about the way that they have been portrayed and disconcerted about having revealed so much of their personal suffering. The ending collapses the boundary between the film viewer and the filmed subject, because of course the audience and the actors are one and the same. But more important is the way that intimacy functions across all body genres, in pornography and melodrama alike: the blurring of the line between film and audience that is blatantly staged here reflects the affective identification such films encourage; the audience feels along with the characters, as if the characters' feelings were their own. To further emphasize this point, after focusing on the family and their reactions to the film, we see that the film crew is still in fact filming. They have been filming all along during the screening and continue to do so as the family leaves the theater. The film's audience is therefore implicated in the affective logics of the film as a matter of structure. The conceit here is not just that the film audience within the film, the Hayashi family, *represents* the audience of *Kazoku Cinema*, but that the film's extradiegetic audience is somehow identical with the Hayashis. By collapsing boundaries between fact and fiction, what's onstage and what's backstage, observer and observed, mediated image and lived experience, the film captures our basic need for something beyond just watching and being watched. Particularly in these films, which double as reconciliation efforts, the director seems to strive for something beyond a mere representation of the Other, something like a sense of profoundly implicated fates.

The double position of the Hayashis, as both viewer and viewed, makes it possible to be both an external viewer of the scene and simultaneously immersed in that scene. That dual position is also prominent in *Asako in Ruby Shoes*, which begins with a tight shot of a calendar image depicting an Alaskan landscape and ends with a shot of U-in and Aya, together in Alaska, looking at the real thing (figs. 1.9–1.13). Standing side-by-side before a beautiful backdrop of forests and mountains, U-in drapes his jacket over Aya's shoulder, and in simultaneous voiceovers, one in Korean and the other in Japanese, both say "This is how our story began." In this third location, neither Korea nor Japan, they mutually take advantage of the tourist gaze, a possibility previously hinted at but ultimately denied. These two first "met" through the medium of pornography, a medium that seems to promise a way to reconcile the breach between visuality and tangibility. But ultimately, of course, pornography cannot fulfill

1.9–1.13 From viewed to viewing together in Alaska. *Asako in Ruby Shoes.*

that promise, cannot offer actual intimacy. Instead, it is tourism that finally delivers the tactile authenticity that pornography offers only in the form of mediated fantasy. Tourism in the film becomes then a realization of the essential fantasy of pornography, an intimacy shared by both the filmic and tourist gaze that Rhona Jackson describes as "predicated on the desire to look, and to possess (by appropriation) what is looked at," and to "pursue a closer relationship."[36] By demonstrating how the tourist and filmic gazes work together, Jackson emphasizes the *feelings* encountered in touristic experiences, which depend on the connection between representation and actual proximity. Both in Jackson's account and in *Asako in Ruby Shoes*, mediated image and lived experience come to coincide. The pornographic camera in *Asako in Ruby Shoes* thus expresses a yearning to restore the sense of touch to visuality.

The film foreshadows the actual contact at the film's ending in an earlier cross-cut scene on two subways: we see U-in on a subway headed for Naebang station in Seoul cross-cut with shots of Aya waiting on a subway platform in Tokyo. The sequence is edited in a way that makes it appear as though U-in is in the train that slows into the station where Aya is waiting. As U-in steps off the train, he bumps in a woman who looks like Aya from the back. He softly exclaims "Aya!" (a pun, since her name in Korean means "ouch"). The camera pauses on Aya's face, which registers recognition, as if she had heard her name called, and then the scene cuts back to U-in, who stops and turns back to look through the windows of the subway car's doors. Despite the clear markers of difference in the two settings—the signage in the respective trains is in different languages, for example—the shot/reverse-shot convention of the scene suggests a chance encounter, even though we as the viewer know rationally that such an encounter is impossible. As they "pass" each other, getting on and off their respective trains and then turning around, we see U-in looking toward us from the other side of the closed glass door, and then we see Aya doing the same. They cannot be looking at each other because they are not in the same place. Indeed, the scene registers a kind of uncanny fantasy. Yet the "reality" of fantasy is sustained by the film's end, as their actual meeting occurs by coincidence when both decide to fly to Alaska—and even more improbably, decide to take the same airplane. Fantasy does not so much dissipate at the end of the film, with the beginning of the "real" relationship, so much as it demonstrates, as it does in the subway scene, that the persistence of the fictive is just as likely in relations of physical as it is in virtual ones.

Tourism is no less fantastical than pornography despite the physical presence fundamental to touristic experience, which ultimately is one that seeks to hide the presence of its mediating apparatuses. So despite their simultaneous intercultural, interlingual assertion that the end of the film constitutes a new beginning for their real lives together (as opposed to their earlier fantastical, pornographic engagements), the end of the film seems to signal simply the beginning of another fiction rather than fiction's end. By extension, the new cooperation between Korea and Japan embodied here by the touristic vision of this interethnic couple at the beginning of a romance, doesn't actually represent the end of postcolonial tensions through an actual resolution of weighty historical burdens, but rather a more provisional form of reconciliation, based on shared interests and attuned to the possibilities of market liberalization. Although the sense of a new beginning is inevitably one of possibility, the clear unease between U-in and Aya at the end of the film suggests that possibility and optimism are more coincidental than coterminous.

False Endings

Given this anxiety about the end of one era and the beginnings of another, perhaps it is not surprising that *Kazoku Cinema* and *Asako in Ruby Shoes* contain numerous moments where the films seem momentarily to end, but instead continue on. These moments are signaled by a fade to a black screen, often in the middle of a scene, and by deceptive freeze frames. Reflecting a political moment in which new avenues to economic prosperity seem to outweigh the latent hostilities of the past, the ambiguous moments in these films call into question the finality of closure—the illusion of resolution—representing this hesitation in formal terms. Just as the prevalence of freeze frames in Korean cinema under the military regimes of the 1980s and early 1990s was, as Soyoung Kim has argued, a cinematic articulation of a broader "sense of entrapment, immobility, eternal suspension, like the experience of spectators who live with the history of colonization, partition, and an intensive concentration of industrial capitalist development," the use of these false endings index the political and economic conditions of the late 1990s.[37] These false endings reflect what Richard Neupert has called an "open story" film, in which in contrast to the tighter "closed story" film typical of classical Hollywood, "the *told* is not resolved but the *telling* is concluded."[38]

Kazoku Cinema begins and ends with moments of heightened self-consciousness about its own medium that troubles the boundaries of its own diegesis, and accordingly it is never quite clear when the scenes of the film within the film begin and end. In fact, it is only the opening scene of pornographic filming in which such distinctions are clear: the beginning of the scene is marked by the direction to roll film and the clapper indicating the scene number, and the end indicated by the male actor who peeks out from behind Yoko and signals "okay" with his fingers and calls it a wrap. In contrast, the moments lacking such distinctions are far more numerous. One very explicit false ending occurs at Mr. Hayashi's house, where the father cooks an elaborate meal. Compared to the cluttered mess of Motomi's studio, the house is virtually empty and the rooms lack furniture, and as resistant as the family was to settling their bitter past in Motomi's house, here they are open about their feelings and pain. While Kiyoko sits on the toilet, massaging her hurting breast and talking on her cell phone about negotiating a way to mortgage the house, the father assembles the children at the traditional Japanese table over sushi and sashimi and formally seizes the opportunity to ask for his children's forgiveness. At a later opportune moment, when Kiyoko comes to the table, he apologizes to his wife and begs for her forgiveness. With resolution of the family drama seemingly imminent, Yoko freaks out at the prospect of premature reconciliation and thus an early end to the film. Here, appropriately, the screen goes black, but only temporarily. The diegetic reason offered is that the roll of film has come to an end, though the audience can still hear the sounds in the room; in the darkness the food in the oven starts burning, and chaos ensues. When a new roll of film is finally inserted, things settle down and we see the family reassembled around a table, calmly eating fruit, but this time they sit at a different, raised, Western table. So the film does not so much resume after the break as much as it begins anew with a new situation and setting, which emerge at precisely the moment when reconciliatory closure threatens to end the narrative.

Most clearly, the end of the film troubles the possibility of clear and clean endings. Not only does the filming continue even after the diegetic film stops playing (on the screen in the theater where the Hayashis are watching), the film crew follows the family out into the lobby of the theater with their cameras still rolling, ignoring the mother's plea to "kill the camera." The camera continues to roll, shooting the faces of the family in close-up even as credits roll over them, until finally, we see three successive shots of the family standing motionless looking back at the camera, the last of which, of the mother and Motomi, freezes and then fades to black.

In *Asako in Ruby Shoes*, Aya yearns for the ultimate form of closure. As she describes early in the film, and then attempts unsuccessfully later, she wishes to die by holding her breath (her preferred, if naïve, mode of suicide) while flying above the International Date Line, a place that is "neither yesterday, today nor tomorrow." Her actions throughout the film are motivated by anticipation of this moment of death, and when we finally see her holding her breath in the plane near the end of the film, the screen blacks out, suggesting that she has succeeded. But after a long beat, the image of Aya returns. She begins to cry, and draws the attention of U-in, who is sitting on the far side of the plane. Though he does not yet recognize her, this moment marks the first time he has seen her without a screen in between. Another fade to black. Then we see them both gazing out the window at the airport; they glance sidelong at each other before she walks away. His moment of recognition—he whispers, "Asako!"—is captured in a freeze frame with her behind him. The scene then resumes as he chases after her. He runs, the frame freezes again, then fades again to black, then opens again on a road seen through a windshield, from the point of view of the passengers in the front seat—a repetition of the film's opening sequence, but with a crucial difference. There is yet another fade to black, this time followed by a shot of snow-capped mountains over the tree line of a forest, a shot that U-in and Aya soon enter, to enjoy the vista. As we ride in the car with them, we hear a voiceover from Aya and then U-in, each in different languages, explaining that this is how their story begins. The film fades to black one last time, and it is only when the credits start to roll that we can be confident the film has indeed ended.

In the context of cultural liberalization and cooperation, these false endings signal both the implicit desires of these policies as well as the unspoken fears that form their limits. If these governments aspire toward flourishing of interaction and mutual production, then the falseness of these many would-be endings looks backward to that which remains unresolved about the past, that which remains elided instead of determined. The dissolution of any resolute closure, while drawing attention to the possibility of closure, also suggests the impossibility of a final stability; hesitations and doubts continue to linger, even in these moments of apparent of cooperation and good will, unable to be contained by any simple ending.

Conclusion

The tourist imagination that drives both *Kazoku Cinema* and *Asako in Ruby Shoes* toward their provisional forms of closure thus reflects both the efforts at regional conflict resolution as well as the significant but invisible tensions that remain once that work has been deemed complete. Perhaps then, taking the final joint assertion of *Asako in Ruby Shoes* seriously—that this is how the story begins—the real content of these films is that which only begins to emerge in their dying moments. The era's new East Asian cooperative arrangements only work by suppressing, or at least containing, the region's history of conflict; against this instinct of avoidance, these films confront the tourist imagination with the limits of its own, often utopian, aspirations. These limits are made clear by coupling the desires and premises of the tourist with those of pornography, a disturbing mimicry of the history of postcolonial sex tourism.[39] What emerges from this thought experiment is an affective sense of unease that bleeds out of otherwise optimistic formulations. Though we appreciate the intercultural sentiment in the final line of *Asako in Ruby Shoes*, voiced at the same time in different languages, we also must wonder whether or not Aya and U-in can ultimately speak a shared language. In hindsight, the cultural initiatives that enabled bilateral cooperation between the Korean and Japanese film industries after decades of restrictions were pivotal in ushering in a new era of high-budget, multilateral, interregional coproductions, and reveal how cultural tourism came to play a role in the Korean film industry's larger East Asian ambitions.

Intimacy in these films, the absence of which is made all the more palpable by the profound loneliness pervading the characters, is reestablished through joint spectatorship (as in *Kazoku Cinema*) or through a simultaneous voiceover (as in *Asako in Ruby Shoes*). In a sense, the bookended framing of these endings that signal new beginnings and resolution by modifying the opening shots is not unlike the joint declaration of the dawning of a "new history" and "cultural sharing" made by Kim Dae-jung and Keizo Obuchi. As Alexis Dudden has suggested, the rhetoric and rubric of "cultural sharing" used in the joint declaration echoed Japan's "cultural rule" in colonial Korea in the 1920s, when official policy on cultural activities was softened to pacify and divert anticolonial protests following the 1 March 1919 Independence Movement. But these resonances with the colonial past were quietly glossed over, both by the government leaders as well as the public press, in light of prospects of military and business cooperation.[40] The halting endings of these films register uncertainty about the commensurability of new beginnings and the nature of the permitted intimacy.

If the absence of any explicit reference to hallyu in these reconciliatory films despite their production and release during what are regarded as the seminal years of hallyu now seems conspicuous, it alerts us to how disconnected cultural tourism as promoted by the two governments seemed to be from what actually drove people to travel. In a scene in *Asako in Ruby Shoes*, U-in is watching a Korean television show that seeks to "find out what young Japanese are like these days." In its motive, the program is in line with the "people-to-people" on an everyday level thematic being advocated at the time in Korea-Japan cultural exchange. We see Rie, Aya's friend who used to work as a dancer in a bar, appear on the show as an example of a random Japanese young person. Asked where she would like to go to spend the impending millennium's eve, 31 December 1999, she replies "Egypt," which is where she has always dreamed of going. Like U-in's fantasies of traveling to Alaska, the "young people" staged in the film and within the film itself desire to travel beyond Asia, beyond Korea and Japan. For Rie, it is because Egypt "just seems mysterious," and also because "the guys are so gorgeous there." Travel to South Korea, which Rie suggests when she realizes she is on a Korean show, brings to mind nothing more than "skin exfoliation" spa packages, in which Japanese travel to Korea to get their dead skin cells sloughed off their bodies. U-in's brother-in-law abruptly changes the channel to a documentary on hyenas in the wild, but his reaction to this segment is revealing of how it is not registered or interpreted as hallyu. In later years, such statements are read as an indication of hallyu's increasing popularity and reach. If the political desire is for intimacy to grow between the lonely, isolated young people of Korea and Japan through cultural tourism and on an everyday level, the progression of these reconciliatory films from 1998–2000 make apparent that in order for this to occur, a change in the underlying motivations for travel must occur, from motivations associated with exoticism, fetishism, and escape to those that have to do with more genuine, or at least less historically determined, forms of intimacy.

As I suggest in the following chapter, films like Hur Jin-ho's 2005 *April Snow* (following on the huge success of the television drama *Winter Sonata*, a cornerstone of the hallyu phenomenon) begin to register how film goes from merely *telling* about the desire for intimacy through travel to *showing* how affective labor has come to work in the relation between visual image and spectator to give rise to alternative sources of intimate feelings, namely through the displacement of affective images onto affective sites. It is this kind of self-reflexivity regarding the growing phenomenon of hallyu at the time that constitutes what I am calling hallyu cinema. The aforementioned travel-show segment is telling, because just prior to this scene, U-in has just been rudely interrupted from accessing Asako on the pornography site www.winterwanderland.com by his young niece, who appears out of nowhere and shocks him by touching his bare thigh; as his attention turns to the television show, we see Aya behind Rie with her back partially turned to the screen. This diegetic, intertextual displacement from one medium to another and the shift from the pornographic image to travel image linked by the shock of touch lack causality because, like the "Smile Campaign" photo at Kyŏngbok Palace dating back to 1998, they refuse a recognition of connections. In *April Snow* establishing connections between travel, feelings, and places become crucial, not just within the film but also in its reception. And the thwarted possibility of intimacy in *Asako in Ruby Shoes* and *Kazoku Cinema* become more fully realized in the affective tourism spurred in Hur Jin-ho's films. If pornography functioned in the earlier films as a model of intercultural intimacy that might redress historical tension, then affective tourism in these later films becomes a means of constructing a more radically conjoined intercultural sensorium that might give rise to connections, not just at the level of individual interaction, but more broadly in terms of a larger body politic based on the transnational consumption of cultural products.

2. AFFECTIVE SITES

Hur Jin-ho's *April Snow* and *One Fine Spring Day*

2.1 Signpost for *April Snow* filming locations in the city
of Samch'ŏk. Photo by author.

In the last scene of Hur Jin-ho's *April Snow* (*Oech'ul*, 2005), In-su and Sŏ-yŏng, one of the two adulterous couples at the heart of the film, are driving together into an improbable April snowstorm. The two have started an illicit affair of their own, after their cheating spouses got into a car accident and each fell into a coma. At this point in the film, they haven't seen each other for several months, separated in order to deal with the particular complexities of their lives: In-su, to settle his relationship with his wife, who has reawakened from her coma, and Sŏ-yŏng, to move past the death of her husband. As they drive, Sŏ-yŏng asks, "Where are we going?," and In-su replies, "Where should we go?"—an echo of their conversation at the beach café just prior to their first hotel tryst: "What shall we do?" "What do you want to do?"

Though these reticent characters, who only met because their respective spouses were themselves having an affair, make a decisive choice to stay together even amid their respective familial upheaval, they remain uncertain at the end of the film about what to do or where to go together. In this last scene, the point-of-view shot we see is from Sŏ-yŏng's perspective in the passenger's seat, as the camera looks out onto the pale landscape passing by and then toward the road in front. The scene closes with the same frame that opens the film, in which In-su drives through a similar snowstorm in the dark after getting the phone call notifying him that his wife has been in a car accident. The contrasting lighting in these two road scenes, from darkness to a muted light, suggests an emotion change—from despair to guarded hope, perhaps, and from solitude to incipient companionship. But the similarity between the two scenes reminds us that when their cheating spouses got into their accident, the weather—and their circumstances—were not all too different.

Echoing the framing device of *Asako in Ruby Shoes*, *April Snow* uses these shots of the road and surrounding scenery from the car passenger's point of view in order to make a subtle suggestion about filmic travel (figs. 2.2–2.3). As the film unfolds, the film itself becomes the space of travel. In this particular brand of travel, the actual geography is not all that important; it seems somewhat arbitrary in *Asako in Ruby Shoes* (Alaska) and uncertain in *April Snow* (where shall we go?). However, the exceptional spaces depicted on-screen (Alaskan mountains, snowy roads) are not so much particular destinations as they are emblems of suspended time; these scenes invite us, the audience, to occupy the same viewing position of the characters, looking at the scenery or the road ahead, as if to indicate not a representation of specific travel, but a

2.2 "This is how our story began."
The road at the end of *Asako in Ruby Shoes*.

2.3 "Where should we go?" The road at the end of *April Snow*.

more overarching structural connection between the filmic medium and travel in general. In addition, implicit in In-su and Sŏ-yŏng's uncertainty about where to go, once they commit to stay together, is a suggestion about the link between travel and intimacy; their as-yet-undecided destination represents their as-yet-undetermined intimate relationship. And since travel and filmic form have already been strongly associated, the end of the film implies the formation of a tripartite assemblage: travel—film—intimacy. In this context, the unprecedented tourism of predominantly Japanese tourists to *April Snow*'s film locations on the eastern coast of Korea in the years following the film's 2005 release seems to have been foreshadowed in the film's self-reflexive awareness of its own implicit invitations to what I call affective tourism, that is, tourism in which travelers seek not just the experience of a place, but also the feelings associated with it, which are in this case inspired by filmic representation.

Hur Jin-ho's *April Snow* is often considered a vehicle for actor Bae Yong-joon, designed to extend the popularity he gained through the television drama *Winter Sonata* (2002), a huge hallyu phenomenon that was extremely popular in Japan. That same fan base presumably was a primary reason that the subsequent filming locations for *April Snow* became popular tourist destinations. Yet considered alongside the reconciliation films *Kazoku Cinema* and *Asako in Ruby Shoes*, which paired the themes of travel and intimacy, *April Snow*'s conscious rumination on the relationship between image, corporeality, and intimacy, all under the umbrella of affective tourism, suggests that the film itself fosters an attraction to travel as part of its own logic. It is a film, in short, that embeds tourist experiences within the filmic experience, such that the ensuing literal tourism to the locations where the film was shot seems like a natural extension of the initial experience of watching the film. I therefore examine *April Snow* alongside its film locations to argue that the film both portrays and encourages an affective relationship between visual image and its consumer. Furthermore, this relationship between the cinematic image and tourism confuses filmic and tourist geographies such that the destinations of tourism might be understood not as literal places, but as locatable within filmic imaginaries. The underlying conceit of the film tourism inspired by the film, as imagined by the organizers of tour sites, is that tourists were to imagine themselves not so much as traveling from Japan to Korea as they were to imagine themselves traveling into the film itself.

The local, regional governments in Korea invested heavily in this period to entice film and television dramas to film in their provinces. Between 2000 and 2005, about thirty-one film sets were built in twenty-six different cities in the rural counties, with government investment totaling forty-nine billion Korean won (approximately fifty-two million U.S. dollars).[1] The primary reason for building these sets was tourism income, the hope of a stream of tourists that would continue long after the film was released.[2] Many of the provinces benefited from the increasing popularity of tourism induced by films and television dramas by both foreign and domestic tourists. That increase was especially important because of a dismaying decline in tourists from other countries in these opening years of the twenty-first century, due to fear of SARS and the uncertainty caused both by the Iraq War and the ongoing North Korean nuclear controversy. The Korean tourism industry, aided by the government, had by 2001 noticed the unexpected popularity of hallyu across

Asia, and launched an aggressive campaign to exploit it. By March 2005, when Japan reignited latent postcolonial hostilities by asserting territorial claims over the uninhabitable island of Takeshima (known to Koreans as Tokto), the unforeseen success of hallyu tourism to Korea, in particular to Kangwŏn Province, was at an all-time high. The controversy over the empty island, and the attendant nationalism it provoked on both sides, threatened to stall the remarkable momentum of reconciliation between the two countries. Starting in 1997, the tourism industries in both countries had worked together to sponsor a range of programs to encourage tourism, such as the "Visit Korea-Japan Year," the "Visit Kangwŏn Province Year," and the "Korean Wave Tourism Campaign." And at first glance, it would appear that it did.

As many feared, the various political controversies seemed to be dampening travel. Yet that initial impression hid an interesting detail. As the Korean Tourism Organization would surprisingly report in its *2005 White Papers*, released at the end of the year, the number of inbound tourists reached 6 million.[3] An estimated 1.2 million of those were tourists whose prime destinations were film sets, up from the 1.12 million recorded in 2004.[4] Figures for particular locations in Kangwŏn Province were even more astonishing. Tourism to the city of Samch'ŏk, for example, where *April Snow* was filmed, recorded an unprecedented 298.9 percent increase in 2005, compared to the year prior. Kangwŏn Province as a whole recorded a 10.2 percent increase in foreign tourists from the previous year. And it also saw a 10.4 percent hike in domestic tourists, bolstered by the continually growing popularity of themed tour destinations in general, of which film tourism was the most popular, in contrast to the decline or stagnancy seen at the usual tourist destinations such as beach resorts.[5] Hostile rhetoric notwithstanding, regional political tensions did little to curb the enthusiasm of film tourists.

These emerging intersections between film and the tourism it inspires were part of an effort to create new regional "structures of feeling" with the potential to diffuse historical political tensions and thus to help construct a new Asian order based on collaboration and cooperation. If *Asako in Ruby Shoes* offered Alaska as a neutral site of reconciliation—neither Korean nor Japanese, unfettered by the colonial past—*April Snow* offers the imaginary space of the film itself, which becomes denationalized and characterized instead by affective identification. As a highly concentrated point of attraction for tourists from all over East Asia, and closely associated with hallyu and the circulation of Korean popular culture throughout Asia, the film locations in Kangwŏn Province, I believe, function as a stand-in for all of East Asia within

Korea. In this context, even domestic Korean tourism to these sites can also be seen as partaking in a form of a regionalized East Asian experience. The continued and heightened appeal of these film sites, in spite of contradicting political tensions, requires that we move beyond the interests of tourism institutions and their marketing strategies, and identify the critical underlying factors that make these sites inspire travel regardless of the political climate.

Here I will focus on the Korean director Hur Jin-ho's *April Snow* (*Oech'ul*, 2005), a filmic melodrama which was hugely popular in East Asia. Starring Bae Yong-joon and Son Ye-jin, it was filmed in the city of Samch'ŏk, also a popular coastal tourist destination in Kangwŏn Province, and as mentioned, tells the story of the attraction between a man and a woman who meet at a local hospital where their adulterous spouses lie comatose after a car accident while in Kangwŏn Province for an illicit weekend together.

Examples of a later and now highly self-conscious hallyu cinema, Hur's melodramas inspire tourism by privileging *affect* over effect and *bodies* over words. I thus treat film here not just as "the manifestation of fixed structures," in the words of the cultural geographer and film scholar Giuliana Bruno, but as "an expression of restless energies" involving "the position and movement of body in space," and in which the spectator is seen not merely as a "*voyeur*, but a *voy(ag)eur*."[6] In *April Snow* the film sites encourage film tourists to relive the intense, almost involuntary, embodied affective experience of watching the films by inhabiting places that were previously only seen. The result is that at such film sites, the tourist gaze becomes a kind of belated filmic gaze. Inspired to travel to these locations because of the film, the tourist travels as if he or she were in the film.[7] The films I discuss, as well as their corresponding sites, attempt to *move* the film spectator-cum-tourist in both senses of the word, emotionally and physically, beyond conventional spaces of cinema spectatorship into the actual spaces of the film's making, consequently collapsing the distinctions between filmic and tourist gaze, filmic and tourist experience.[8]

Affect, Body, and Tourism

Hallyu star Bae Yong-joon, known to his Japanese fans as "Yonsama," recognized early the affective role of hallyu and tourism in Asia and its potential during times of political conflict. When pressed by irate local critics to declare Korea's sovereignty over Tokto in March 2005, Bae, at the time filming *April Snow* in Samch'ŏk, released a statement on his website.

Tokto is Korean territory, which I think calls all the more for a rational response. There is also a need to consider from a remove what actually gets changed as a result of arguing about the territorial rights over Tokto, and whether this contributes to finding a real solution. It is my earnest desire that people from both countries do not get hurt by letting their *feelings* [*kamchŏng*, 感動] get involved, thus allowing relations to worsen. . . . If there is a role for me, I wonder if it is not in connecting the *hearts* [*maŭm*] and minds of an Asian family, rather than drawing territorial lines with mere words. As it has been up to now, my heart's [*maŭm*] desire to accomplish something good with our family in Asia remains unchanged. Therefore, I will try to return the undeserved love I have received thus far as an even greater love.[9]

In negotiating this tense issue, Bae resorted to the discourse of emotion to appease his Korean critics, making a telling distinction between "feeling" and "heart." *Kamchŏng*, which roughly translates as "feeling," has in Korean negative connotations of irrationality, and is often used to describe the kind of emotional turmoil that threatens political reconciliation. Fierce forms of nationalism are associated with this sentiment. The bodily heart (*maŭm*), however, is perceived as distinct from nationalist sentiment and capable of overcoming political relations and territorial claims. Bae's role, as he sees it, as a Korean hallyu star and as a promoter of tourist attractions, is to connect to hearts all over Asia.

In Korean film tourism, emotion is a primary motivator. Emotion (*kamtong*, 感動) is distinguished from feeling (*kamchŏng*, 感情) and heart (*maŭm*), in that it entails the ability to move emotionally or be moved, by acting upon, or impinging upon another body. As such, "affect" might be a better translation than "emotion" for *kamtong*, as a means to describe what can be elicited by watching a film. Kim Sun-kŭn's popular guide, *Screen Tours*, published in 2002 at the ascent of the hallyu phenomenon, gives us a good sense of how the term underlies film tourism. According to Kim, kamchŏng differs from person to person at most of the places that tourists go. In contrast, literary, filmic, dramatic, and historical memorial sites enable tourists to remember how they were moved when they encountered the original piece of art or learned about the historical moment. The emotion (*kamtong*) felt at these sites "is a kind of 'organized emotion,' thus making literary, film and drama tour destinations different from other tourist destinations. Even though it may be a destination you have been to several times, historical events, drama and film locations have an additional 'spice' that still gives it a sense of novelty and difference every time. If we are to seek a tourist destination more than once, there must be something that moves you."[10] Feelings (*kamchŏng*) at tour sites differ depending on the tourist. The emotion (*kamtong*) at film sites, on the other hand, is described as outside of personal experience, that is pre-personal, affecting all tourists in an organized manner, and as moving and intense. These aspects of the term *kamtong* resonate with the term *affect* used in Western philosophical discourses of emotion that make distinctions between feeling, emotion and affect.

In his discussion of Deleuze and Guattari's definition of affect, Brian Massumi distinguishes these overlapping terms. Emotion is differentiated from affect (or "intensities," to use Massumi's term), in that it designates feeling given "function and meaning": "An emotion is a subjective content, the sociolinguistic fixing of the quality of an experience which is from that point onward defined as personal. Emotion is qualified intensity, the conventional, consensual point of insertion of intensity into semantically and semiotically formed progressions, into narrativizable action-reaction circuits, into function and meaning."[11] We can understand these three terms as existing along a continuum. First, feelings are personal, drawn from a set of previous experiences that differ from person to person. Next, emotions are feelings that conform to social convention and consensus. Last, affect is difficult to represent in linguistic terms and lies before and outside of consciousness, thus making it the most abstract of the three terms. According to Massumi, affect is "unformed and unstructured, but is nevertheless highly organized and effectively analyzable (it is not entirely containable in knowledge, but is analyzable in effect, as effect)," that is, registered corporeally and not necessarily linguistically.[12] Affect, then, is a bodily function, defined in the broadest sense to include the mental and ideal bodies, and arises within the energies of a particular situated context; it "doesn't just absorb pulses or discrete stimulations; it infolds contexts."[13] This corporeality of affect is perceived as being easily aroused, but difficult to control. Most crucially, affect determines sensation, giving feelings their intensity.

Film tourists who visited the sites of Hur Jin-ho's melodramas in Kangwŏn Province did not so much seek authentic experiences or second-hand proximity to the celebrities they admired, but rather this sort of corporeal affective experience. Both the film itself and the place it was made thus become complicit in producing what I call *affective tourism*. What moves the tourists and that which they seek at film locations is not content or the meaning derived from the visual, but the intense sensation and emotions acted upon the body while viewing the film, which they hope to relive by traversing the physical space of film location.

In this sense, *April Snow* belongs to what Linda Williams calls "body genres" of excess. The viewer in Williams's account is not an abstracted viewer, but an embodied one. According to Williams, the three body genres—horror, melo-drama, and pornography—are conducive to spectatorial embodiment and thus elicit a bodily response from spectators, such as fear, tears, and arousal. In the films that fall within these body genres, there is first "the spectacle of a body caught in the grip of intense sensation or emotion."[14] Like the portrayal of the orgasm in pornography or of violence and terror in horror, the body spec-tacle is featured in melodrama through the portrayal of weeping. Second, such genre films are marked visually by "a quality of uncontrollable convulsion or spasm—of the body 'beside itself' with sexual pleasure, fear and terror, or overpowering sadness" and aurally by "recourse not to the coded articulations of language but to inarticulate cries of pleasure in porn, screams of fear in hor-ror, and sobs of anguish in melodrama."[15] Third, these films urge a particular viewing experience: "The body of the spectator is caught up in an almost invol-untary mimicry of the emotion or sensation of the body on the screen."[16] The audience lacks any "proper aesthetic distance" between the spectator and the representation on the screen, and instead feels "a sense of over-involvement in sensation and emotion."[17] Not only do body genres emphasize bodies as they experience intense sensation, but these bodies on-screen become models for the body of the spectator, who is urged to feel in correlating ways; indeed, a primary goal of such films is to produce parallel sensation in the bodies of the voyeuristic spectator. Film tourism would then seem a more radical extension of this logic. Not only does the spectator wish to feel along with the characters in the film's diegesis, the spectator also wants to do so in the literal space of the film.

Hur Jin-ho's films place an emphasis on bodily experience by undercutting language in favor of other modes of expression and experience. *April Snow*, in particular, privileges the physical over the spoken. Its emphasis on extralin-gual, bodily expressiveness manifests Hur's larger attempt to transmit affect. From the very first moment of *April Snow*, we encounter wordless images of the body gripped by intense sensation. In-su's heavy breathing and immo-bility, registering physical shock as he stands backstage at a rock concert, is followed by Sŏ-yŏng's anxious wringing of hands as she rocks catatonically.

According to Eric Shouse, "Every form of communication where facial expressions, respiration, tone of voice, and posture are perceptible can transmit affect," and Hur's staged images use all of these measures.[18] In-su and Sŏ-yŏng's relationships to the comatose bodies of their spouses, to whom they have to tend at the hospital, is linked in turn to the gradual awakening of their sensory capacities as they start an affair of their own.

A few scenes into the film, we see In-su cleaning his wife's naked body with a towel. He begins to talk to her. Where he had, in the days after the accident, wished he could replace her body with his, he now wishes her dead. Though their spouses' bodies lie still in comatose, it is through the effect the intimate images they have left behind on their phones and cameras have on them that In-su and Sŏ-yŏng slowly come to realize what makes them feel. Hur's depiction of the affective relationship In-su and Sŏ-yŏng have with the images of their comatose spouses mirrors the relationship we are to have while watching the embodied images of Hur's film. This relationship to the lifeless bodies of their spouses contains a metaphoric, but gut-wrenching, parallel to how we as viewers relate viscerally to the bodies on-screen. After the accident, In-su and Sŏ-yŏng discover that a cell phone and camera recovered from the accident contain photos and videos of their spouses' affair. Even as those spouses lie lifeless on their hospital beds, the mediated images of their passion inflict visceral physical responses. When In-su first sees the videos on his wife's camera, he is alone on his bed. The video, filmed by his wife, is of her in bed with her lover, shot in close-ups and medium shots, and we see both the video itself as well as In-su viewing the video as we hear the audio from the video. After a while, In-su gets up, places the camera on the bed, and leaves the frame; soon after, we hear him vomiting violently as the sounds of the lovers laughing and kissing continue (fig. 2.4).

As In-su and Sŏ-yŏng's relationship progresses, their relationship to the comatose bodies also changes, as does the state of the bodies themselves (In-su's wife awakens, Sŏ-yŏng's husband dies). In several scenes the two go on dates to popular tourist sites; each of these scenes is punctuated by a visit to the body of their spouses, next to which they each sit and wait for some sign of life. They are in turn shocked, disgusted, and inspired by these bodies to feel again. The comatose bodies, in turn, function like a medium through which images of intimacy are conveyed. The videos and photographs that they see of their spouses on the road and in bed together, which initially cause bodily revulsion, are later ironically mimicked by In-su and Sŏ-yŏng in their own affair, shot by Hur Jin-ho in close-ups as though it were a video they were tak-

2.4 The intimate video taken by In-su's wife with her camera.
April Snow.

2.5 In-su and Sŏ-yŏng start their own affair. *April Snow.*

ing of themselves (fig. 2.5). But where the bodies in the found videos exude pleasure and joy, In-su and Sŏ-yŏng's relationship is mostly physical, and their mimicry of their spouses' acts initially lacks genuine attraction.

This repeated invocation—of intimate, affective images and the effect that these images have on the viewer—is not limited to found images of cheating spouses, but applies also to general affective images viewed on television. In one scene, Sŏ-yŏng lies in her room flicking through TV channels, lingering a moment on a pornography channel. Though we cannot see clearly what she is watching, the pornographic image is visible in the bed's mirrored headboard, which forms the background of the shot, and the erotic sounds are audible (fig. 2.6). Switching the television off, she turns to the window, where she sees

In-su (fig. 2.7). We see her reflected in the window, watching him from her room, and we see him on the sidewalk below, also in reflection; the camera position focuses on the windowpane outside her room, thus containing them both in the same shot, but only as reflections on a split screen (fig. 2.8). The in-between shots that produce a reflected image (in this case via the window-pane) within the film's frame mark moments of belated cinematic affect, that is, instances in which the affect from an image transmitted from one screen to its spectator (in this case, the pornography that Sŏ-yŏng watches on the TV screen) is displaced onto another, related act of visual consumption (Sŏ-yŏng watching In-su through the window, and the audience watching both Sŏ-yŏng and In-su on-screen) (fig. 2.9).

If *April Snow* foregrounds physical over spoken communication, *One Fine Spring Day* (*Pomnalŭn kanda*, 2001)—which is sometimes considered part of a trilogy that includes *April Snow* and *Christmas in August* (*P'alwŏlŭi k'ŭrisŭmasŭ*, 1998)—favors silence over sound.[19] Though less successful than *April Snow*, the earlier film, by way of comparison, reveals Hur's depth of interest in the capacity of cinema to produce affective experiences that ulti-mately define not only the relationships between characters, but also between film, audience, and eventually tourist. With its typical use of long, slow shots that reflect the value Hur places on sensory expression, Hur's films also ex-periment with sound as part of a larger concern for extralingual affective ex-pression. In *One Fine Spring Day* Hur fills the space of his screen with figures of palpable aurality. Filmed in the city of Tonghae on the northeast coast of Kangwŏn Province, *One Fine Spring Day* (a joint production between Korea, Japan, and Hong Kong) follows a divorced radio journalist (Lee Young-ae/Yi Yŏng-ae) and a younger recording specialist as they start a relationship while producing a program on nature sounds in Kangwŏn Province.

Throughout the film, the sound recorder, Yi Sang-u, attunes the radio pro-ducer, Han Ŭn-su, to the rhythms and sounds of nature, creating associations between places of nature and their nature sounds with stages in their bud-ding relationship. For example, at the Tonghae bamboo forest (the location most frequented by tourists as a result of this film), Sang-u and Ŭn-su stand quietly listening to the sound of swaying leaves as it envelops them in content-ment. Later, they go to Maengbang Beach to record the lapping of waves, an aural experience that seems to estrange them. Like the sound of the waves that crash and then recede, their affair, which began so well in winter, now starts to fall apart. Before spring has passed, Sang-u is forced to resort to his record-ings to re-elicit the body memory of the emotions contained in them. In this

2.6–2.9 After lingering on a pornographic TV channel, Sŏ-yŏng initiates a more intimate encounter with In-su. *April Snow*.

manner, music and sounds are central to the film, and are a critical factor in encouraging intense bodily sensations. In contrast to the act of conversing, the more sensual sounds in *One Fine Spring Day*, be they musical or natural, aim for the same kind of affective expressiveness that physical bodies obtain in *April Snow*, one that encourages the forms of intimacy represented in the film's diegesis as well as the extradiegetic sense of connection felt by the members of the audience, many of whom later became film tourists.

Affect and Affectation

Even though Hur Jin-ho's films may not have been created with the tourist enterprise in mind, they can nevertheless be said to have been imagined in touristic terms. Hur is well-known for eschewing the constructed film set, opting instead for real places where, as in both *April Snow* and *One Fine Spring Day*, he barely alters the location. Filming actors in a real space, he has said, elicits distinct, natural, and unexpected elements, all enabled by that space, which he then aspires to capture with his camera.[20] In our terms, I would say that Hur seeks out the affective energies of a particular place. His fans have said that in order to appreciate his films, one must view them not with the eyes, but with the heart (*maŭm*). The success of Hur's films thus depends on the extent to which the bodies of the actors reflect and express the spaces within which they work. Furthermore, these places, selected by Hur, are intentionally not carefully engineered tourist sites. To the contrary, they are places, like Samch'ŏk or Tonghae, that maintain what he calls a "junk style," meaning that they contain the traces of time and change that a place has undergone naturally. Just as Hur expects these disembodied places to elicit certain bodily responses from the actors, so we can expect the places themselves, even without the characters on-screen, to elicit affect from spectators-cum-tourists. In multiple ways these are affective sites.

By *affective sites*, I mean the places featured in melodramas that elicit such an emotional reaction that the viewer is spurred to visit, in hopes of recapturing, through acts of mimicry, the emotional states prompted by the film. This notion draws on Anne Rutherford's concept of "affective space," which is characterized by corporeal intensity. Such space is not only "inscribed with a palpable cinematic image . . . with traces of the forces that play around the body in space," and a place where not only "mimicry of physical movement or a simulation of motion perspective" occurs, but also one that represents "the possibility of the spectator's dissolution, or loss in the movement."[21] Rutherford's concept is particularly useful in understanding the relationship between cinematic affect and tourism, because unlike Williams's aesthetics of cinematic embodiment, which relies on the on-screen "display of the human body," Rutherford proposes an "aesthetics of embodiment" in which "the tensions and dynamism of the surface of the image can effect a bodily agitation" just as well.[22]

Affective tourism, exemplified here by the *April Snow* and *One Fine Spring Day* tour sites, operates through an imaginary conflation between the bodily qualities of the cinematic experience in relationship to filmic images and the embodied experience of the tourist at the tour site. In most cases, the individual site is marked by a still image from the film on a sign depicting the characters caught in a moment of experience. Entering and touring the site becomes for the tourist a moment of mimicry of the physical movement of the film.

The affective tourism of *April Snow* and *One Fine Spring Day* works because both films were shot in locations that are all accessible to the tourist, and it is possible to visit most of the locations of one particular film in a relatively short amount of time. Film-location tours in Manhattan, Hawaii, or Los Angeles, in contrast, often show tourists one or two locations from several different movies, because in most cases, although the exterior shots of the city are shot on location, the interior shots are usually filmed on sets elsewhere. Rather than seeing an exterior of a particular shot from a scene as detached from the overall context, film spectators here at the *April Snow* and *One Fine Spring Day* sites are able to experience the tour in a manner analogous to that in which they view the film because of the convenient proximity and organization of the tour sites, and this ability to follow the map laid out by the film also affords an accompanying form of emotional mapping, recreating the affective content of the film in the same way that the tour sites allow reenactment of the characters' literal movements. Epitomizing affective tourism, the tour offers thus not only a behind-the-scenes view of where the film was made, but also an opportunity to enter imaginatively the world of the film itself. The film tourist is drawn into the scene and the moment of experience by way of a cinematic image that activates the memory of the emotion and energies conveyed through the bodies of the depicted characters, whose spatial frame the tourist now shares instead of viewing it from a remove.

The film *April Snow* is reproduced spatiovisually onto the city of Samch'ŏk by way of strategically situated maps and signs throughout the city (figs. 2.10 and 2.11). These signs direct tourists to the various individual sites, which are numbered and sequenced to correspond to certain scenes in the film. In

2.10 *April Snow* film location signpost in Samch'ŏk. Photo by author.

2.11 Map of *April Snow* locations. Photo by author.

contrast, the self-guided tour for *One Fine Spring Day* is less obviously scripted because the locations are all exterior sites and all in the countryside, set further apart from one another. More confined to a central location, the *April Snow* tour takes about three hours (a time period that is just a little longer than the film itself) if the tourist walks, which a careful viewer of the film might regard as the preferred method of touring given that the main characters list walking as one of their favorite activities. Each site along the tour is inscribed with a matching still from the film, as in the sign outside Somang Pharmacy, where In-su and Sŏ-yŏng run into each other in search of sleeping pills. The maps, and the various written guides on websites or printed brochures, on the other hand, present the sites without contextualization with respect to the film. For example, the Samhŭng Motel, one of the locations, is pictured on the Korea Tourism Organization's website (visitkorea.or.kr) and in free tour maps that guide tourists from one destination to the other. The photograph includes no bodies and depicts only the place as it is. By contrast, when the tourist gets to the location itself, he encounters not a generic photo of that location, but a still from the film. That is, first, the spectator views the film (fig. 2.12). Second, the spectator-cum-tourist reads the map and views the photos of the destinations, either online, in printed guides, or on the street maps within the area (fig. 2.13). Third, at the destination, the tourist encounters the film still that links the space to the tourist's memory of the relevant scene in the film (fig. 2.14).

If we consider the precise location and function of the cinematic image in the film tourist's experience here, as well as the nature of its content, it is possible to discern a tourist experience closely linked to the experiences of cinema spectatorship. For instance, in the hotel room used as In-su's room, a photo of the scene in which In-su gets sick watching the video on his wife's camera of her with her lover is placed directly above the bed on which In-su was sitting. A number of scenes in the film take place in room 205 of the Samhŭng Motel; thus, many parts of the room are marked with stills from the corresponding scenes, framed and hung near the relevant places. Some of these stills even reference related scenes, thus helping the tourist make the emotional connections to other parts of the narrative that contextualize the particular scene. The large film still hanging on the bathroom wall in this room is from a scene that prefigures a psychological turning point in the film: In-su and Sŏ-yŏng suddenly realize the illicitness of their relationship and the emotional pain they will potentially inflict on each other when In-su's father-in-law unexpectedly knocks on the door. In-su grabs Sŏ-yŏng and shoves her into the bathroom to

2.12 In-su and Sŏ-yŏng run into each other at Somang Pharmacy, unable to sleep. *April Snow*.

2.13 Photo of Somang Pharmacy in the "Filming Locations" guide for *April Snow* on the VisitKorea website.

2.14 Somang Pharmacy's tour-site marker depicting images from the corresponding scene in *April Snow*. Photo by author.

hide her. The urgency of this scene, especially after the director had just lingered on the shot of them having fruit and touching each other, is disquieting. The inscription of cinematic images into the bathroom space resonates with Sŏ-yŏng's initial shock and fear as the door closes on her, the relief when In-su returns after shaking off his father-in-law, and the tenderness and gratitude he expresses toward her as she forgives him. The tactility in this film scene functions to produce a sense of spatiality by occurring not in the actual space but in the mirror reflection of the image. The bodily experience, it suggests, is perceivable only in the relationship between real space and image. At the site, when one looks into the tiny bathroom, the tourist's position at the doorway looks directly onto the poster of the scene from the film, which is also reflected in the mirror (figs. 2.15 and 2.16). Looking in the mirror, one might almost feel that the characters were in the bathroom as bodies, not as images on a poster. The spatiality of the two-dimensional image in which Sŏ-yŏng is doubled in the mirror, reflected again in the bathroom's real mirror, creates a three-dimensionality that "infolds" the spectator-cum-tourist into the bathroom scene; we are bathed, so to speak, with the original emotions of shame and tenderness that we likely felt when first watching the film. This bathroom scene and its attendant location provide an example of how image and site become complicit in producing a distinct film-touristic experience; that experience involves the tourist's body in physical space and completes the act of film spectatorship with all of its projections on and identifications with images that only looked real. By eliciting cinematic affect at the film's location, the tour sites recreate in material terms the cinematic forms of embodied affect that might otherwise be confined to diegetic spaces.

Furthermore, the involuntary mimicry of corporeal sensation is invited through voluntary imitation of the characters' physical movements within each location, to the extent possible. These affective sites, in short, evoke affectation, that is, a studied and ultimately artificial rehearsal of behaviors and affects that the tourist had earlier witnessed in the role of film viewer, but one that, because inspired by a moving film rather than the tour site, realizes the more powerful cinematic emotional reaction. Unlike visitors to Universal Studios Hollywood theme park in the United States, tourists at the *April Snow* sites are invited not only to the place where the movies are made, but as if into the diegetic and affective space of the movie itself. Like the double structure of *April Snow*, in which the shots of In-su and Sŏ-yŏng's affair in its intimate moments seem to imitate the images of their cheating spouses, drawing our attention to their mimicry of their spouses' affair, here tourists are invited to

2.15 Hiding in the bathroom. *April Snow.*

2.16 The bathroom in room 205, Samhŭng Motel. Photo by author.

mimic the characters' movements and to relive the memory of the embodied affect elicited during the initial viewing experience. For example, in Samch'ŏk, tourists interested in *April Snow* can sleep in the same room as the characters in the film, eat the same foods, sip coffee at the same table, and walk the same streets. Similarly, on the *One Fine Spring Day* tour, visitors to the bamboo forest at the base of the mountain go past the side of the elderly couple's house to stand in the forest, just like the characters (figs. 2.17 and 2.18).

Despite the highly artificial environments at the tour sites, the reenactments of the tourist are imbued with an aura of authenticity that subsumes the fictionality of the filmic settings. Although closed to overnight guests and open only for tours when I last visited the site in the summer of 2012, Samhŭng Motel's rooms 205 and 210, both of which are featured in *April Snow*, used to be available to tourists wishing to stay there. The Palace Hotel's room 1407, which also appears in the film, remains open for guests. In addition, the Samhŭng Motel rooms have preserved everything from the clothes In-su and Sŏ-yŏng wore, to the bags they carried, and even to the hairspray and lotions she used in the scenes beside frame-by-frame images of the scenes as they played out, placed in the room next to the precise locations. They also have in glass displays license plates and awards given to the actors and film producers in gratitude for the tourism the film has generated for the city (fig. 2.19). The set of Somang Pharmacy, provided for purposes of the film by the city, has also been preserved in part, as have the cafés, restaurants, and other locations associated with the film, with the quite understandable exception of the Samch'ŏk hospital, where their spouses lay comatose (fig. 2.20).

In *Transmission of Affect* Teresa Brennan suggests that there is "no secure distinction between the individual and environment."[23] As opposed to individual feeling, affects for Brennan are the basis for social interaction. In similar terms, we recall that Massumi defined *affect* not only as the ability to affect, but also to be affected. One body's experiential state can be passed to another, inducing that body's capacity to act. This transmission of affect can occur because affect, unlike feeling and emotion, is unformed, unstructured, and ubiquitous. What happens at these tour sites, at least in their idealized form, is a transmission of affect that arises when the individual tourist engages with his or her highly scripted environment, but it is one that furthermore completes a prior, presumably affecting cinematic experience. These affective sites thus bring to tourist locations the affective power of film, which is buttressed by the aura of authenticity that comes with material presence.

2.17 Road sign for a popular *One Fine Spring Day* filming location.
Photo by author.

2.18 The bamboo forest of *One Fine Spring Day*. Photo by author.

2.19 In-su's Samhŭng Hotel room from *April Snow* preserved.
Photo by author.

2.20 The café from *April Snow*. Photo by author.

Of course, the tourist apparatus that promotes this sort of experience has the relatively brief shelf life that characterizes the trajectory of many consumer products and popular culture phenomena, and ironically, the very features that lend these tour sites the aura of authenticity are also the ones that, as time passes and dust gathers, cease to function as markers of the recent presence of characters and movie stars, and become instead musealized artifacts of an ever receding past. By the time of my most recent visit to the site, in 2012, the excitement over the film had passed and only the occasional tourist stumbled onto the individual locations, now more in the mode of idle curiosity than inspired fervor. At a certain point, the process of enshrining becomes counterproductive to the production of affect at tour sites and can be seen as a sign that a film location is beginning to lose its appeal and effect as affective site.

Conclusion

Though the period of transnational cooperation and coproduction covered by the films examined here from 1998 to 2005 was eventually overwritten after this period by state-sponsored nationalist agendas that sought to appropriate earlier hallyu discourse, the reconciliatory films *Kazoku Cinema* and *Asako in Ruby Shoes* are clearly identifiable as intermediate prototypes of hallyu cinema, whose logic becomes more self-conscious and fully realized in films like *April Snow*. These films examined in part I exemplify the way in which the commercial promise of hallyu manifests itself not just as a marketing strategy, but as a set of aesthetic characteristics. Beginning with *Kazoku Cinema* and *Asako in Ruby Shoes*, the reconciliatory films tentatively gestured toward a sense of transnational intimacy that would be brought about by cultural exchange, including cultural tourism. This intimacy, though expressed in the films as hopes of interpersonal romance and the desire for touch, speaks to larger questions of transnational commerce and exchange, limited as they are to some degree by the historical specter of colonial exploitation, which is manifested in the interest of these films in pornographic logics. Later, in films like *April Snow*, the scale of intimacy broadens, becoming tied to an awareness of hallyu's growing cultural and economic impact, which becomes highly visible specifically in hallyu tourism, which was one of the prominent epiphenomena of the television drama *Winter Sonata*'s immense popularity throughout Asia after its initial airing in 2002. As a result, the earlier focus on the reconciliatory possibilities enabled by interpersonal intimacy shifts with *April Snow* to a more general preoccupation with formulating an aesthetics of intimacy that might help consolidate a transnational audience of consumers for Korean cultural products. In this context, film locations cease to simply provide backdrops. Instead, they become a more essential part of the story that is being told and indeed themselves products to consume. In this more self-conscious iteration of hallyu cinema, films like *April Snow* attempt to imagine in the broadest of terms how intimate visual images might move people, emotionally to tears or geographically to travel. My central argument in part I is that, in hallyu cinema, these are related phenomena.

This prioritization of location in films that were made immediately around *April Snow* can thus be regarded as a formalistic internalization of the unanticipated touristic impact of the phenomenal reception of *Winter Sonata* and of other unanticipated successes of the early, unselfconscious hallyu period. The television drama *Winter Sonata* single-handedly increased Japanese tourism to Korea by 40 percent from January to October 2004 compared to the previous year, as millions of fans sought out the filming locations following the show's first airing on Japanese television, in 2003.[24] *April Snow* is not only conscious of this fact; this fact is also at the core of the film's logic. If we remember in the opening and ending scenes of the film, the question of destination ("Where shall we go?") becomes both the existential conundrum of its cautiously hopeful characters and also an uncanny rallying cry for the crowds of tourists it invites to otherwise quiet towns on the eastern coast of Korea. As these films become more self-conscious, hallyu as a commercial phenomenon also becomes increasingly central to their aesthetics, and a good number of these films thus pair an interest in affective expression with an interest in travel.

Toward the end of *April Snow*, there is a scene in which In-su sets up the stage lighting for a K-pop concert outdoors. The onstage performances that follow comprise footage from an actual concert that was staged for the film as "Concert *Oech'ul* [the Korean title of *April Snow*]: Super Live," which was held at Yonsei University's Outdoor Theater on 24 April 2005, a few months before the film was released. The thousands of real fans who came to the concert venue, in anticipation of the release of the film and curious about a "live" preview of the film and its production, are thus part of the final scene. Remarkably, the film's own marketing efforts are actually represented in the film itself, and for this reason, the scene might be highlighted as a kind of signature moment for hallyu cinema. The performance included popular K-pop artists Jo Sungmo, Lee Min-woo (Shinhwa), SG Wannabe, Loveholic, Clazziquai Project (also known as Clazziquai), and Leessang, among others, whose performances get blended seamlessly into the concert within the film, which the character In-su, played by Bae Yong-joon, is purportedly producing. The concert closed, self-reflexively, with a screening of the making of the film and key scenes before the live audience, with close-up shots of Bae Yong-joon watching it along with the concertgoers. In the scene that documents the shooting of this live preview in the DVD documentary of the production of *April Snow*, which was released just before the film's release, close-up shots show that Bae is visibly emotional as he watches. And though it is unclear if he is in character or being himself, what remains certain is that this scene renders the theater a place in which the film scene and tour site converge wholly, that is, as an example of the kind of spaces the film *April Snow* will go on to generate after its release. Thus, the intimacy that gets foregrounded here in this complex self-referential movement is a circulation of affects to and from the visual to the actual, from the screen to the site; the fans embedded in the film itself thus become inseparable from the hallyu product and essentially move with it in its transnational circulation.

I opened part I with Korea-Japan coproductions in order to probe the possibilities of *intimacy* as the affective precondition for a reparative sense of intercultural closeness that functioned initially to redress historical tension and later as a critical optic that helped make clear the logic of regional economic circulation. I now turn to an examination of a Korea-China co-production, where questions of intimacy modulate into problems of *amity*, and relations modeled on erotic connections shift to relations based on friendship and camaraderie. In the context of China as an emerging global powerhouse, the inquiry into amity helps highlight possibilities of cooperation as national interests transform into regional interests, a shift that is mirrored by a parallel renovation of emotions once understood in a strictly national context, which now become retrofitted for new transnational contexts.

PART II

AMITY

3. PROVISIONAL FEELINGS

The Making of *Musa*

3.1 "*Musa* Staff, Fighting!!!" Souvenir photo of the Korean and Chinese film crew of *Musa*. Still from the supplementary DVD special features.

In the late 1970s, the Hong-Kong based director King Hu filmed the vast land-scapes and scenic temples so central to his Buddhist- and Taoist-themed mar-tial arts films, *Legend of the Mountain* (*Shan zhong chuanqi*, 1979) and *Raining in the Mountain* (*Kong shan ling yu*, 1979), in the northern mountains of South Korea.[1] Since filming in China was restricted by Cold War tensions, filming in South Korea offered an alternative to the constraints of Hong Kong's stu-dios, which King Hu sought to escape. *Legend of the Mountain* alternates be-tween breathtaking wide-angle shots of mountains and seas with a heavy use of zooms. The mise-en-scène of *Raining in the Mountain* captures the same vast mountains and bodies of water that have inspired Korean landscape painting traditions such as *sansuhwa* (mountain and water painting) as far back as the Chosŏn period (1392–1910).[2] As in these paintings, the Korean landscapes King Hu employed to stand in for China reflect the desire for an idyllic state of being, unaffected by the suffering and pain of urban life. The interchangeability of Korea and China in this affective representation extracts and abstracts physical space into the emotional and spiritual state of the film's characters, subordinating geographical coordinates to affective ones.[3]

Twenty years later, this process of national-emotional abstraction was reversed. Mirroring King Hu's earlier search for ersatz landscapes in South Korea, the Korean director Kim Sung-su sought to film *Musa* (2001), a martial arts epic about itinerant Korean warriors caught between the warring dynasties on mainland China. The film is set in the late fourteenth century, just after the Chinese Ming dynasty has defeated the Mongol Yuan dynasty and reestablished Han rule. Amid this great upheaval, relations between China and Koryo (ancient kingdom of Korea) sour after a Chinese envoy is killed; Koryo dispatches its own envoys to China in hopes of reconciliation. According to the historical record, Koryo sent four groups of diplomatic missions to Ming China (1368–1644), which had driven out the Mongols, ending the Yuan dynasty (1271–1368) in 1375. Relations between Ming China and Koryo were souring due to the chaos following the assassination of Koryo King Kongmin and the accession of King Wu, as well as the murder of a Ming envoy to Korea. The first group of envoys was confined; the other three were not heard of after their arrival in Nanjing. After the amelioration of Ming-Koryo relations, several of the envoys returned to Koryo, but there were also those who vanished. The film speculates about what might have happened to this group of men.

In Kim Sung-su's telling the Koryo envoys arrive at the Chinese court, only to be arrested, then sent into exile across the desert. Led by General Choi (Joo Jin-mo), his aide Lt. Ganam (Park Jung-hak), and Daejung, the leader of the people's army (Ahn Sung-ki), the group tries to make it to the coastal Shandong Province, and from there by boat to Korea. Tension builds between General Choi and Yŏ-sol (Jung Woo-sung), a slave bodyguard of the vice-envoy who was recently liberated following his master's death, when they find themselves in a love triangle with a Ming princess, Furong (Zhang Ziyi), who says they will be rewarded if they get her home safely. The group is soon further saddled with a group of Chinese claiming loyalty to the princess, and conflict erupts as the Korean delegation is torn over whether they should sacrifice their safe return to Korea for the sake of the Chinese.

In August 2000, after five years of lobbying and preparation, Kim Sung-su's South Korean crew arrived in Beijing to start filming. Along with the crew for *Anarchists* (*Anak'isŭtŭ*, 2000), Yu Yŏng-sik's film about Korean nationalist independence fighters exiled in early twentieth-century China, they were one of the few South Korean crews ever to film on location in China. In Beijing they joined a local team of four hundred Chinese crewmembers, some occupying parallel positions to the Korean staff to oversee the Chinese side, and flew to Zhongwei (called Chungwi in Korean), in central China. From there they began the trek that takes up the bulk of the trek at the center of the narrative: across ten thousand kilometers of desert to the coastal region of Liaoning Sheng (Yonyongsong), in the southern part of the northeastern province. The trek took five months. The crew suffered everything from the sweltering heat of the barren desert to the plunging subzero temperatures of the frozen terrain as winter set in along the coast. The scene of great slaughter at the hands of Mongol forces that ends the film is thus apt, in that it also marked the crew's long-awaited end of the grueling experience of onsite filming.

When one of the few survivors of the final battle, a Korean emissary played by the veteran actor Ahn Sung-ki, bids his Chinese fellow travelers farewell near the end of the film (after having cremated his massacred delegation on the icy shores of the sea), the film's diegesis mimics the experience of the film crew, who would also soon say their goodbyes. The final shot of the small boat journeying home to Koryo thus marks the end not only of the film but also of the crew's travels. As the "making of" documentary (hereafter MOD) on the supplementary DVD reveals, the entire process of travel plus filming was remarkably arduous.[4] A mash-up of B-roll footage and onsite interviews documents the vast emotional arc of the film shoot: the initial excitement of the actors and crew about traveling to China; the highly anticipated differences in both locale and locals, heightened by the sense of displacement caused by the film's historical setting in the late fourteenth century; the impact of the harsh desert landscape in forming their particularly "severe and intense" experience; the respectfully forged friendships between the Koreans and their Chinese co-workers; and the pervasive homesickness. Last but not least, the footage depicts the sense of responsibility felt by the cast and crew, the hope that their collaborative project might pave the way for future collaborations between the two nations. Alongside a film based on tensions between nations, the documentary suggests a deep connection between the film's explicit themes—interethnic conflict and intercultural cooperation—and the conditions of its production.

Kim Sung-su's film *Musa* parallels the transformation of the genre in the Taiwanese director Ang Lee's *Crouching Tiger, Hidden Dragon* (2000). Lee's film was hugely successful around the world and burst open the genre of martial arts film, but just as important was that he infused that genre with the concept of *qing* (情). Gary Xu describes *qing* as denoting "various forms of feelings, emotions, or love. In traditional Chinese narrative, fictional or nonfictional, qing is often coupled with *yi*, the Confucian principle of righteousness and self-sacrifice. Qing and yi complement each other: strong feelings—heterosexual love, camaraderie or homoeroticism between male friends, admiration, sympathy—ensure the desire for justice and self-sacrifice under the direst of circumstances; righteousness and self-sacrifice in turn evoke and deepen feelings in various relations."[5] Stephen Teo suggests that Lee essentially tweaks the genre into something like martial arts romance, by downplaying the tenet of yi (righteousness, "with its attendant themes of friendship, loyalty and betrayal")—upheld only in the purest sense by King Hu—and emphasizing instead the romantic tradition of amorous love (*yan qing*) or knights-errant in love (*xia qing*) found in the literary examples.[6] For Gary Xu, the qing of Asia's "global affective cinema," exemplified in the films of John Woo, differs from that of traditional Hollywood because it emphasizes the "intensification of feelings" and the effect of this intensification, "not what is intensified."[7] Xu ascribes to qing a flexibility because it is "always associated with the innate human nature that *gives rise* to emotive expressions such as *xi* (happiness), *nu* (anger), *ai* (sadness), and *le* (joy)," as well as "ethical expressions that include *yi* (righteousness) and *li* (reason, the organizing principle of the cosmos)."[8] In short for Xu, qing is a historical, culturally coded affect.[9] The compounding power of qing (phoneticized as *chŏng* in Korean), which makes it malleable as an affective element, as well as its ability to bind to other emotions, reminds us of the formative power of affect as it circulates within society—what Sara Ahmed calls "affective economies."[10]

The relationship between *Musa* and its supplementary MOD gives form to a very particular emotion associated with the bonds of compassion that arise in the course of travel. This emotion, referred to in Korean as *yŏchŏng* (旅情), conjoins the character for *qing/chŏng* with the character for *yŏ* (traveling). The compound signifies both the weary heart of a traveler as well as the bonds formed with other travelers through shared experiences associated with traveling, such as longing, trepidation, and enduring hardships. *Yŏchŏng* begins to stir only at the onset of travel, and then intensifies, as the bonds of compassion are established, tested, and sustained over time and space. Yŏchŏng abounds in *Musa*, whose narrative is defined by hardships of every sort. Doubly relevant, the yŏchŏng in the film is paralleled in the film's documentary, which emphasizes not only the joint-production process but also the intense emotional experiences of the actors and crew. Though the yŏchŏng of the film and documentary alike is associated with nationalism, due to the implicit desire to return home embedded within the emotion, the particular manifestation of yŏchŏng becomes denationalized in the joint Korea-China collaboration, when home is unattainable.

The bonds of yŏchŏng are provisional, both sustained for the duration of the journey and constituted by it as well. In this case, the provisional feelings of yŏchŏng—exemplified by the collaborative production of the film and represented diegetically within it—reflect a sense of shared fate, both artistically and economically, between these countries. From Korea's perspective, economic cooperation has been a cornerstone of relations with China, but also a source of vulnerability due to the imbalance in trade dependence.[11] In *Musa* yŏchŏng speaks to the contemporary economic relationship between Korea and China, by reimagining these economic relations in affective terms. The affective mechanism of yŏchŏng, as an interpersonal emotion emphasizing the bonds between individuals, is utilized to humanize the joint-production process. Accordingly, the fictional plight of the transient Koreans and Chinese in the film becomes what Kathleen Woodward has called a "liberal narrative of compassion";[12] this serves to create an affective understanding of cooperation whereby compassion becomes an indicator of how socially progressive both nations have become in their relations with one another. In turn, compassion here is understood not as "an organic emotion," as Lauren Berlant describes, but rather as "a social and aesthetic technology of belonging."[13] As such, it models the shared affect not only of an international film crew traveling and enduring together, but also the broader possibilities of inter-Asian cooperation in regional economic endeavors.

During the Korean War, China supported North Koreans against the South Korean and United Nations forces. After 1953, China's alliance remained with the Communist North, while South Korea's Sino-relations focused on Taiwan, impacting not just political exchange but also economic trade. Korea and China reestablished diplomatic relations in 1992. During these heady years of China's growth, China's primary trade focus was with the United States, since Korea in this equation was not economically or politically important enough to warrant significant attention.[14] But as both nations emerged as global economic powers during this period, the geographic neighbors also came to see the advantages of cooperation. Cooperation did not come without problems: the political scientist Chung Jae Ho noted in 2013 that the increasing economic and political interaction of the two countries has been accompanied by the amplification of frictions based on trade disputes, ideological disagreements, historical and territorial conflicts, and policy differences with respect to both North Korea and the United States, and so on.[15] *Musa* was produced amid great anticipation in Korea of an economically interdependent future with China. Particularly with the success of hallyu cultural products in China during the 1990s, both sides came to regard Korean popular culture as a welcome and integral part of the process of overwriting Cold War history and forging friendly economic cooperation, in part through a discourse that accentuated "cultural similarity" and "cultural synchronization."[16] *Musa* was explicitly marketed as a binational coproduction shot on location in China and as a demonstration of the resumed regional consolidation efforts between Korea and China; the film's supplementary footage is very conscious of its political and economic role.

As with Korea-Japan coproductions, examining Korea-China coproductions at the intersection of film and tourism exposes inherent processes of reconciliation and cooperation involved in joint film production between the participating nations. As in the Korea-Japan films, the geopolitical realities of Korea's relationship with China became inscribed within *Musa*. As with Japan, Korea's cultural interactions with China reflected a ready compliance with China's shift in foreign policy toward "confidence, reconciliation, and flexibility," and away from "vulnerability, contention, and rigidity."[17] Both the coproductions with Japan and with China engage with discourses of reconciliation and a cosmopolitanism exemplified and celebrated through tourism in the spirit of the times. But in contrast to Korea's anxieties concerning Japan as an imperial power in the early twentieth century and its "return to Asia" at the turn of the millennium, Korea's anxieties regarding China involved its ascent as an Asian power in the twenty-first century, which was articulated and negotiated in the joint production of popular films between Korea and China by visually representing the conversion of mutually beneficial economic relations into affective terms.

Whereas the first reconciliatory Korea-Japan coproductions proceeded relatively smoothly, the Korea-China collaborations were more fraught. Unlike the Korea-Japan productions, which tended to divide the labor along national lines, with minimal interaction between the two teams, Chinese regulations on coproductions and the appeal of filming in China necessitated the close intermingling of Korean and Chinese film crews. Though intended to encourage a useful exchange of skills benefiting the film project, working together also involved constant frustrations with differences in language, culture, and industry practices. The discord underlying the joint production process is blatant in the MOD, and its account of working with Chinese and Hong Kong cast and crew members does not attempt to elide the friction, instead bringing into focus the provisional aspect of an emotion borne in itinerancy. The Korea-China coproductions were thus ventures into inter-Asian productions in the fullest sense.[18] The relations between Korean and Chinese film workers and their travails in the course of traveling, as represented in the MOD documentary film, can be read in relation to the primary film, which not coincidentally emphasizes journeys and personal relationships between people of different Asian ethnicity. The ease with which the *Musa* MOD slips between footage from the feature film itself and the film crews' journey during the making of the film reflects the film's deeply self-reflexive nature. Read together, the film and the MOD provide an invaluable glimpse into the external realities of inter-Asian joint production as well as insight into how this touristic mode of approaching on-location joint production, embodied by the experiences of the actors and film crew, opens the possibility of transnational solidarity and negotiates interregional problems.

The Golden Market

Whereas Korea's cultural reconciliation with Japan necessitated actual policies that gradually phased Japanese popular culture into Korea, Korea's relationship to China called for different tactics. Bolstered by a growing spirit of global East-West rapprochement, and driven by a convergence of economic interest between the two developing economies, China emerged as a crucial partner to South Korea in the early 1990s. The distance between Beijing and Seoul had narrowed after the 1986 Asian Games in Seoul, and even more so after the 1988 Seoul Olympics and the 1990 Asian Games in Beijing. Several historical shifts and cultural evolutions also had profound impact. Since the end of the Korean War, China and North Korea had been locked in a rigid Cold War alliance against South Korea. But following events such as the Tiananmen Square massacre, China's full economic liberation, and the collapse of global communism, the rigid triangulation became a bit more fluid: China was able to disengage partially from its allied relationship to North Korea; South Korea began to distance itself somewhat from Taiwan; and both started dealing directly with one another. Bilateral exchanges proved mutually beneficial on many fronts; China provided Korea with low-cost labor and a profitable overseas market, while Seoul provided China with much-needed capital and technology with few strings attached. Semi-governmental trade offices were established in 1991, and diplomatic normalization was achieved in 1992. By 2003, when the two nations announced their "comprehensive cooperative partnership," China had already replaced the United States as the largest export market for Korea and the primary destination for its outbound investments.[19] China had become a golden market for Korean industry of all kinds, culture included.

This gradual change in cultural climate, punctuated by a series of sudden shifts, enabled China, as Ch'oe Wŏn-dam puts it, to "break its fantasy about the West and turn to Asia after the mid-90s."[20] China's cultural presence in Asia was notably different from that of South Korea, in that, according to Gilbert Rozman, China retained "a strong sense of their own identity and did not regard Japan as a cultural great power."[21] China was "not worried about the cultural dangers of regionalism" and had remained relatively open to cultural imports from Hong Kong, Taiwan, the United States, and South Korea since the late 1990s, indicating that neither Japan nor these other Asian cultures were considered a threat.[22] In contrast to South Korea, where Japanese popular culture was regarded with caution due to residual postcolonial tensions, China's "turn to Asia" occurred in the mid-1990s with the popularity of the Japanese Wave.[23] By the time Korean popular culture in the form of hallyu began to supplant its Japanese precedent, China had already loosened its regulations in various sectors of culture, and it continued to do so after its entry into the World Trade Organization, in 2001.

Just as the lure of a golden market accelerated bilateral economic relations, the number of tourists taking advantage of open national borders following the normalization of diplomatic normalization increased dramatically. By 2001, the number of people traveling on China-South Korea airplane routes had exceeded the number of those on U.S.-South Korea routes.[24] In addition, China had usurped the United States as favored tourist destination for Korean tourists, and by 2002, middle-class Chinese tourists taking advantage of relaxed restrictions on travel abroad were "flooding" the rest of Asia, constituting "the largest contingent of visitors to descend on Korea from any country."[25] The Korean government and businesses alike tried to capitalize on

China's enthusiasm for Korean cultural products and on the surge of tourists as a means to promote the country's national image, using the success of Korean visual media in Japan, Taiwan, and Hong Kong as a model.

However, in 2002, a study conducted by the Korea Culture and Tourism Policy Institute suggested that unlike tourists from Japan, Hong Kong, and Taiwan, Chinese tourists were not attracted to filming locations, either of dramas or of films.[26] Korean films overall were not very successful in China. Korean film producers hoped that hallyu would boost the popularity of Korean cinema in the Chinese market, but such hallyu-inspired interest was limited to films that starred actors from popular TV dramas and pop music.[27] Furthermore, although the marketing juggernaut of hallyu made it easier to get other cultural products into China, the Korean tourism industry still had difficulty getting permits to set up offices in China, necessary to promote the drama and film locations so popular among other Asian tourists; and in the rare moments when these permits were attained, these businesses faced the challenges of restrictive laws and inadequate publicity infrastructure.[28]

Yet the difficulties in accessing China's byzantine bureaucracy did not dim Korea's enthusiasm. After the decline of Hong Kong's film industry in the 1990s, the Korean film industry attempted to fill a perceived gap in the Asian film market, as a way to enter larger foreign markets. Moviemakers in Hong Kong and China had both filmmaking "know-how" and name recognition in the United States, both of which Korean producers valued. In addition to using coproductions as a way to utilize the experience of the movie industries in Hong Kong and China, Korea also began to invest directly into Chinese film production, seeing it as a viable way of jointly exporting films and reaping the benefits.

As China reformed its economy, Korea saw an opening as it realized that the Chinese film industry's production base was in dire need of capital. The Chinese government, eager to promote on-location filming in China and to attract foreign capital, decided to ease its long-standing insistence on censoring scripts and to facilitate cooperation between local and foreign production companies. These circumstances played a large role in enabling *Musa* and other early coproductions between Korea and China.[29] In this new arrangement, a script, along with information on production and potential film locations, had to first be submitted, with a fee, for potential censorship with the Ministry of Foreign Trade and Economic Cooperation of the People's Republic of China. If the script was approved, Korean producers had to go through film studios in China, including Cinerent, Salon, and ARRI, that provided services from preproduction to postproduction, in order to facilitate the process of coproduction. Considerable customs costs for bringing in film equipment also made it much more efficient to work through these studios. Korean filmmakers quickly found it easier to bring only essential equipment while renting the bulk from local Chinese companies.[30]

As a result, the first joint Korea-China film productions—such as Yu Yŏng-sik's *Anarchists* (*Anak'isŭtŭ*, 2000), Kim Yŏng-jun's *Pich'ŏnmu* (also known as *Bichunmoo/Bicheonmu*, 2000), and *Musa*—started shooting in China in 1999. These first productions, in other words, took place simultaneous to an unprecedented surge of tourism between China and Korea, as well as to an explosion in Korean popular culture consumption in China that, in 2001, would be marked in hindsight as the onset of hallyu. To take advantage of these conditions, Korean filmmakers made efforts to engage China through various coproduction models and partnerships formed across inter-Asian film networks of cooperation, often in the form of martial arts films.[31] The first coproduction, *Anarchists*, was initiated through the Korean Film Commission's foreign-film promotion department (*yŏnghwa chinhŭngwiwŏnhoeŭi haeoe chinhŭngbu*) and through the city of Pusan's international exchange division, which had connections to the city of Shanghai, where the film was set, and to the Shanghai Film Studio. It featured main actors from Korea and employed Koreans for its core production staff, while working with Chinese staff in Shanghai on set design and production and with extras supplied by the Shanghai Film Studio. Despite this unprecedented cooperation, *Anarchists* was from the start intended for the Korean domestic film market.

Pich'ŏnmu was the first coproduction cofinanced by both Korea and China; in addition, a film studio in Hong Kong oversaw the technical aspects of the film and the hiring of artists for the choreography of the martial arts action. Although Korea and Hong Kong had cooperated on films decades before, in the 1960s and 1970s, in a partnership between Hong Kong's Shaw Brothers and Korea's Shin Films, the resumption of such efforts was suffused with a new ambition: to assert a distinct Korean style of filmmaking while setting a solid foundation for future collaborations. A major point of contention in the collaboration on *Pich'ŏnmu*, according to the postproduction interviews conducted by the South Korean Ministry of Culture and Tourism, was that the Hong Kong martial arts team was conflicted about the Korean directorial designs due to a fundamental difference in action aesthetics. The "exaggerated and showy style" of Hong Kong martial arts direction was felt to be incompatible with Korean sensibilities (*chŏngsŏ*) and affective emphasis.[32] According to the postproduction reports, the Hong Kong staff was often embarrassed and befuddled, but even this vexed relationship was better than the problematic relationship between the Hong Kong staff and Chinese staff working on this film.[33]

Reflective of the Korean movie industry's "China Shock" and "Chinese Fever," as China made itself felt in global politics and economics, both *Musa* and *Pich'ŏnmu* are considered to be relatively successful joint China-Korea projects.[34] For comparison, the collaborative efforts behind *Dream of a Warrior (Ch'ŏnsamong*, 2001), coproduced between Korea and Hong Kong around the same time, and *Time Travel to the Root of Samurai (Saulabi*, 2002), a coproduction in the swordplay genre between Korea and Japan (with choreography by Takakura Eizi, a collaborator of the legendary Akira Kurosawa), were less successful. However, these small successes and relative failures together offered cumulative lessons: it could be argued that precisely these tentative strands of bilateral cooperation enabled, just a few years later, full-blown inter-Asian collaborations on a spectacular scale, which combined the full resources of Korea, China, Hong Kong, and Japan. These subsequent, multinationally produced films equally focused on martial arts and intimate personal relationships, such as Chen Kaige's *The Promise (Wú Jí*, 2005), Tsui Hark's *Seven Swords (Qī Jiàn*, 2005), and the Hong Kong director Jacob Cheung's antiwar epic set in ancient China, *A Battle of Wits (Mò Gōng*, 2006). These forms of swordplay and martial arts films reveal the processes of cultural reconfiguration by which local film industries negotiate, construct, and situate themselves in what Arjun Appadurai calls "imagined worlds," more specifically transnational "mediascapes," which foreground the transnational distribution and interconnection of disparate images through media, but without completely effacing national identities.[35]

MODs and Mapping Affect

With the growing sales of DVDs in the mid- to late 1990s came a parallel growth: the rise of "bonus material" accompanying the film itself. Though such extras vary widely depending on the production's budget and genre and the enthusiasm of its makers, the "making of" documentary is one of the most common, and central, features. And essential to these documentaries are some combination of film excerpts, location footage, interviews with the cast and crew, and other miscellaneous material. With certain films, the "making of" material constitutes a text in its own right, particularly in cases in which the conditions of production are exceedingly technical or otherwise difficult.[36] As a text about a text, the MOD has been recognized as "an ideal postmodern idiom."[37] Coinciding with the growing popularity of home theater systems and the release of special edition DVDs such as the Criterion Collection—which legitimated the home as "an important alternative space for film spectatorship and analysis"—the MOD positions a film in its industrial context, according to Craig Hight (referring specifically to the MOD for *The Lord of the Rings*), but with "little exploration of wider political or economic contexts."[38] For Hight, the DVD's extended version of the film alongside its copious supplementary material effectively created a new text, "one perhaps offering a distinct experience for home audiences."[39] What *The Lord of the Rings* MOD and the *Musa* MOD have in common is the revelation that, among the crew, the production of the film was itself a journey that doubled the diegetic journey of the characters depicted in the film itself.[40]

The MOD as a form has been traced to Hollywood behind-the-scenes documentaries in the 1960s, which served as promotional material and television filler.[41] It could be argued that the earliest Korean MOD, although not recognized or marketed at the time as such, was actually a narrative film, *Spring on the Korean Peninsula*, directed by Lee Byeong-il and released in Korea in 1941, then under Japan's imperial rule. The film centers on the goings-on backstage during the making of the film *Chunhyang*. These behind-the-scenes "actualities," featuring the actors Kim So-yeong and Kim Il-hae, offer a rich depiction of the era's film technology, and thus the film has proved invaluable in understanding Korean studio conditions under Japanese rule. When *Musa* was released in 2001, MODs were just starting to become a common feature in DVD releases, and their presentation of material was relatively primitive. Pak Hui-jun's *Dream of a Warrior* (*Ch'ŏnsamong*, 2001), for example, which starred Hong Kong's Leon Lai and South Korea's Lee Na-young, released stills and promotional information as additional material on its DVD, but the MOD of behind-the-scenes footage was released separately, and only on the film's website, just before the release of the film.[42] But as coproductions grew—both as a vehicle for profit and for cooperation—the MOD became a useful promotional vehicle not only for the film itself, but for the new bonds of mutual cooperation and collaboration required to make such a film.

Musa's MOD was not lost on critics, who were just beginning to take note of this material as a genre in its own right. The Korean film magazine *Cine21* singled out *Musa*'s MOD as one of the more appealing DVD supplements ever released, along with the special features of Francis Coppola's *The Godfather* box set, Alfred Hitchcock's *The Birds* (1963, Collector's Edition DVD released with supplements in 2000), and John Cameron Mitchell's *Hedwig and the Angry Inch* (2001).[43] The article noted the *Musa* MOD's particular emphasis not just on the physical but on the emotional toll of film production, as well as the bond of camaraderie formed between the Korean and Chinese crew members.[44]

Presented to the viewer using an interactive map, the *Musa* MOD is framed by the film crew's journey: as we know, the Korean crew flew into Beijing, headed west by train to Zhongwei, and from there proceeded 10,000 kilometers back east across the desert to Liaoning Sheng. Organized by the various filming locations, the MOD's title page displays a map in which each location is identified by the film crew's emotional state at that particular juncture in the filming process: Beijing is associated with excitement (*hŭngbun*), Zhongwei with fervor (*yŏlgi*), Yinchuan, the capital of the Ningxia Hui Autonomous Region, with homesickness (*hyangsu*), Pukt'aek with anticipation (*kitae*), and lastly, Liaoning Sheng with reminiscence (*ch'uŏk*). The result is a cartography that links geography to affect, and an interactive interface that resists narrative and structural linearity. With each location—and emotion—accessible through a click, the MOD encourages a journey through an emotional rather than strictly geographical terrain.

Early in *Musa*, the envoys and warriors draw a rudimentary map of China—coarse lines in loose sand—to mark the desert that the warriors must traverse to make it back home to Koryo. The same landmarks that situate the desert within the film for spectators, the Nanjing castle and the fort in Shandong, mark the points of their departure and arrival, and also the beginning and end of the film. Facing warring Yuan troops to the north and Ming troops to the south, the Koryo delegation is forced to forge a path through the treacherous desert "in-between." This desert remains untouched by either side because it is considered unconquerable. Yet for this reason, it is also the safest and shortest way for the warriors to get back to Koryo. Their planned route, however, is changed unexpectedly when they come across a kidnapped Ming princess, played by the actress Zhang Ziyi (who, by the time of the DVD's release, was a global sensation thanks to her role in Ang Lee's *Crouching Tiger, Hidden Dragon*). When the delegation stops amid a group of traveling central Asian tradesmen and sees the captured Ming princess, General Choi is stirred to action by her beauty and seductive cry for help. General Choi commands that they reverse course and accompany the princess home to Nanjing first and, at the same time, fulfill their diplomatic mission. Hoping that the promise of the princess's safe return will gain them entry into Nanjing castle on more favorable terms, and perhaps restore their diplomatic status, the Koryo delegation decides to head to Shandong (where they will be given a boat, promises the princess, as a sign of gratitude by the Ming army who will meet her there and accompany her the rest of the way), instead of Koryo, so that they can restart their journey to Koryo with honor. This departure from the original route, which is motivated by sudden emotion, strangely mimics the terms in which a viewer might engage the MOD's interface. The original linear journey is scrapped, and the travelers are instead led by their emotions. Later, at the fortress where the film reaches its climax, the decision about whether to continue helping the princess return to Nanjing or abort their mission and continue their original plan to go home to Koryo divides General Choi and the slave Yŏsol, both of whom are in love with the princess. Travel becomes determined by affect, a point magnified by the film's persistent visual contrast: vast desert landscapes, each largely indistinguishable from the last, contrast with the film's sharply articulated representation of the characters' affective states.

Unlike the diegetic maps in films such as *Raiders of the Lost Ark* (1981), *Casablanca* (1942), and *Les Amants* (1958), all of which use maps to situate characters geographically and to represent travel between places, the interactive extra-diegetic map in *Musa's* MOD functions to direct viewers as if we were tourists entering the virtual space of the film.[45] So, rather than travel vicariously through the itinerancy of the film's characters—as we do when we are swept up in a film's plot—viewers of the MOD seem to travel in their stead. In contrast to films in which maps locate and fix the viewer in acts of "global positioning," *Musa's* emphasis on indistinguishable locations—epitomized by makeshift camps, by abandoned fortresses, and perhaps most strongly, by the desert itself—signals its interest in a more flexible mode of viewer positioning, one that the MOD makes explicit.[46] Thus, though the film itself seems intent on denying the specificity of global positioning, it seems to do so in order to focus instead on the progressive bonds formed between the characters as strangers become friends, especially across national lines. Both *Musa* and its MOD ask that viewers relate not to nationally located characters per se, but to the bonds forming between them, and thus the map charts not the movement of bodies through space, but the dissolution of national boundaries within new affective formations.[47] Drawing on Lev Manovich, Hight suggests that viewers of such DVDs are not viewers at all, but rather "*users*, navigating our way through menus and following the pathways they provide."[48] Organized by the exploratory logic of the database rather than the delineated arc of narrative fiction, the DVD with all of its added features requires the viewer's participation in order to create order out of the otherwise fragmentary nature of the information presented therein, in a similar way that the interactive narrative allows for multiple narrative possibilities within a discrete text.[49]

Labor, Logistics, and Affect

In his interview included in the DVD's special features, an independent component of the "extras" DVD, the actor Ahn Sung-ki remembers the most extreme aspects of the filming experience. Beginning with how he felt on reading the script, Ahn proceeds to talk about moments of great suffering (kot'ong) and hardship (kosaeng), as well as his most absurd (hwangdang) and most regrettable (ashiun) moments while filming. Ahn recalls that his role in Chung Ji-young's Nambugun (1990), a film about North Korean POWs, had been the most difficult in his career, but that the physical and mental toll of Musa was far worse. Learning Chinese, along with martial arts training and horseback riding, all of which he began prior to his trip, was trying, but these were nothing compared to the challenges of life on location in China. He describes, for example, the blistering chill coming off of the frozen sea as they filmed the final scene, and the inconvenience of unpredictable water shortages while showering. Despite these difficulties, however, Ahn remembers the experience fondly: "I kept thinking it was hard then, but after time, it became a precious memory of unforgettable and great stories. Good things—working together and getting to know great Chinese crew, and amongst our staff, the friendly bonds [uchŏng] formed beyond the roles was palpable and very good." Despite the physical hardship suffered by himself as well as the other members of the film's cast and crew, the bonds formed as part of the experience of joint production becomes a substantial reward, constituting indeed a kind of yŏchŏng.

Ahn's positive memory of past suffering offers a model, both in the film and across the extras DVD, in which we see a parallel process at work: we learn how the film resolves the historical hostility between the Chinese and Koryo people and how the difficulties and tensions faced by the mixed production crew transformed into yŏchŏng through the collaborative film-making process. The MOD tracks this conversion by focusing in particular on what have been termed meta-emotions, or "evaluative thoughts and feelings about emotions."[50] They are what allow, for example, viewers to enjoy filmic representations of otherwise undesirable emotions. We can enjoy watching a tearjerker, for example, as Mary Beth Oliver suggests, if "the viewer's metaemotions [sic] associated with the negative sentiments are favorable."[51] As is the case in the film itself, it is intercultural cooperation in the MOD that overcomes individual suffering by giving it meaning, by making that suffering part of a valuable collective effort. Both texts self-reflexively document the coproduction process and model future possibilities of China-Korea collaborations by staging, in often melodramatic terms, the fact of shared labor and toil, of the sort that creates lasting bonds of camaraderie that sketch out the terms for broader scale exchanges between nations. What we find here is that compassion (and I am thus categorizing yŏchŏng as a kind of compassion) is the preferred meta-emotion of joint cultural and economic collaboration. By rehearsing and documenting what it felt like to enact tragic circumstances under conditions of physical duress, the MOD offers the experience of the production crews as a model for broader cultural and economic exchanges; this model yokes the interpersonal meaning of compassion—the sense of suffering together—with Kathleen Woodward's notion of a geopolitical compassion that indicates how socially progressive the two now friendly nations have become.

The resonance of compassion is evident even in the filming itself, and in particular in the use of CinemaScope to capture the awe-inspiring Chinese landscape.[52] CinemaScope refers to the anamorphic camera lens used widely from the 1950s until the mid-1960s to shoot widescreen movies. Though the lens became obsolete, CinemaScope's anamorphic format stayed. In 1954 Roland Barthes described CinemaScope's capacities in relational terms, as "a new dialectic between men and the horizon, men and objects," one that would constitute "a dialectic of interdependence and no longer one of décor."[53] The aesthetic proximity afforded by the technology would allow the audience to sit in "the balcony of History," in which one might imagine oneself "in front of *The Battleship Potemkin*, no longer stationed at the end of a telescope but supported by the same air, the same stone, the same crowd: this ideal *Potemkin*, where you could finally join hands with the insurgents, share the same light, and experience the tragic Odessa Steps in their fullest force."[54] Barthes sees in the expansive space of CinemaScope the possibility of awakening a different mode of political consciousness. *Musa* attempts to inscribe, into this capacious visual world made possible by CinemaScope, the mechanisms that enabled its production, specifically a compassion borne of cooperation, using the technology's ability both to close distance between the Chinese and Koreans diegetically and to shape a more visceral experience for the viewer, in the way prescribed by Barthes, in order to further its collaborative logics (figs. 3.2–3.7).[55]

The descriptive copy on *Musa*'s DVD packaging emphasizes the film's "most real and touching action" as well as its "most real and brutal martial arts action." Such claims are only partial hyperbole. The film's liberal use of spectacular widescreen shots of vast landscapes establish a visual panorama almost too enormous to comprehend, while extreme close-ups, such as the jarring shots of the horse and envoy moments before they fatally succumb to the desert, infuse this brutal landscape with a desperate sense of struggle, both between humans and between humans and nature. CinemaScope's widescreen capabilities are thus used in conjunction with close-ups as a way of embedding the viewer visually and affectively in the landscape. The film critic Derek Elley has observed that the action sequences, particularly toward the second part of the film, "have a melancholic viscerality."[56] This visceral depiction of action is something that *Musa* consciously attempts to represent by alternating between hand-to-hand combat scenes in tighter views and wider shots of horseback battles that occupy more space, the latter culminating in a spectacular scene of hundreds of warriors on horseback descending barren desert slopes, which was filmed under the supervision of Korean, Chinese, as well as Mongolian martial arts choreographers. But even the abundance of wider shots is consistently interspersed with lingering close-ups of death by arrows, severed limbs, and decapitations, all filmed in a measured, realistic tempo.

The film culminates in a failed defense of an old abandoned fortress, which pits the protagonists—a polyglot cast of characters divided by affiliations and priorities—overmatched against a much larger and more powerful Yuan army. They are overwhelmed and many of the principals die, but the survivors, including the princess, are spared at the last moment when the opposing leader is killed in battle. In their doomed effort to defend the fortress, the group has to rely on each other, dividing the various tasks to defend themselves as efficiently and effectively as possible. In short, they have to work together. Because their position is so weak and overwhelming, the battle itself becomes reimagined as the division and sharing of labor; the task of meeting a powerful foe in battle becomes reimagined as a long list of practical details that must be addressed. The work of collaboration not only characterizes the film's production history, but is explicitly thematized in the film itself.

The "extras" features, too, highlight this vision of atomized labor. The segment titled "Documentary by Producer," for instance, begins with shots of filming in the summer of 2000 that establish the number of extras involved, China's participation in terms of sets and actors, the distance covered, and the temperatures under which the filming took place. The segment also discusses aspects of the production process in relation to individual scenes, such as the numerous decapitation scenes, by taking the viewer through the computer

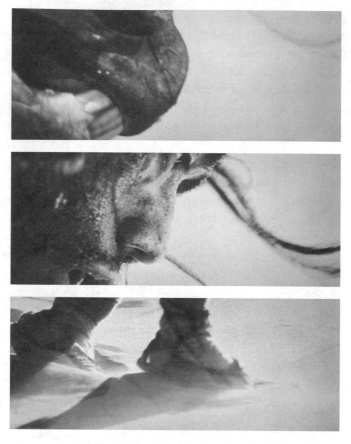

3.2–3.7 (*above and opposite*) CinemaScope in *Musa*.

graphics, dummies, the animation techniques, and the piercing and lancing. Documenting the complexity of the film's production, the MOD focuses on the myriad underappreciated tasks that go into each scene, for instance, shots of the equipment that had to be set up and the extras that had to be organized. Doubling the final scene of the film, the brutality of battle is reduced to a series of logistical problems. And as if to foreground this transition, the demystifying behind-the-scenes accounts are juxtaposed in the MOD with the actual scenes from the film. In both cases, beyond the high drama of the scene itself, what we are witnessing is work.

Pertinent here is the fact that the word *yŏchŏng* contains a double meaning. It is an emotion associated with travel, but it can also refer to a travel itinerary. Both senses seem relevant to *Musa* and its MOD. They are concerned

both with the emotional bonds formed through prolonged travel and with the logistics of travel: itemized, broken down into a series of days, hours, minutes, places, and locations. Perhaps this is because the intensity of the feeling of yŏchŏng becomes measurable in these little details, and these details, in the context of the MOD, coincide precisely with the details of work. Accordingly, the slickly edited MOD fashions a parallel between narrative progression and behind-the-scenes production: scenes from the film blend seamlessly with shots of the filming, as the MOD's editing collapses feature-film footage with video format into a coherent whole. Without belying its disjunctive constitutive parts, the intermedial editing of the MOD depicts the production process of the film as an extension of the film itself and the logics that govern it.

So when director Kim Sung-su suggests in the MOD that the film is ultimately about the internal enemies faced by the traveling warriors, rather than about their external adversaries, these internal enemies seem self-reflexive embodiments of the adversities experienced in the film's production. Similarly, the "excitement" the Beijing portion of the MOD captures is the enthusiasm of the initial moments of a large, carefully planned project—before the immensity of the task really sets in. We see the crew shooting the first scenes juxtaposed with preproduction sketches and wide-angle shots of the production enterprise en masse. In the filming of the sandstorm scene in the "Zhongwei/Fervor" section, the forces of nature are continually recoded as challenges to work. The MOD shows the crew struggling in an actual sandstorm (rather than one generated by electric fans) cross-cut with scenes from the film in which the envoys endure the very same elements; there is even a close-up of a character reaching out his hand to another traveler, followed by a shot of the film staff doing the same.

Conclusion: Provisional Feelings

In this context, *Musa* itself, like its MOD, might be read as an allegory for the increasing overlap of Korean and Chinese cultural and economic interests. In this respect, *Musa* itself functions as a kind of MOD. Both work to expand the category of yŏchŏng to include not just the affects that arise from joint travel, but also broader relations between countries. That expansion is evident in the plot of the film itself: the first half of the film is dominated by the internal antagonisms between individuals vying for leadership and the attentions of the princess, whereas the second half of the film depicts group solidarity that is forged after the negotiation of shared interests. The motley band, making their way past battlefields littered with corpses and across a never-ending desert to Shandong, consists of Koryo Yongho soldiers assigned to guard the diplomatic envoys, members of the Koryo people's army, Koryo interpreters, and a freed Koryo slave. A Ming princess, a Buddhist monk, and a Yuan prostitute formerly in service of the Mongol warriors later join the travelers, and at Hwangho River, they are further joined by a large group of Chinese civilians driven out of their villages by the plundering Yuan army. But despite all the divergent interests of the group, eventually they unite in the final battle and work together, if only, for many in their party, to die a heroic death.

The yŏchŏng developed among the group of beleaguered travelers helps them create a provisional unity in order to accomplish pressing tasks. This provisional quality suits the general ethos of the film, which seems far from nationalistic or xenophobic. Loyalties, and boundaries, between good and bad are temporary and ambiguous. Alliances are provisional and forged based on ever-changing circumstances. The Koryo envoys initially align themselves against the Ming, but then assert their impartiality between the Ming and the Yuan in the market scene where they stand by in the observance of Yuan burial rites for Yuan warriors. Once the Ming princess is in their midst, the Koryo delegates shift their hopes to the Ming army, from whom they hope to gain protection against the Yuan on their return to Koryo.

One provisional commonality shared by the disparate travelers in the film and as well by all the members of cast and crew in the MOD, regardless of nationality, is homesickness. Everybody in *Musa* is a traveler far from home. The battling Yuan and Koryo warriors are all far away from their homes—the Koryo warriors are on a journey home, while the Yuan warriors want to complete their mission so that they may return to the prairies. The separation from home and family is the main source of conversation around the campfire. Princess Furong is far from home, and having barely escaped death in enemy hands, she is determined to stick by the Korean warriors in order to make it back to her palace. The Mongol warriors constantly long for the plains and struggle with the urge to leave the princess behind rather than obey the orders of their leader. Even the Yuan general mourns the fading dreams of Genghis Khan, a leader who for him embodies home, revealing this longing as his weakness one night over a drink too many.

In similar fashion, the segment of the MOD entitled "Yinchuan/Homesickness" (*hyangsu*) opens with establishing shots that seem anathema to the idea of home, specifically shots of vast landscape with the filmmakers' caravan of vans and tracks moving along the horizon in a thin line toward Yinchuan. We eventually see the crew at their night camp, listening to opera music on a CD player that Ahn Sung-ki turns on. We see them smoking together and commenting on how such music at this location feels like a fantasy. Despite their efforts to make the best of the situation, crew and cast members alike profess their homesickness and longing for the family and food that await them when they return. One moment focuses on the Korean actors on Ch'usŏk, the Korean harvest festival and traditionally a time when Koreans visit their families. Missing home, they speak wistfully about missing the holidays and even apologize to their parents, using the MOD itself as a means to transmit their feelings, wishing those back home a happy Ch'usŏk while they work. Homesickness is a universal emotion on the set and thus gives way to the construction of provisional familial ties, for example, through gleeful celebrations of birthdays, the cultivation of friendships, and the kind of playful joking around that comes with such environments. Laughter outtakes in fact are quite prominent in the MOD, demonstrating the camaraderie experienced among the cast and crew, despite—and indeed because of—the difficult circumstances. In an interview Zhang Ziyi emphasizes the shared effort: "It was as if this schedule was a process of training our wills, from the actors to everyone."

As it progresses toward its conclusion, the MOD increasingly focuses on the Chinese collaborators; it documents the growing camaraderie between the Koreans and Chinese. And as filming draws to an end, the interviews become more wistful. The final chapter of the MOD, "Liaoning Sheng/Reminiscence" (ch'uŏk), coincides with the filming of the climactic fortress scene. By now, it is winter. Here, beginning with the film crew's arrival at Liaoning Sheng (shown in video format) and the point toward *Musa*'s end where the travelers arrive at the fortress (shown in film format), the MOD periodically alternates rapidly between the film and video formats, effectively re-creating parts of the scene in a way that essentially erases the boundary between film and filmmaking. In pulling the MOD camera back from the film scene to reveal the film cameras, lighting, and crew members standing by—especially in the making of the scenes in which characters we are emotionally invested in are killed— these scenes not only make the process of labor inextricable from the affective scene itself, but also highlight the coming to an end of the provisional feelings. The focus eventually turns to shots of laughter as Koreans and Chinese working on the film are captured in the midst of acting, shooting, setting up equipment, and discussing the process of filming the scene together. As a Chinese song from *Musa*'s soundtrack plays, we see a sequence, in which Zhang Ziyi waves goodbye to the MOD camera and various configurations of the crew take pictures together. That laughter is followed by another sequence of scenes from the fortress night scene, scenes of killing and the filming of those scenes. We then shift to the last day of filming. Zhang Ziyi is sad because they have all spent so much time together. Again blending dramatic scenes from the ending of the film itself with production footage, we see everyone expressing wistfulness now that filming is drawing to an end, the crew gathering to take a group photograph, and a farewell shot of Zhang Ziyi waving, saying, "This film, for which I had to endure longing and suffering, is therefore dear."

In demonstrating the yŏchŏng cultivated throughout the arduous filming process, the final sequence of the MOD culminates a narrative of cooperation and bathes it in sentimental affect, producing what amounts to a melodrama of coproduction. It is no coincidence then that this section of the MOD features scenes from the climax of the film at the ruined fortress, which is suffused by the same affective sensorium constructed in the MOD's final moments. If the cast and crew, sharing a collective sense of homesickness, began to behave as a kind of provisional family, then the fortress in the finale takes on the function of a de facto home. Despite the disparate political and national interests of the group, its generational and religious divisions, everyone puts aside his or her own interest for the benefit of the group, as it comes under the vicious attack of the Yuan army. Within the crumbling walls of the fortress, a new baby is born, and as near-certain death encroaches, mothers hold soldiers and call them son, while old men feebly pick up swords in defense of young women. Warriors put aside rivalries and conflict in order to fight against a common enemy, sacrificing their own lives to protect people they barely know. In this way, the climax of the film mirrors the work of the DVD, which is to stage collaboration itself and to articulate possible points of contact with strangers. Such an imagination requires compassion, an ability to feel together. And it is this affective foundation of compassion on which the new alliances and cooperative endeavors that define hallyu cinema aspire to reshape East Asian cultural and economic relations.

If *Musa* and its MOD work to build this affective foundation of shared affect through compassion borne of traveling together, then *Daisy*, a 2006 collaboration between Hong Kong's Andrew Lau and South Korea's Kwak Jae-yong, demonstrates how interregional collaboration can produce not just shared affect between individuals from different nations, but more radically, the layering of disparate traditions and complex histories into what I call an affective palimpsest. Between these two films, the new amity between nations that were recently antagonistic moves from being rooted in interpersonal cooperation to being based on a sense of discursive cooperation. More than different people working together, affective palimpsests encourage less provisional models of feeling together, modes that elide their initial national contexts and instead attempt to produce new transnational syntheses out of historically divided interests. In this manner, hallyu cinema functions to produce an interregional audience that not only shares feelings, but also imagines itself as somehow part of a single entity.

4. AFFECTIVE PALIMPSESTS

Sudden Showers from Hwang Sun-wŏn's "Sonagi"
to Kwak Jae-yong and Andrew Lau's *Daisy*

At the Sonagi Village tourist attraction in Yangpyŏng, South Korea, which
opened in 2004, artificially manufactured rain falls three times a day. These
downpours mimic the sudden shower (*sonagi*) central to Hwang Sun-wŏn's
classic 1952 coming-of-age short story, "A Shower" ("Sonagi") and later to Ko
Yŏng-nam's now equally iconic 1978 film adaptation, *The Shower (Sonagi)*.[1] In
the story, a boy and girl spend a day together, during which they are caught
by a sudden rain shower. Though the rain gives them the opportunity to get
closer together for warmth, the girl gets sick and dies. Referencing one of their
more intimate moments, tall millet stalks lean against each other around the
perimeter of the field, and when the rain falls, visitors run for shelter under
their sheaves. The manufactured scene creates a very specific kind of rain
that speaks to the often deep-rooted, affective association between the sudden showers and a nostalgic intimacy evoked in the original tale (fig. 4.2). In
contrast to the more negative affective states that pervaded postwar Korean
discourse in the latter half of the twentieth century, the affective quality of

---

4.1 Haptic origin of the sudden rain shower trope in Ko Yŏng-nam's
film *The Shower*. Courtesy of the Korean Film Archive.

4.2 Sprinklers regularly re-create "sudden" rain showers at Sonagi Village.
Photo by author.

innocent "pureness" (*sunsu*), embodied by Hwang's rain, persevered through
the tumultuous decades following the Korean War (1950–1953). These "sudden showers" become an important trope in postwar South Korean culture,
linked to a universal affect that was internalized as personal feeling for many
Koreans, a trope that reappears in various forms and contexts from 1952 to
1978 and through to the present. Two-and-a-half decades after the original
short story, Ko's erotic treatment of the material actually intensified, rather
than sullied, the innocence of the love sprouting between the boy and girl
in the rain, revealing a certain element of affective *refusal* inherent in the qualities of sunsu. That insistence on innocence is hardly surprising since the ideal
of "pure literature," with which Hwang Sun-wŏn was aligned, lay consciously
outside the bleak reality of a Korea occupied by the U.S. military. Postliberation notions of pure literature—which had Japanese and colonial origins
going back to pre-1945 debates with proletarian and commercial literature that
can be characterized as art for art's sake vs. art for people's sake—upheld the
earlier convictions of artistic independence and aesthetic autonomy, with an
emphasis on purity and a distinctive Koreanness.[2] However, as before, this apo-
litical tendency and ethnonational particularity also lay claim to humanism
and universalism in its attempt to give form to a new aesthetics of global

humanism bringing together "East" and "West."[3] In other words, for writers of pure literature like Hwang Sun-wŏn and Kim Tong-ni, assertions of "a truly global modern literary spirit" and emotional particularity always set in motion the possibility of a universalist, global affectivity.[4]

Like a fable, the rain of the story instead conjured glimmers of ahistorical, pastoral times. The evasiveness of sunsu that simultaneously gives it its force—a paradox specifically associated here with the sudden downpour of rain—thus entails a denunciation of reality, and by extension corporeality. As such, though the longing for sunsu is potent because of its contrast with the reality of Korea's postwar troubles, it is simultaneously an attempt to articulate an affective state independent of that reality. Like the Sonagi Village itself, the pervasive reproduction of Hwang's sonagi trope between 1978 and today, in films, television dramas, theater, musicals, animations, and theme park alike, has continuously attempted to distill a pure essence that paradoxically remains elusive.

One example of this pervasive reproduction is an inconspicuous scene in the South Korean director Kwak Jae-yong's seminal hallyu film, *My Sassy Girl* (*Yŏpkijŏgin kŭnyŏ*, 2001), which reprises the sonagi affect in comic terms. In a set-piece retelling of Hwang Sun-wŏn's story, the film subverts the ending of this classic tale of innocent love between two schoolchildren in a mock-morbid reenactment. The original tale sublimates the pang of sudden grief and loss that readers would presume on behalf of the half-sleeping boy into a trite conversation he overhears between his parents speaking of the girl's death, especially her wish to be buried in clothes that (only he knows) refer to their day together during a sudden rain shower. *My Sassy Girl*, in contrast, temporally destabilizes and structurally disperses the passively emotive force of this ending: the girl's last wish is not to be buried in particular clothing, but with the boy himself; we see him forcefully dragged and knocked into her grave with a shovel by mourning villagers. Although lighthearted, the film's comically sadistic modification of Hwang's "Sonagi" draws our attention not only to its identification of the sonagi trope as inherent to distinct Korean sensibilities (*chŏngsŏ*), but more significantly to the desire for intimate touch in the trope, which in Kwak's version forcefully demands violent reclamation of bodily rather than representational forms (the stained clothes).[5] Kwak does draw the film's affective energies from the sonagi trope, gesturing to the historical within a structure of layered genres, but only insofar as the tale offers a means for the film to proclaim its desire for material presence, one that is divested of the affect imbued in the stained clothes. In so doing Kwak disaggregates material form from its historical emotional content. The sonagi affect is cited without being felt, experienced as a kind of presence without intimacy.

Kwak's empty materiality thus starkly contrasts the intensely emotive quality of Hwang Sun-wŏn's rain and the version of materiality captured in Ko's 1978 filmic adaptation, which uses physical contact to signal emotional identification (fig. 4.1). In Ko's film torrents of rain simultaneously obstruct our view while activating the vicarious feeling of cold rain prickling the boy and girl's flesh. Here, the moist warmth of the boy's mouth sucking blood from her scraped knee stands in contrast to the prickly droplets of cold rain on their skin, producing a sensorium in which the haptic and the affective overlap. In addition, the film reclaims touch not just as rain on the skin, but also as rain on the film screen, effecting a kind of material contact between film and spectator, analogous to the elaborate sprinkler system at Sonagi Village. In both the film and the tourist site, the artifice compels the observer to feel the rain that once dampened the skin of fictional characters on their own. In both Hwang's and Ko's productions, rain functions as the material conduit for the affect and the memory of an erotic intimacy, a fantasy that emanates from purity and pure desire but is shattered by the violence of modernity. In contrast, Kwak's homage, which persistently averts intimate touch, denies this connection between physical and emotional proximity that downpouring rain has traditionally signified in Korean iconography.

Kwak's preoccupation with the denatured sonagi trope—also found in his *Watercolor on a Rainy Day* films (*Pionŭn nal such'aehwa*, 1989; *Pionŭn nal such'aehwa 2*, 1993) and *The Classic* (*K'ŭllaesik*, 2003)—leads us to *Daisy* (*Teiji*, 2006). Here, he continues in his collaboration as writer (alongside co-writers Gordon Chan and Felix Chong) with the Hong Kong neo-noir director Andrew Lau, who is best known for his *Infernal Affairs* trilogy. While working with Lau, following the success of *My Sassy Girl*, Kwak was at the height of his transpacific visibility as a hallyu filmmaker. It is therefore no surprise, perhaps, that the sonagi trope in this collaborative effort leaves the familiar confines of national cultural production and becomes further removed from Hwang, to become part of what David Howes calls a discourse of intercultural "intersensoriality."[6] If Kwak's *My Sassy Girl* represents a disarticulation of the trope from its historical context, then his participation in this collaborative venture opens further questions about what happens when affect travels. Directed by Lau, written by Kwak, and set in Europe, a locale native to neither, *Daisy* displaces and reincarnates the sonagi trope in a new transnational context.[7] If Kwak's *My Sassy Girl* used the trope to reclaim a sense of intimate haptic corporeality at the expense of an emotionalized historical nationalism, then Lau's *Daisy* takes this decontextualization even further by divesting the story's rain and stain of their original associations in order to foreground instead an inquiry into the tactile nature of the affective image itself. The appropriation begs some questions: what does the creation of a denatured sonagi trope—heretofore quintessential to postwar Korea's nativist return to a "pure" literature—accomplish in this collaborative production? What is the meaning of a historically Korean trope as it travels from Korea to Hong Kong to Europe?

Set in the Netherlands—specifically Amsterdam and Haarlem, the world capital of tulip bulbs—*Daisy* demonstrates Kwak and Lau's shared sense of spatiality along with their penchant for water-centric aesthetics, but also foregrounds their different genre interests and characteristic styles of expression; and it is clear that Lau's preferences, as director, take privilege.[8] First of all, the weather of the location itself in water-bound Amsterdam, namely the endless, mostly nocturnal drizzle, in contrast to South Korea's more evenly spread rainfall, would seem to appeal to Lau's Hong Kong neo-noir sensibilities. Second, the plot is typical of Lau's *Infernal Affairs* films: *Daisy* similarly features the rivalry between a mobster and a cop, blending the triad genre with stylistic and thematic elements associated with the Hong Kong New Wave.[9] What is typical of Lau is atypical of Kwak, who prefers (and indeed, helped to define) the themes and visual aesthetics of Korean Wave romantic comedies, as evidenced in *My Sassy Girl* and the subsequent *Windstruck*.

Daisy uses the sonagi trope to layer aesthetically, affectively, and sensorially the various cultural sensibilities at play in this self-consciously transnational film, which was written by a Korean, was shaped by a Hong Kong director, featured an international cast, and was set in the Netherlands. Reflecting this transnational production, and an interregional aesthetic that foregrounds travel, the film thus manifests what I call *affective palimpsests*. Palimpsests are traditionally associated with writing, in which faint traces of the past remain in the present.[10] By affective palimpsests, I refer both to the layering of various aesthetic styles that have to do with the expression of sensuality, which retain traces in spite of the overwriting, and also to the layering of different cultural sensibilities and national histories that are synthesized in joint productions and disarticulated from their original contexts. In *Daisy* the rain of the sonagi trope, brought to the film through Kwak Jae-yong's participation, functions not as a symbol that imports meaning from one context to another, but as a formal vehicle, a kind of nexus, that allows for the layering of multiple traditions and complex histories. Rain, in this context, allows for the preservation of affective traces, rendering visible the extant stains that constitute the remains of the past, but at the cost of other erasures. Rain thus signifies a certain historical desire for materiality that emerges, paradoxically, when the traditional mechanisms of historical preservation, like national emotive tropes, dissipate. Although helmed by a director from Hong Kong, the film represents a full commitment to the logics of regional commerce and transnational production that characterizes hallyu cinema. *Daisy*'s affective palimpsests are thus symptomatic of the interregional collaborations that made the film possible and of the larger Asianization pressures that inform those collaborations. If *Musa* builds a sense of transnational solidarity by foregrounding the shared affects of unlikely travel companions, *Daisy* imagines a shared discursive sensibility that produces a sense of transnational collectivity that both appropriates from and subsumes older nationalist constructs.

The Sonagi Trope Distilled

Hwang's "Sonagi" story revolves around the nature of chaste, heterosexual love in its first encounter, ways to gain respite from social obstacles that forbid it, and its affective potential to invoke solace when recalled later from a different, usually more difficult, place and time. Almost all of the adaptations across the next half-century draw on several water elements that collectively constitute a particular sonagi sensibility. The sudden rain shower insulates the protagonists from the larger society and its strictures, such as class division, educational pressure, and repercussions of criminal activity. The downpour causes a flowing body of water, initially harmless, to suddenly surge, engulfing and enfolding the body. Protagonists seeking relief from the shower are brought into physical proximity. Last but not least, there is usually a stain marking the passing of that day that is linked to a sense of certain death. A parable about romanticism and nostalgia, the narrative sublimates the prohibition of sexual union and expression into pure reserve and reticence.

The abundant water symbolism in the original coming-of-age tale evokes an association between rain and eroticism as a form of "primitive passion" (*wŏnshijŏk yŏlchŏng*), which lingers in the subsequent texts.[11] Ko's film, for example, hints at this mode of primitiveness in interspersed hallucinatory scenes. At the beginning of the film, a woman scantily clad in a bra and skirt made of leaves appears before the boy in a jungle. Reminiscent of eroticized representations of tropical, South Pacific women, she is nothing like his mother, who always dresses in traditional commoner's clothes (*hanbok*). This apparition steals his clothes, essentially leaving him naked. Later, after the girl's death, a young woman in a white dress appears before him in the same forest, presumably a virgin ghost representing the girl. According to common Korean myth (as told to the girl by her grandmother in the film), virgin men would tremble before virgin ghosts, but the boy proceeds unaffected, yelling with exuberance. In 1978, and perhaps even now, explicitly sexualizing the two children in the filmic rendering would have sullied the original tale and Hwang Sun-wŏn himself, who has so long been associated with "innocence, restraint, and love of nation."[12] The director utilizes nature shots instead, in particular close-ups, to deflect but still hint at a budding sexuality and intimacy.[13] Hidden from sight and unbeknownst to others, the rain shower experience remains unseen. Thus, the sonagi creates an intimate space, in which the characters can explore the surfaces of one another. The haptic emphasis of both the story and the film brings to the fore the vulnerability of adolescence, which is inseparable from the pubescent fascination with the human body and its surface.

For the city of Yangpyŏng, the Sonagi Village provided a way to repair its seedy reputation—based on its remotely located love-motels that rented rooms by the hour—without erasing the city's associations with love. For the literature professors from Kyung Hee University that collaborated with developers of the site, a central problem in the design of the village was how to retain certain literary attributes of Hwang's "Sonagi" that they felt might otherwise be ignored in reimagining a narrative text as a theme park.[14] In particular, conveying the fabled nature of the narrative and its nostalgia for childhood, crucial to the tale's widespread appeal, required a way of actively triggering a visitor's affective response. Hwang's literary style, however, lent itself to a solution surprisingly well. His clear and concise writing frequently employs a repetitive pattern in which a physical description of a scene is immediately followed by a description of a character's emotional reaction to the scene, uncannily corresponding to the structure of a theme park.[15] Furthermore, "Sonagi" is an initiation story structured around allegorical travel that maps easily onto spatial coordinates, making it ideal for a theme-park format. The boy and girl cross a field to the base of a mountain, then go up the mountain, where they eventually get caught in the rain. The area up to the base of the mountain is childhood, and the space of the mountain itself and the

4.3 Wooden face-in-the-hole photo prop for the film *The Shower* at the Hwang Sun-wŏn Sonagi Village. Photo by author.

purple rain that falls there figure the hardship of adulthood.[16] Sonagi Village provides literal forms of these metaphors, physical spaces to contain these experiences.

The design for Sonagi Village embodies the afterlife of Hwang's rain, transposed into a different medium, but still accomplishing the affect prompted by the sonagi trope that the planners deemed crucial. The village is built concentrically. At the center is the sonagi field, ringed by millet stalks along the perimeter; this field forms the core of the village, which is accessible after a walk uphill from the parking lot. At the edge of this inner circular area is a stream with stepping-stones, a path with a bronze cow statue, and large screenshots from the film's rain scenes with face cutouts, where tourists can take snapshots of their own faces on the bodies of characters (fig. 4.3). Encircling these central moments is a narrow walking path with markers symbolizing each of Hwang's various works, thus weaving the "Sonagi" tale into the fabric of his larger oeuvre. The stream flows into a fountain designed to look like millet sheaves, and rising above it at the farthest edge is the museum, which is devoted to Hwang's oeuvre. Though the exterior of the museum is made of glass, it, too, is shaped like a millet stalk.

In this respect, Sonagi Village is not unlike Lau's *Daisy*, which also uses the sonagi trope in relation to both film and painting in order to draw out the trope's affect. In Hwang's tale the boy first sees the girl playing by the stream in the countryside. In *Daisy* a hit man goes into hiding in rural Netherlands after an assignment. There he sees a young woman, Hye-yŏng, on her way to paint a field of daisies, fall into a stream while crossing a log. In lieu of Hwang's stepping-stones, there is a fallen log (and later in the film, two bridges over the Amstel and Spaarne Rivers, which are equally crucial to the plot). Whereas the boy in Hwang's story carries the girl on his back, the hit man secretly builds a bridge for the young woman's safe crossing. In both versions, stains on cloth remain as result of that watery exchange: the stain on the girl's blouse that is transferred from the boy's body as they cross the water in "Sonagi" (fig. 4.4); and an oil painting of the stream that Hye-yŏng leaves as a gesture of thanks on the bridge in *Daisy*. Both leave material residue as a memory token that is later associated with precise moments of death. The girl in "Sonagi" asks to be buried in the stained clothes, while Hye-yŏng in *Daisy* gets shot while holding the canvas, her blood splattering on the depicted landscape (fig. 4.5).

The critical difference, however, between the tour site and *Daisy* is in how the village's structuring of the sonagi narrative preserves the essence of the sonagi trope and Hwang's authorship even while acknowledging the inter-textual associations that have accumulated over the years. In its transnational appropriation by Lau, the sonagi trope becomes severed from Hwang and is more clearly in keeping with Kwak's already denatured appropriation. In terms of interregional cinema collaboration, the circulation of the sonagi trope across genres and interpretive communities implies the same invocation of intimate space and hapticality that we witnessed in the more nationalist context, but the fate of Korean rain on foreign soil becomes an open question.

Shelter from the Rain

Given its subject matter, perhaps it is no coincidence that *Rain* (*Regen*), the Dutch filmmaker Joris Iven's 1929 iconic short documentary, was filmed in Amsterdam. *Rain* is a slick modernist exercise in film technique, register-ing the changes in mood that occur as a looming rain becomes a downpour, then as the sun breaks back through the clouds. Although it purported to represent a "day in the life of a rain shower," the film was actually filmed over four months. Along with *The Bridge* (*De Brug*, 1928) it established Ivens as an important avant-garde filmmaker. Writing of *Rain*, Béla Balázs explains that

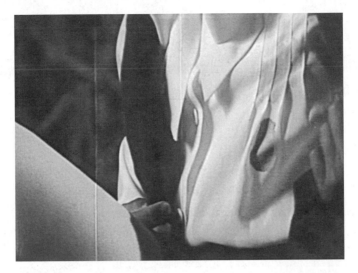

4.4 The girl's stained blouse. *The Shower.*

4.5 Hye-yŏng's splattered blood stains her landscape rendering of first love. *Daisy.*

Ivens watches and magnificently captures how it *looks* when the first drops begin to fall and the surface of the pond seems to shiver with gooseflesh, when a lone raindrop struggles to find a path down a windowpane, when the life of the town is reflected in the wet asphalt. How it looks. We have a thousand impressions—not an object. But only these impressions have meaning in our eyes. The object—the rain itself—holds no interest for us. What such images aim to show is not a state of affairs, but a particular optical impression, in short, an image. The image itself is the reality that we experience and there is nothing behind it, no concrete objective reality beyond the image.[17]

It is fair to say that Amsterdam afforded *Daisy*'s filmmaker similar possibilities for experimentation with the possibilities of wet, haptic imagery and its associations with time, albeit here within the parameters of commercial cinema. As with the rain in Ivens's film, the rain in *Daisy* belies a coherent temporality. The difference between Ivens's rain as observed by Balázs and the rain in *Daisy* has to do with the centrality of the object. The purely formal self-referential image itself of the rain is primary in Ivens's film, in contrast to *Daisy*, in which the rain is important for the possibility of multivalent transhistorical forms. Thus, although it holds true for *Daisy*, as for Ivens's film, that "no sense of time or space" holds the impressions left by rain—after all, the postwar context of the sonagi trope and the Hong Kong post-1997 (that is, after the "handover" of Hong Kong back to China, ending British rule) neo-noir sensibilities are drastically displaced here onto Amsterdam—there is a recombinant temporal and spatial specificity attributed to the rain in *Daisy* that is necessary for its affective force. This is also different from the particularity and deliberateness of rain that Laura Marcus has described, in contrast to Balázs's analysis of *Rain*; rain for Marcus retains the sense of consisting of visual impressions and maintains ocular centrality. Marcus draws our attention (by way of rain in Brussels, as described by the film reviewer Robert Herring) to the particular situatedness of rain, "as 'one particular rain, which fell somewhere, some time'—it drips 'with deliberation' from the Brussels Metropole's awning—but there is also a sense that this is a world composed entirely of 'visual impression' and that the optical effects of the rain in the Brussels city square and the images that might be projected on the Berlin city screen are indeed one and the same feast for the eye."[18]

The rain in *Daisy* consists of affective impressions in a repetitive framework that betray a preoccupation with preserving sunsu, that notion of "pureness" that here only exists in a time that is always already past. Sunsu suggests the purity and innocence of a relatively presocial moment in life, typically identified at the cusp of adolescence, a time felt to be most palpable just before its loss; that moment in life becomes appropriable by different contexts precisely because its own palpability is inseparable from its disappearance. Yet in the sense that the film repeatedly returns to a specific rain and singular event bound by numerical repetition within a temporally ambiguous structure that gets initiated by Hye-yŏng's admission of purity (that is, her inexperience of first love), time operates in a Deleuzian interrelationality of different times. In his gloss of Deleuze, James Williams suggests that temporalities are multiply co-implicated, in terms that resonate with my notion of affective palimpsests: "The past and the future are not simply realms we might be able to visit, they are processes fully implicated in our present ones. They are not only present as mediated, in imagination and memory, but directly in all present processes. . . . For him, past, present and future are not separate parts of time. Instead, they alternately treat each other as dimensions, where to be a dimension means to be a subsequent process."[19] For Deleuze, according to Williams, affective actors attempt to be worthy of the past, but because of an inevitable tension between the contingency of singular events in relationship to the pure past, the individual actor engages the pure past as if a time traveler: on one hand, he is incapable of mastering this engulfing past, but on the other hand he cannot help but to alter this past because it is always already implicated in the singular passing present.[20] The Deleuzian model also helps to figure the palimpsestic nature of pure sunsu time, which like the Deleuzian pure past cannot be captured by subsequent enactments, but is nevertheless changed by new upstart time travelers.

The director's cut version of *Daisy* is framed by a pair of nearly identical scenes that stage a version of the sonagi trope, in which Hye-yŏng, the painter, finds shelter from a sudden rain shower. In between these frames, the film consists of three interwoven narratives told from the perspective of three different characters, first by Hye-yŏng, then by the Interpol officer Chŏng-u, then by the hit man Pak Ŭi. Each segment begins self-reflexively establishing time and perspective, then flashes back to the person's memory of how they met the other two characters. The final shelter-from-the-rain scene, in which Hye-yŏng (in a voiceover) speaks of her hopes of experiencing first love, repeats the opening rain scene that comes after the opening credits, which is notably omitted in the theatrical release shown in Korean theaters. While the narrative here seems initially forward-looking in terms of her aspirations for love, it is ambiguously rendered backward-looking in that her story shifts to one of relating an encounter and event that has already happened. The opening rain scene thus ceases to function as a beginning but instead becomes a Proustian remembrance that is abruptly marked by the precise recollection of the specific time of her first meeting of Pak Ŭi, at 4:15 p.m. The precise time, and later the date (15 April), punctures the film periodically as if insisting on the persistent stalling of time in spite of the temporal and narrative progression of the film's forward-moving plot.

The repetition of the shelter scene at the end of the film in the director's cut follows what we assume to be the death of Pak Ŭi at the hands of his boss. In a transition from offscreen sound to on-screen image, the echoing gunshots converge with the sound of thunder materialized in sudden rain, at which point we see Hye-yŏng running under an awning for shelter. The act of waiting under the awning implies a brief respite, where she is untouched by the rain and by the time that passes outside of the space of shelter. The film repeatedly insists on a specific time and date—15 April, 4:15 p.m.—but only as compulsively repeated signifiers, just as the rain that falls is a repetition of a rain that has already fallen or will fall again in the film. The film's overarching frame thus destabilizes time, such that a specific time marked by a specific event essentially becomes indefinite. In so doing, the play of time in the film here resonates with Todd McGowan's notion of an "atemporal cinematic mode," in which filmic technique disrupts linear experiences of chronological time in order "to introduce spectators to an alternative way of experiencing existence in time—or, more exactly, a way of experiencing existence outside of our usual conception of time. Time in these films doesn't bring about a different future but instead an incessant repetition."[21]

An atemporal logic seems to surround these shelter scenes. The opening shelter scene anticipates an event, then quickly slips into a recollection of an encounter that has already occurred. The last rain scene is preceded by a shootout that proceeds only to be rewound and re-proceed in reverse: the assassin, Pak Ŭi, is seen heading into a building where he is met by bullets and a statue falling from several stories up. The Virgin Mary shatters on the floor, then is shown being pieced back into a whole, rapidly, as the film reverses the same sequence of shots. The shooters seem to retreat, as does Pak Ŭi. Whereas the opening scene had not zoomed in on Pak Ŭi under the awning, in the end scene we see him here, in a tight shot/reverse-shot with Chŏng-u, but unacknowledged by Hye-yŏng who leaves as soon as the rain ceases. That all three are dead at this point in the film also renders this scene posthumous and ghostly, further complicating the film's already atemporal coordinates.

But the point of atemporality in the film is not just to add complexity. Time compulsively repeats, but repeats with a difference, such that the various layers of the rain trope within the film double the larger acts of appropriation in which the film engages, with respect to the history of the sonagi trope. Even more than the Korean theatrical version, which in the shelter scene appears only in the end, the director's cut foregrounds an atemporal ethos right from the beginning of the film. Above the awning is a sign, "No matter what, the future can be changed," which the cop reads aloud before the camera turns to Pak and his pot of daisies, which he holds up to the sky as the screen turns to color format. This is in contrast to the Korean version, in which the billboard reads "Wings of Happiness" over a pictured butterfly. In this version, the monochrome segment foregrounds only the flesh of people's skin and the thick green and white of Hye-yŏng's oil painting bleeding onto the sidewalk and into Pak Ŭi's pot of daisies. As the rain ceases, color from the pot of daisies spreads throughout the screen. Pak Ŭi exchanges gazes with the Interpol cop, who stands on the other side of Hye-yŏng, and she leaves. As Pak Ŭi holds the pot of daisies up toward the rain, the monochrome scene turns into color.

In both versions, however, the scene reframes its own acts of signification, inviting the viewer to engage the material presence of (now decontextualized versions of) tropes that have been central to the film—not just rain, but also oil paints and daisies in flower pots. Through the texture of the seeping oil paints and the presence of figures that we now know to be deceased, the film in both versions is thus able to lend materiality to the affect of first love via a set of now iconographic objects. Not only is the film engaged in a historical trajectory of affective palimpsests—one layer within this history of sonagi— but as a discrete film, it also reveals itself to be layered in a similar way.

Within the persistent repetition, we see a good deal of more subtle repetition, and this is where the operation of the affective palimpsest becomes most apparent. The scene of Pak Ŭi's mugging of the Interpol agent, Chŏng-u, during a sudden rain shower, for example, is framed by a repetition of this shelter-from-the-rain scene, shown before and after the mugging. It is supposed to be Hye-yŏng and Chŏng-u's second meeting for an oil-portrait session when it suddenly starts to rain. Hye-yŏng ducks for shelter at the entrance of a building, leaving her easel and paints on the square. The camera zooms in on her oils, which bleed into the wet cobblestones, in a shot reminiscent of the film's framing scene. Even her voiceover emphasizes repetition and substitution, commenting that the rain is coming in place of Chŏng-u. Meanwhile, Chŏng-u is there on the square under a statue, as is Pak Ŭi, who is standing outside the Korean store, both unbeknownst to Hye-yŏng. As in the main frame's ending, they exchange glances from which Hye-yŏng is totally excluded. The three occupy separate frames, until Pak Ŭi ducks into a dark alley and Chŏng-u takes chase after him. The handheld camera shakes as the rain obscures our view, ending with a visceral punch as the camera swings 180 degrees to show Pak Ŭi's fist fly into the camera representing Chŏng-u's face. We see Pak Ŭi going through Chŏng-u's belongings to learn his identity. The scene then shifts to Hye-yŏng still waiting for the rain to pass. In a later version of this scene, retold from Chŏng-u's point of view, we see Chŏng-u waiting in the rain first. Whereas in Hye-yŏng's segment, she had been staring into space, and Chŏng-u's gaze had been on Pak Ŭi offscreen, here Chŏng-u's gaze goes to Hye-yŏng. It is then that he sees Pak Ŭi and follows him. Instead of returning to Hye-yŏng, this telling of the mugging in the rain here returns to Chŏng-u as he gets up off the street, relieved that he was merely mugged and (he wrongly assumes) that his cover wasn't blown.

The complex layering of scenes extends even further, to a layering of genre. Amid the relationships between different strands of a repetitious plot, elements of the sonagi trope—and its melodramatic fixation on first love—exist alongside aspects of Lau's brand of Hong Kong neo-noir aesthetics—with its preoccupation with alter-egos. And those styles foment within atemporal frames that return us to already visited sites and already seen scenes.

In Slavoj Žižek's reading of Deleuze, these structures of repetitions and difference allow for a reenvisioning of the relationship between past and present that, paradoxically, makes possible something truly new: "What repetition repeats is not the way the past 'effectively was,' but the *virtuality* inherent to the past and betrayed by its past actualization. In this precise sense, the emergence of the New changes the past itself, that is, it retroactively changes not the actual past—we are not in science fiction—but the balance between actuality and virtuality in the past."[22] James Williams extends this reading, suggesting, "Intensities come into relation with each other through repetition," which in turn "allows us to explain the relation of virtual events to actual events and vice versa. Put simply, this means that signs acquire fixity."[23] The fixity of rain as a sign in the affective palimpsests I have been describing reorients the relationship of the past of a nationalist Korean trope into the present of transnational coproduction. If Lau's task is to rewrite a decades-old aesthetic that he obtains through Kwak, then we see this transaction/translation in the film as an act of repeated rescripting. In Ko's 1978 film, rain acts like a thick monochromatic shield, an undifferentiated and expansive mass, from which shelter is a space of respite made possible by enclosure. Rain in *Daisy*, in contrast, both exposes and erases layers, giving fixity to that which gets dislodged and reoriented by rain. Instead of seeking shelter, the film embraces it as a mode of materializing new intensities unburdened by historical baggage.

Facial Landscapes and Spatial Portraits

In the following excerpt from Hwang's "Sonagi," water becomes the surface in which faces appear; this ephemeral fluid becomes the natural surface of portraiture.

> The next day, he arrived at the stream a little later. This time he found her washing her face, sitting there in the middle of the stepping-stones. In contrast to her pink jumper with its sleeves rolled up, the nape of her neck was very white. After washing her face for a while, she stares intently into the water. She must be looking at her reflection. She makes a sudden grab at the water. Perhaps some baby fish were swimming by. There is no knowing if the girl is aware or not of the boy sitting on the bank as she goes on making nimble grabs at the water. But each time to no effect. She simply keeps grabbing at the water as if for the sheer fun of it. It looks as though she will only get out of the way if there's someone crossing the stream, as on the previous day. Then she plucks something from the water. It was a white pebble. After that, she stands up and goes skipping lightly across the stepping-stones. . . . One day, the boy sat down in the middle of the stepping stones, just where the girl had sat playing with the water. He dipped his hand in the water. He wiped his face. He stared into the water. His darkly tanned face looked back at him. He hated it. The boy grabbed at the face in the water with both hands. Several times he grabbed at it. Then he suddenly sprang up in surprise. Why, the girl is coming, walking in this direction! "She was hiding, watching what I was doing." The boy started to run. He missed his step on a stone. One foot went into the water. He ran faster. If only there was somewhere he could hide.[24]

Hwang's "Sonagi" draws an association between water and mirrored reflection that speaks to the affective and haptic potential of portraiture.[25] The boy in the story expresses a desire to touch the reflection in the water and to extract something tangible from the water, a white pebble as white as the nape of her neck. In a reversal of the Narcissus myth, the boy's own reflection in the same spot, however, returns something that he hates, filling him with self-loathing, and the same act of reaching into the reflection is one that effects erasure, rather than the retrieval, of something concrete from a fluid form. The self-hatred he directs toward the reflection takes on the form of anger, then humiliation and shame as he becomes aware that the girl, whose actions he had been reenacting, is watching. This self-loathing is doubled by the character Pak Ŭi in *Daisy*, who plants daisies, which he associates with Hye-yŏng, as compensation for his life as a hit man: "If I pretend I'm her, I feel like my soul is pure, at least a little bit." As in Hwang's story, this desire to be like someone else is born of the recognition of one's own indelible impurity, which is impossible to redress, whether by planting flowers or imitating a pure being at the water's edge.

The particular preoccupation with the representation of the face in Hwang's story becomes a preoccupation with painted portraits in *Daisy*. Because of a series of coincidences and misunderstandings, Hye-yŏng comes to believe that Chŏng-u (and not Pak Ŭi) is her secret admirer, with whom she has become intrigued. Based on this misunderstanding, she paints a series of portraits of Chŏng-u's face, which refer ironically to Pak Ŭi's affections. So while a good deal of affect is invested in these portraits, they depict the wrong love object. This problem of facial (mis)signification is somewhat reminiscent of John Woo's *Face/Off* (1997), in which a criminal and federal agent get reconstructive facial surgery in order to impersonate one another. As a "double-protagonist" film by a Hong Kong director lured to Hollywood (and in turn, leaving behind an industry and nation struggling under the "one country, two systems" policy inaugurated by the handover of Hong Kong to the People's Republic of China), *Face/Off* questions the adequacy of a single male to fulfill his duties.[26] Traces of this idea—the face as the site of a historical burden—can be seen in *Infernal Affairs*, where the cop undercover with the Triad bemoans how the passing years get written into his face and the audience sees an old identity card as a measure of time past. In contrast, *Daisy* recasts the historical in relation to landscapes, but also, at the same time, reimagines the portrait, along with the face it depicts, along these lines, as if it were a landscape, which also becomes the site of affective historical matter. After all, though Hye-yŏng paints portraits for money on the public square, her real artistic interest is in landscapes. This transformation is effected through a kind of palimpsestic process, a kind of facial layering.

Facial layering occurs in *Daisy* through the confluence of portraits in various media contained within a single frame—for example, a montage of portraits that functions to question the relationship between image, object, and how and where emotion gets articulated. Hye-yŏng works as a street portraitist in Haarlem's Grote Market, under the gaze of a statue of Frans Hals, the legendary seventeenth-century Haarlem painter who was inspired by Rubens and was famous for his use of the visible brushstroke. The disconnect and dissolution of the relationship between image, object, and emotion is established early on with the portrait sessions in the market square, when Chŏng-u sits down for a sketch. We learn later that he is actually covertly watching suspects and that the portrait session provides him cover as well as a good vantage point. Hye-yŏng is startled by the daisies that he places beside him—also a coincidental part of his cover—and what proceeds is a sketch motivated by her emotions toward the person who secretly leaves her daisies (whom she loves), when in fact it is someone else. Thus, the portrait being drawn is not really that of Chŏng-u, and he himself is preoccupied by what is occurring behind her. We also learn later that Pak Ŭi was observing this scene from his apartment window, complicating the network of unmet gazes. Because Chŏng-u must abruptly leave, Hye-yŏng completes the portrait in his absence later in her studio from memory, and the painting becomes a record of lost presence and the inadequacy of representation: her touch of the portrait's cheek in her studio is later repeated on Chŏng-u, when she brushes the pencil off his face.

This act of portraiture, in which the subject being drawn is not fully the subject being captured on paper, as a result of emotive deflection, occurs again in a later scene that comes shortly after Chŏng-u has been killed. A year has passed, and in a voiceover Hye-yŏng narrates her act of sketching portraits in her studio, explaining it as a way of dealing with her loneliness whenever she thinks of Chŏng-u. When she misses Chŏng-u, she feels bad, so her response is to sketch. But we see that the face being sketched is actually of Pak Ŭi, and the scene is followed by Pak Ŭi's appreciation and a shot of a number of other portraits of him she has given to him: "She sketches me probably only because she feels sorry. But still there I am within her reach." The emotion of painting in both of these examples turns on the disparity between portrait and referent; Hye-yŏng never seems to paint whom she is thinking about.

The layering of faces, and the persistent confusion over whose face belongs to whom, effectively dislodges the face as reliable signifier and destabilizes the relationship between faces and the emotions that the recognition of a particular face engenders. The dislodging of face as signifier becomes even clearer in the scene in which Hye-yŏng visits Pak Ŭi's boat; he turns on an episode of the television drama *Eyes of Dawn* (*Yŏmyŏngŭi nuntongja*, 1991–1992).[27] He pauses it on a close-up, with large Chinese subtitles: "Do you understand, I have only you." Showing Hye-yŏng, who has lost her voice in an earlier shoot-out, that he can read lips, he mutes the television and proceeds to demonstrate his new skill. In this scene, we see behind him one of Hye-yŏng's portraits of him, then the close-up television screen shot of the male character Ch'oe Tae-ch'i (from the television drama they are watching). But the sound on the television is muted, and the camera reverses on to Pak Ŭi to show him speaking the words instead. The layering here is of three media, with the emotional content displaced from the television scene onto him and the portrait we know to be Chŏng-u in conception but Pak Ŭi in perception.

The emotive mimicry that Pak Ŭi is engaging in here is something he does habitually, having rented an apartment overlooking the market. From his window, we see in a montage sequence how he mirrors Hye-yŏng's every move, raising his glass to her, moving his hand with her wave. Thus, as with the montage in which the window separating them creates a space of haptic force between them, through the act of mimicry, here in this scene, where his face and likeness substitutes for Chŏng-u and his words speak for a television character, Pak Ŭi's face comes to literally embody emotive deflection. In terms of reading emotion, Hye-yŏng for Pak Ŭi is no different from the TV drama image. Given the film's emphasis on his undying love, the faces here are oddly interchangeable.

With the failure of language signaled by Hye-yŏng's violent loss of speech, the film resorts to landscapes as prime means of conveying emotions. In the process, faces themselves are rendered kinds of landscapes, reminiscent of the way in which Deleuze and Guattari describe the face in relation to topographies of signification, a face which carries out "the prior gridding that makes it possible for the signifying elements to become discernible, and for the subjective choices to be implemented. . . . A language is always embedded in the faces that announce its statements and ballast them in relation to signifiers in progress and subjects concerned. Choices are guided by faces, elements are organized around faces: a common grammar is never separable from a facial education."[28] In his discussion of these ideas, Richard Rushton suggests that Deleuze and Guattari reserve their "harshest criticism of the face for that which reduces the face purely to its nominal register," and that a broader view opens onto the virtual potentialities of world making: "It is the face that opens up the world as an experience of possibility; it is the very conception out of which worlds are born. . . . The elements of the world are organized around faces; the face carries out a preorganization of the world upon which experiences are made possible: the face is virtual, while the experiences are actual."[29] In this context, the task of portraiture in *Daisy* is to demonstrate how faces access these kinds of topographies, which the film specifically figures in the ideal of landscapes, thus implicitly expanding the trope in Hwang's story, in which the face becomes legible within the land, into a broader conceptual formulation in which faciality comes in contact with landscape topography in a manner that registers with Deleuze and Guattari.

Pak Ŭi first had first seen Hye-yŏng crossing a log and falling into a stream, a scene that the film represents in a flashback, when he was hiding out in the countryside after his first assignment. Retrieving her painting supplies, which have flowed down the river, he returns these to her anonymously by leaving them on a bridge that he constructs out of the log. Hye-yŏng repays this act of kindness with an oil painting of the field of daisies nearby which she leaves in the same place. Notably, this is the only landscape painting she gives him, unlike the series of portraits. Inspired by the painting, Pak Ŭi further reciprocates by regularly leaving potted daisies for her without being seen, so the original painting comes to prompt ritualized repetition. Impressionist in style—which Pak Ŭi (as hit man turned art critic) glosses as "characterized by concentration on the immediate visual impression produced by a single scene and by the use of unmixed primary colors and small strokes to simulate actual reflected light"—the painting provokes in Pak Ŭi a kind of impressionist behavior, his own small gestures honoring the single scene that triggers his initial infatuation and surreptitious courtship.

Later in the film, the painting of the field of daisies appears again, this time in a dissolve, in which the painting is superimposed onto Hye-yŏng's face. Significantly, the shot marks a moment of revelation, the moment when Hye-yŏng finally realizes that her secret admirer is Pak Ŭi, not Chŏng-u as she has thought all along. Pak Ŭi has left a note with the painting on a table on the porch, and as Hye-yŏng reads it, we see a flashback of the initial bridge scene, now accompanied by the contextualizing force of the note, which we hear voiced by Pak Ŭi in a voiceover. A moment that explicitly unites portraiture and landscape, the dissolve literalizes the kind of palimpsestic layering that we have seen at work in other registers of the film, all under the rubric of love story, which brings us back to Hwang's original story (fig. 4.6). Hye-yŏng's

4.6 Affective, palimpsestic layering of portrait and landscape. *Daisy.*

belated recognition of Pak Ŭi's love becomes realized visually as the recognition of the landscape painting, here a quintessential affective palimpsest, as in fact the portrait of a face, which reflects back to the love object the fact of love. Finally realizing what has happened, Hye-yŏng rushes back to the public square, the site of her portrait work, where Pak Ŭi is engaged in his last assignment, bringing the painting with her as a sign of her belated identification. When she is finally killed by the sniper's bullet meant for Pak Ŭi, her blood splatters onto the painting of daisies, converging with paint, a representational medium, literally giving blood to a landscape painting. In this transference, landscape painting acquires a kind of corporeality. What remains in her death, as with the original sonagi trope, is a stained piece of cloth, which is here figured by the sullied canvas (fig. 4.5).

In Ko's film adaptation of "Sonagi," there is a comparable scene, in which the camera follows the boy carrying the girl across the stream, falls out of focus, then retreats into a bed of daisies that comes into focus in close-up. Nature, as elsewhere in the film, affords them privacy for physical intimacy, and this closeness results in a stain. As the boy carries the girl on his back, her blouse gets stained, close to the area where her heart would be, by some blood that was on his back. She wears this blouse when they meet again after her illness, unbuttoning and peeling back her red vest as if spreading apart her ribs to show the boy the stain, and we learn later that she wishes to be buried in it when she dies. The stain is central, belatedly arousing the hapticality and physical intimacy between the two children in terms of the affective power evoked by representation. Ko's stain scene attributes permanence to the stain in its resistance to numerous washings, a durability in spite of the fact that it gets hidden (under her vest) and later buried (under the ground). Stains are an integral element of the sonagi trope from the original "Sonagi" tale that gets reformulated in *Daisy*'s treatment thereof, and as in Ko's film, stains retain their affective traces, even when additional layers render them invisible. Marking the affective value that accrues in palimpsestic layering, these stains are material traces. And as Pak Ŭi tells us, describing his work as a hit man, "Leaving traces means death." Indeed, traces have consequences in the film, but equally important are the materiality of those remains. Although Pak Ŭi fears traces and uses a revolver and a type of ammunition that does not leave shells, the smell of gunpowder remains, despite his attempt to erase it by planting the daisies Hye-yŏng paints. We see him gripping the soil, rubbing it into his fingers, then tasting the dirt; what we see is not exactly the persistence of memory, but more specifically, the way that material traces resist elision, the ability of reality to linger in the layers.

The scene in which Hye-yŏng's blood stains her landscape painting reformulates the bloodstain on the girl's clothing in both the original story and in Ko's film. The reinscription of the painting resonates with a prominent stylistic feature in *Daisy* that we saw in the scene of Hye-yŏng's belated recognition of love, namely the use of dissolves. Dissolves, in which the end of one shot is briefly superimposed onto the beginning of another shot, might be understood as bringing to a scene a "different segment of time, space and pictorial information," and a "different graphic configuration."[30] In *Daisy*, the dissolves insert difference into fields of sameness—as, for example, the endless field of daisies in the beginning of the film that the camera pans across with seamless fluidity, infolding one shot of the field into another as it continuously moves forward. By using dissolves, Lau visually incorporates the painterly styles of impressionism and post-impressionism, which Hye-yŏng also adopts in her artwork. Pak Ŭi, in fact, diligently studies Monet and Van Gogh, among others, in order to understand her work. In particular, the film incorporates the post-impressionist practice of layering and bright colors as a means to prompt emotional effects.[31] Through the use of dissolves, Lau creates a similar layering effect, which synthesizes disparate fragments into unities of space, color, and time, particularly in the case of landscape sequences, which suture together panning shots of nature scenes with dissolves so as to compress space and time into smaller, more digestible entities. Connected by dissolves, these natural montages create the semblance of depth in an otherwise flat image by crystallizing and erasing possibilities into a more singular and discrete image. Furthermore, in line with the impressionist influences, the film itself tends to bathe the exterior landscape shots in bright, natural light and colors. This increases the sense of flatness while eliminating shadows, which are relegated to the contrasting urban landscapes that wind through narrow streets, the scenes, that is, more reminiscent of Lau's previous work.[32] More important, these filmic modes of layering—namely dissolves and montage, in which one images bleeds into another image—speak to the palimpsestic nature of affective production and haptic images.

In a different configuration of layering through the insertion of a post-impressionist painting on canvas into a filmic image, Lau superimposes throughout the film one medium onto another, like a montage, where the inserted post-impressionist painting fills space inconspicuously by enfolding the same or what lies beyond the scope of the frame but only in different media, or as intervention, in which the post-impressionist painting serves to interrupt and interject by invoking an affective, here sunsu, moment. Particularly striking are the shots in which we see Hye-yŏng's hands physically inserting the impressionist painting into the shot, and the rendering of this act as a landscape itself in which the subject is visible (figs. 4.7–4.9).

These insertions of post-impressionist paintings are associated with that first sighting at the bridge after Pak Ŭi's first hit assignment, when he sees Hye-yŏng fall off the log, and become a means of transporting the sonagi trope that is woven into the *Daisy* narrative. Read along with the blood that gets splattered onto the painting, the film attributes a distinct corporeality, perhaps even a haptic capacity, to the painting itself: the image seems capable of being touched. Pak Ŭi sets eyes on the painting placed on the bridge, but subsequently touches it, then reviews the landscape in its larger context, through the touch of his hands. In addition to dissolves and superimpositions, Lau also uses bleeds and bleeding in multiple senses of the word, both the bleeding of the oil paint as it is washed away in the rain as well as the blood trickling from gunshot wounds (fig. 4.10). The conflation of paint with blood further lends corporeality to the oils used in painting, suggesting a life to the painterly image that is necessarily coopted by the filmic image to harness its corporeal powers.

Conclusion: Sonagi Montage and Transnational Affectivity

In Hwang Sun-wŏn's tale, we overhear talk of the girl's death, but we do not "see" her corpse. News of her death is not communicated directly to the boy, who merely overhears his parents talking about it. Because the girl and boy had played together in secret, no one else knows of their association with one another. It is only the boy who understands that the stain marks his intimate

4.7 Post-impressionist painting on canvas inserted into a similar filmic image. *Daisy*.

4.8 Sunsu moments associated with post-impressionist paintings intervene in neo-noir film sensibilities. *Daisy*.

4.9 Inserting Pak Ŭi into the landscape of the paintings. *Daisy*.

4.10 Blood from Chŏng-u's head wound trickles onto the street like red paint. *Daisy.*

association to her and her body. The stain of his blood and sweat—dried onto the fabric of her clothes with the rain—is, crudely put, a sort of affective imprint materially inscribed on her body, which becomes buried in death. The burial then covers not just her body, but also knowledge of the event and the affect embedded in the clothes, both of which will remain invisible and unknown, despite the irrevocable presence of the imprint. In Ko's film, the boy's mourning occurs at the bridge, where he returns to cry in private, maintaining the film's spatial isolation of affect. But in his defiant attachment to his own grimy shirt—reminiscent, for him, of what he had with the girl, but inexplicable to his parents—we recognize a transference of the girl's affective attachment to her blouse; we conflate the shirt on the boy's body with the girl's blouse, which is now presumably underground. Accordingly, the grime that the boy refuses to have washed off takes on the affective weight of the stain on the blouse. This act of reiteration, absent from Hwang's original tale, signals the material afterlife of affect displaced onto another body. That reiteration is analogous to the intersensorial displacement of the sonagi trope under Lau's direction, which—through the procedures of affective palimpsest—constructs a kind of transnational affect. The sonagi trope in *Daisy* activates an otherwise absent and forgotten affective materiality that imports a formerly nationalist emotion, enabling it to gestate in new environs while it fuses with other elements to produce hybrid forms.

The question of the imprint we make, and indeed, of our own visibility, culminates in *Daisy* as a composite of readily identifiable, generic fragments from the sonagi trope and from Hong Kong neo-noir. This composite stages a crisis of auteurship in transregional coproduction, which mimics the kinds of competitions and antagonisms lingering beneath the more overt cooperative stances of Asianization. The film stages a self-reflexive auteurship that attempts to assert itself in affective fragments, through montage and palimpsests that lurk beneath the image. The jumble of these many pieces, and the effect of watching the cumulative product, reminds us of Roland Barthes's famous essay "The Death of the Author," in which he writes that "a text is made of multiple writings, drawn from many cultures and entering into mutual relations of dialogue, parody, contestation, but there is one place where this multiplicity is focused and that place is the reader, not, as it was hitherto said, the author. . . . A text's unity lies not in its origin but in its destination."[33] Juxtaposed here, *Daisy* brings out Barthes's attraction to the sense of possibility that comes from travel, and the dialogic aesthetics, which includes contestation, speaks anachronistically in the present to the new logics of transnational exchange. *Daisy* relies on the juxtaposition of affective fragments, using the logic that Lev Kuleshov famously associated with montage in his experiments with film editing, where he juxtaposed an expressionless face with various images designed to elicit emotional reactions, namely the ability "both to break down and to reconstruct, and ultimately to remake the material" in order to remake emotion itself.[34]

Yet if we identify in *Daisy* a postmodern montage of commercial genres, an ambiguity remains: does the montage-like structure of *Daisy*, and the displaced reformulation of the sonagi trope, embrace or deplore the conditions of postcolonial transregional production? This ambivalence emerges especially when considering Kwak's role in the film's production. On the one hand the film is unquestionably imprinted by Lau's directorial style, but on the other, the invocation of the sonagi trope and the casting of Jun Ji-hyun—who has come to be closely associated with Kwak's films—for the role of Hye-yŏng leave the question of authorship open.

The film, which perhaps not coincidentally is in part about the rivalry between two men, contains a subtle nod to the complex dynamics here: in the Haarlem square where Hye-yŏng works as a portraitist, there is a statue of Laurens Janszoon Coster, a local inventor of movable type, whose statue claims "I made this"—that is, before Gutenberg. The statue is visible in the background of a number of shots. Another statue, that of the nineteenth-century Dutch anticolonialist writer Multatuli (a.k.a. Eduard Douwes Dekker), presides over the film's climax, which consists of a violent neo-noir shoot-out transplanted onto the bridge in Amsterdam, which invokes the bridge that Pak Ŭi built for Hye-yŏng at the beginning of the film. Furthermore, as Hye-yŏng and Pak Ŭi face each other in the center of the bridge, a "real American" hot-dog vendor, his cart emblazoned with the American flag, is in the background on one bank of the river. Then, a few minutes later, the death of Hye-yŏng occurs at the foot of Multatuli's statue itself. The presence of various imperial or hegemonic modes in this scene, be it Dutch colonialism or soft American power, at once invokes a broader historical context while sublimating that big picture within the drama of the scene. After a montage accompanied by melodramatic music, Pak Ŭi cries out—in anguish and to no avail—"We'll start again," as the camera pulls back to a bird's-eye view of the scene.

But what does it mean to start again, especially in the new transnational context within which the film emerges? If, following Barthes, we are concerned not with origins, but destinations, then how does one make sense of the new interregional constructs and power configurations in an era of reconciliation, in which history remains only in material traces? Hwang Sun-wŏn's legacy has become fractured and intertextual: the subject of a theme park, and in Kwak and Lau's hands the vehicle for a popular inter-Asian collaboration that threatens to dissociate fully from the original context. The fragmented and composite nature of *Daisy*, which was released in different versions for different markets, dovetails with Barthes's emphasis on the spectator rather than the auteur as giving unity and meaning to the fragments of a film. But if audience becomes the arbiter, what becomes of history? Like Kuleshov's montage, in which the emotionally bland face acquires affect through juxtaposition, affective palimpsests in the film mobilize elements of the sonagi trope and Hong Kong neo-noir to both provoke and preserve emotional states. But *Daisy* assembles not just images in relation to affect, but, more complexly, material traces in relation to histories of affect, the global circulation of which, paradoxically, accesses a wider audience for a story that seems to diminish with its circulation. Affective palimpsests are thus a distribution aesthetic.

Amity, and the configuration of what constitutes amicable relations, became more multifarious and multilayered as Korea looked to China (with whom relations were complicated by its relation to North Korea) and to Hong Kong (which was in a complicated relationship with China) for collaboration in film production. In the years of diplomatic amity in Korea-China relations starting in 1992, and following the assimilation of Hong Kong into China, in 1997, as a "Special Administrative Region" under a "one country, two systems" approach, hallyu cinema played a transformative role in how amity was visualized in the face of negotiating shifting sovereignties. In *Musa*, Koryo is presented as a tributary state of the Ming empire, as "China's number one ethnic younger brother," although the represented concerns are clearly of contemporary political and economic relations between two sovereign nations.[35] Amity is visualized in this context as arising in human relations in spite of enmity between rulers, and amicable relations take on the form of benevolence and compassion that transcend political and social differences. The bonds that get formed are provisional and conditional to the displaced circumstances, but nevertheless result in sincere connections between people. Produced in 2001 just prior to the full emergence of an explicit hallyu discourse, *Musa* represents the idea of amity as encoded within political discourse, metatextually prescribing a connection between travel, as a means of closing distance between peoples and homes, and friendship.

As hallyu seeped into Korea-China relations, in the late 1990s, and into Korea–Hong Kong relations, post-handover Hong Kong cinema was in a slump and struggling with the after-effects of the Asian financial crisis, not unlike the Korean cinema industry at the time.[36] Through joint production and collaboration, hallyu provided Hong Kong cinema with an alternative means to expand its market, by tapping into hallyu's network and possibly into hallyu's mainland China market, which was considered crucial to the survival of the Hong Kong film industry; from another perspective, it also gave hallyu cinema the chance to bank on Lau's success, especially from the *Infernal Affairs* installments. Since the handover, Hong Kong films were no longer considered foreign imports in mainland China, and Lau had consciously worked on implementing changes in his filmmaking since his *Infernal Affairs I* (2002)— which had been deemed unsuitable and did not do well in the mainland—to his *Infernal Affairs III* (2003), to better appeal to the mainland Chinese market.[37] The total box-office gross for *Daisy* in South Korea around the time of its release was US$5,864,872, compared to a mere US$416,956 in Hong Kong a few months after its release. In China, by the end of 2006, *Daisy* had grossed US$1,280,000.[38]

Though it cannot be said that China was the singular concern of *Daisy*'s producers, it is fair to say that the Chinese market figured indirectly into the *Daisy* collaboration, considering the significance the Chinese market has for both Hong Kong and hallyu cinema. In this context, amity in *Daisy* becomes discursive and less provisionally associated with circumstances, seemingly separate from the overt political and ethnic forces seen in *Musa*, thereby recalibrating relations and tropes so that they seem to lie outside the representation of historical circumstances. The now aligned interests of Korean and Hong Kong filmmakers manifest in the film as the construction of a deep sense of shared affect, which instead of being connected to a contingent experience like a journey, as it was in *Musa*, now becomes the result of a broader effort to imagine a new single entity out of once disparate interests. If *Musa* staged the discovery of shared interests and cooperation within a motley crew of factions and ethnonationalist divisions, then *Daisy*, through the use of its affective palimpsests, imagines amity by attempting to elide difference itself. It is not just the characters that travel in *Daisy* as Asians living and working in Europe, but perhaps more important, it is the tropes, affects, and ideological positions that constitute discourse that prove to be moveable across national boundaries. *Daisy*, in short, imaginatively dehistoricizes and synthesizes Hwang Sun-wŏn's nationalist rain with Andrew Lau's sensibility such that we can imagine the showers in both texts as consisting of the same water.

In the first two parts of this study, I have looked at South Korea and its neighbors and the effort to build a transnational sense of affectivity that might abet the forms of transnational commerce that emerge at a moment of Asian regionalization. In part III, I turn to South Korea's most historically fraught, complex relationship with a neighboring country, that with North Korea. In this context—a dominant one in postwar Korean discourse—the challenges for the kind of empathetic and cooperative dispositions implied in intimacy and amity become subordinated to a more fundamental task: the effort to get beyond the past must be preceded by an attempt to understand it. Hence, *remembrance* (which constitutes not just memory, but more specifically feeling about memory) becomes the key affective category for reimagining Cold War geopolitical formations in a new era of transnational commerce.

PART III

REMEMBRANCE

5. POSTMEMORY DMZ

Joint Security Area, Yesterday, and *2009: Lost Memories*

Since it was established in 1953, the demilitarized zone (DMZ) between North and South Korea has remained suspended in a kind of tense stasis, which both testifies to the past violence and bloodshed that made the DMZ necessary, and hopefully anticipates the possibility for future reconciliation. Nowhere are these meanings better captured than in the 1965 semi-documentary *The DMZ* (*Pimujang chidae*) by Pak Sang-ho, which was filmed in the demilitarized zone under the auspices of the Eighth U.S. Army Commission and the Neutral Nations Supervisory Commission (NNSC) just twelve years after the truce. Presumed lost until 2005, when a copy was discovered, *The DMZ* captures the

5.1 South Korean tourists on the North Korean side of the Demarcation Line between North and South Korea, as reproduced at Yangsuri Film Studios' *Joint Security Area* film set. Photo by author.

dormant state of the truce line, as well as Pak's own sense of obligation to do something to revive public interest in this deserted zone as part of a larger effort to explore not what the DMZ has been in the past, but what it will mean in the future. The result is a fusion of documentary footage and an allegorical story of two orphans who scavenge the DMZ's rusting war remains to still their hunger and sense of loss. Pak would later write, "I try to film life and society with a victorious future. . . . I dare to appeal in pain to the nation and the world with this one film. Bless the free and unified future of my nation."[1]

Standing in between its bloody past and hopeful future, the DMZ as a symbol—despite numerous incursions, infiltrations, and breaches—has morphed over the years into a kind of timeless figure of waiting, ossifying into the spatial coordinates it inhabits (more or less the 38th parallel on the Korean Peninsula). It has thus become increasingly removed from the history for which it serves as an interstitial figure of pause, that is, of war held in abeyance.

It has even become a tourist destination, a fate that Pak had specifically hoped to prevent by making his film.[2] Pak feared that the DMZ would become itself an object of curiosity, a site "full of thrills and suspense"—a bizarre kind of amusement park—rather than a real boundary between opposing factions. This is the worry that a material historical site of military and political significance might be reduced to mere metaphor or trope. Contemporary representations of the DMZ demonstrate that Pak's fears were justified, that the symbolic resonance of the DMZ has indeed changed over the years. I look specifically at the way in which the DMZ is represented in South Korean cinema in the period that coincides with the rise of hallyu, which in the present context was characterized by three overlapping phenomena: the increase of political contact between North and South Korea, most clearly instantiated by the so-called Sunshine Policy, which attempted to soften historical antagonisms through economic cooperation and other forms of increased interaction between North and South; the gradual emergence of an Asianization discourse that downplayed South Korea's relationship with the West in favor of a focus on inter-Asian relations; and the rise of popular South Korean cinema, particularly in the form of blockbusters. In this context, it is no surprise that so many South Korean films in the period dealt with relations between North and South, and with the DMZ in particular.

An important theoretical notion that underwrites my argument is the idea of postmemory as articulated by Marianne Hirsch, which describes "the relationship of the second generation to powerful, often traumatic, experiences that preceded their births but that were nevertheless transmitted to them so deeply as to seem to constitute memories in their own right."[3] In other words, postmemory is the memory of something that was never personally experienced, but via national or cultural tradition has come to feel vital or lived by the following generations. Undeniably, the trauma caused by the Korean War is still felt today, roughly sixty years after the fact. But Hirsch's notion, which she uses to think about the legacy of the Holocaust, helps us consider how the forms of this trauma change over time. Especially influential in this change is the rise of Asianization, which demands that the past be settled in order for formerly antagonistic nations to move toward new relationships of cooperation and mutually beneficial enterprise. It is my contention that the DMZ, as a highly symbolic site that marks not only the border between nations but also between temporalities, serves as a particularly fertile ground for investigating the afterlife of memory because the representations of the DMZ, which themselves must be read historically, help demonstrate how postmemory works in generations increasingly removed from the original event.

In 1999, following the release of Kang Je-gyu's (Kang Chegyu) blockbuster *Shiri* (*Swiri*), films about national division found a secure foothold in the South Korean film industry by appealing to popular memory and imagination.[4] Themes of national division and reunification were a savvy way to appeal to a national market that already had such issues on their mind, but the success of these films was aided by contemporary political developments. Since the 1960s, Hollywood films had dominated the South Korean market. To protect a struggling native film industry, the government introduced a screen quota system in 1966. It was not fully enforced until 1993, when Hollywood was granted permission for direct distribution in Korea rather than being required to go through Korean film companies, which oversaw production of local films as well as import of foreign films. The screen quota system required Korean local theaters to screen films made in Korea at least 146 days a year, a restriction that was later reduced to 73 days a year (in 2006). But by the late 1990s, Hollywood studios demanded that South Korea abolish the screen quota system as part of the free trade agreement.[5] Filmmakers like Kang Je-gyu considered the standoff between North and South Korea on the peninsula and the nation's history of struggle for reunification as something uniquely Korean, and hence came to regard the "Korean blockbuster" as a particularly appropriate vehicle for treating at once the struggle against Hollywood hegemony, the nation's simmering anti-American sentiment, the realities of national division, and the hopes for reunification.[6] Thus, the emergence of the South Korean blockbuster coincided with a "memory boom," a new fascination with the subject of memory—be it the settling of memory, the purging of memory, or the imagination of lost memories.[7]

The association of the blockbuster genre with "popular culture" and entertainment differentiated it from the more politicized "mass culture," defined by the underground avant-garde South Korean cinema and video of the 1980s, which critiqued postcolonial nationalist narratives.[8] Packaged in a relatively depoliticized form of entertainment, and with the potential to garner high box-office numbers and recognition from the international film community, the North-South narrative was able to elide government censors, at least to a certain degree. The blockbuster could take on a politically sensitive topic and push for new ways of engaging with it, while also reflecting social moods on the matter. The stories, usually in the form of murder mysteries and criminal investigations, transform real political circumstances into fictive reverie. The cinematic narrative of North-South Korean relations, as told through the depositions of suspects and investigators' reports against the background of believable historical circumstances, thus constitutes a history of the ways that popular culture has imagined these political relations. When popular art is bestowed with the serious task of transmitting historical material, conditions become ripe for transformations, distortions, and realignments, all spurred on by the work of postmemory.

Six blockbuster films—Jang Jin's *Spy Li Ch'ŏl-chin* (*Kanch'ŏp Yi Ch'ŏlchin*, 1999), Park Chan-wook's *Joint Security Area* (*Kongdong kyŏngbi kuyŏk*, 2000), Lee Si-myung's *2009: Lost Memories* (*2009: Rosŭtŭ memorijŭ*, 2002), Chŏng Yun-su's *Yesterday* (*Yesŭtŏdei*, 2002), Kim Hyŏn-chŏng's *Comrade* (*Ijung kanch'ŏp*, 2003; a.k.a. *The Double Agent*), and Kang Woo-suk's *Silmido* (2003)—formed a group released immediately after *Shiri* that addressed, explicitly or implicitly, North-South Korean relations. With each successive film, restrictions on engaging with the subject of North Korea and North Koreans eased as the political climate shifted. By 2003, the depiction of the North Korean leader or the integration of superimposed North Korean stock film footage was possible, whereas such images would have been impossible in the half-century prior. Thus, these films can be seen as occupying a continuum across the popular South Korean filmic imagination, an increasingly complex depiction of national division and reunification. It is no coincidence that the actors who first appeared together in *Shiri*, thus inaugurating the contemporary North-South narrative—Han Suk-kyu, Song Kang-ho, and Kim Yunjin—

would go on to each carry another blockbuster about Korean division and reunification, further supporting this sense of a continuum.[9]

Blockbusters about North and South Korea reflect an ideological development shaped by generational changes as well as changes in Korea's national identity and historical subjectivity that arose as the war became a more distant memory. The divided Korea in *Joint Security Area* (*J.S.A.*), for example, is a crucial part of a global world order, playing a central role alongside the United States and the West in general. The reunified Korea as imagined just three years later in *Yesterday* and *2009: Lost Memories*, by contrast, is more concerned with its place in an Asian world order. *J.S.A.*, addressing discourses of globalization, imagines relations in broad geopolitical terms and acknowledges the dominating presence of America's military and culture; *Yesterday* and *2009: Lost Memories*, which were intended solely for the Asian movie industry amid a scheme of recentered globalization in a more regional context, and fantasize about relations in the future, are based on a serious reworking of the past in which America and the legacy of the Cold War becomes less relevant.[10]

In light of the growth of these narratives over the span of less than five years (1999–2003), all revolving around the desire for reunification, we must consider the shift across these films, from globalization to Asianization, alongside shifts in narrative time and memory. By looking at how these films utilize the passage of time, we can better understand the shifting transnational orientation of these films. Temporality in the discourse of globalization associated with the United States stressed linearity as it moved toward an unknown future. Films like *J.S.A.*, for example, were primarily concerned with the procedural recovery and reconstruction of past events, as a means to prevent future changes that could have political ramifications. In contrast, temporality in the discourse of Asianization associated with China and Japan re-engaged with the region's re-emerging problematic past in the early twentieth century as part of an effort of looking toward the future, thus accounting for its cyclical and synchronic structure and preference for films set in the future such as *2009: Lost Memories* and *Yesterday*. I suggest that in the historiological shift from a U.S.-centered globalization to Asianization and from national division to reunification, we see a shift from an emphasis on history to an emphasis on memory, as the two become distinct from one another. Amidst the shift from a global world order to an Asian world order, this chapter looks at the development of tropes about North Korea and representations of the DMZ. It is my intention to show how what Alain Delissen terms a "memory-nation," located materially in time and space, is produced differently depending on whether the film is informed by discourses of globalization or Asianization.[11]

Neutral Time: The DMZ in the Unspecified Present

The film *J.S.A.* takes place at Panmunjŏm, the iconic border point on the DMZ where the 1953 Korean Armistice Agreement was signed and now something of a tourist attraction, on October 28 of an unspecified year. After hostilities break out in the DMZ following unexplained murders and a joint North and South Korean investigative effort fails, suspicions grow that North Korea has a nuclear weapon, and U.S. Navy vessels start advancing into the East Sea. Faced with a U.S. military threat, both North and South agree to allow a Neutral Nations Supervisory Commission (NNSC) investigation, led by the Swiss-Korean officer Sophie Jean (Lee Young-ae). The trope of the detached, impartial detective is here rendered in near-literal terms as the entrance of a neutral nation in this tense political environment. But the ideological neutrality enforced by the Swiss and Swedes, who constitute the NNSC, is contradicted by the insistence on the impossibility of neutrality asserted by the South Korean general stationed there. This neutrality is presumably defined and determined by the NNSC's investigative ability to chronicle in minute detail the circumstances and events leading up to the murders at the border, in the precise order of actual occurrence. The considerable documentary apparatus that surrounds the investigations doubles this precision: detailed legal documents, video cameras, cross-examinations, and so on. In addition to an insistence on chronological order and continuous progress toward answers, *J.S.A.* reinforces the singularity of truth and the existence of only one version of what really happened, which Sophie insists on discovering even after she is relieved of her duties. Hers is painstaking work that depends on a persistence aimed at reconstructing past events as they happened, an attitude that is enforced in the film by the many extradiegetic time signatures on the screen that chronicle for the filmic audience a clear narrative of events.

Time, thus, ironically becomes intimately bound to the notion of neutrality. Within the space of the DMZ, where time has virtually stood still with concerted global efforts since the Armistice in 1953, time must be recorded as progressing with events, as if central to the very act of investigation was the act of bearing witness to time itself. Typically, we think of history as defined by a sequence of events, yet the history of the DMZ is defined by the impossibility of events; it is a place where time, like the stoic guards on both sides of the tense standoff, stands still. *J.S.A.* reasserts history onto the DMZ by rendering it a site of an event and thereby imposing time back on it, thereby allowing it to occupy a dimension where time can proceed forward. Interestingly, the structure of time that is imposed on the DMZ mimics the standards of a criminal investigation. As Sophie's superior tells her, what is most important in this investigation is not outcome, but *procedure*.

J.S.A. chronicles the unlikely friendship between North and South Korean soldiers stationed at the DMZ, and the bloody outcome when the fraternizing is discovered. The plot revolves around events—in this case illicit fraternization, accidental exchange of gunfire, and ensuing murder and suicide—that have or had potential to change history and must be prevented from doing so. The logic of Panmunjŏm as a demilitarized and neutral zone, according to Sophie's commanding officer, is predicated on "hiding the truth": what both sides want "is that this investigation prove nothing at all." Rather than resolution, the process itself is imagined to have ameliorating effects. Witness accounts of events are interrogated, then organized into a narrative of truth that approximates the past. History, according to Pierre Nora, is how modern society, forgetful through so much change, organizes the past in reconstructions that are always problematic and incomplete. Aware of its own potential shortcomings, history thus "binds itself strictly to temporal continuities, to progressions and to relations between things."[12]

In *J.S.A.*, the "thing" to which history binds, and through which it gains its authority, is the DMZ itself. Furthermore, the Korean soldiers in the film (on both sides) have desires and natural inclinations that seem to oppose this historical authority, eventually leading the characters into what is regarded by their superiors as criminal behavior or betrayal. While the soldiers transgress literal borders and injunctions of conduct by befriending would-be enemies, the DMZ, as a manifestation of historical authority, is reconstituted by the processes of criminal deposition and narrative reconstruction—processes which aspire to impose temporal continuities on events that exist fully only in characters' memories. From the point of view of the higher-up military authorities on both sides in the film, the investigation intends not to gain an accurate historical picture of the events as they transpired, but to reaffirm the force of the DMZ itself, further reifying its authority and rescuing it from any sense of ambiguity or arbitrariness. Against this attempt at reaffirmation, the DMZ in *J.S.A.* becomes a crime scene. Both in the film and in modern Korean history, the DMZ acts as "third zone" (*che 3 chidae*) to the first and second zone of

North and South Korea. Turning it into a crime scene thus becomes a way to probe this already interstitial condition.

Furthermore, the DMZ in *J.S.A.* is of course not the actual one but a cultural reconstruction, since there is no possibility that the scenes set there could have been shot on location. One of the most expensive sets in Korean cinematic history at the time, the authentic, 90 percent scale model of the Panmunjŏm border village cost $1 million, nearly a third of the total $2.7 million budget it cost to make the film.[13] The film set as a representation of the real acts as an additional doubling, since the actual DMZ also has its own double, as a manifestation of the historical past in the Korean national imaginary. That doubling is further echoed in the film itself, in a small table-top model of the North Korean guard house where the shootings occurred, which the officials construct for investigative purposes. A clear parallel is drawn between the characters and the cardboard figures in the model throughout the duration of the film. Just as we, the viewers, are equipped with the filmic reconstruction of the DMZ as a crime scene and privileged to witnesses' and suspects' accounts, the investigators in the film rely on the model reconstruction of the DMZ in order to visualize the crime scene and deduce what happened. Viewed in this light, we sense the layers of artifice through which we view history, not the least of which is the original DMZ itself. Like the model in the film and the offsite film set constructed for filming, the DMZ itself is a kind of construct. It is as if, in fact, the DMZ itself were inseparable from such artifice, as if there was no thing itself under all these layers of discourse and representation. Significantly, while we finally do learn the truth at the end of the film about what happened in the North Korean guardhouse, it is a truth that exists only in the memory of one of the characters, Yi Su-hyŏk (Lee Byung-hun). That truth is visualized on the screen just before he commits suicide. At this point of the film, Sophie has long been relieved of her investigative duties, and her efforts are unofficial, off the record. So while the film does insist on completing the investigation and in providing the truth about the past, it does so in such a way as to make this truth exist independently of the investigation that aspired to bring it to light, demonstrating ultimately a gap between official history (what is recorded for posterity) and memory (which dies with Yi).

The real object of investigation in the film, then, is not the crime itself, but the transformation of its location. By turning it into a crime scene, the DMZ, no longer a relic of history, becomes markable space which can be inscribed with new stories, like that of the soldiers on opposing sides who become friends. In the film the DMZ as a crime scene includes the barley fields, where Yi Su-hyŏk first steps on a landmine and seeks the help of two North Korean soldiers, breaking the prohibition of communication. The Bridge of No Return also becomes a crime scene when Yi crosses it, following a joking invite received via illicit correspondences thrown back and forth over the border. In a cross-examination scene, both North and South Korean suspects are seated at a table in the little building at Panmunjŏm that bisects the line between the two sides. The investigator is seated in between the two suspects. The model of the watch house where the murders occurred is in front of her on the table. She begins to explain what she assumes to have been the proper order of past events. She also has a video camera, and a video recording of the other suspect's suicide attempt, which Yi happens to witness during his interview with Sophie—Yi sees his friend falling through the window of the room in which he is being interrogated. As the crime scenes proliferate within the larger umbrella of the DMZ as the overarching site, we begin to see the DMZ not as static, but as a place that exists within time and indeed within history—however murky, opaque, and unknowable that history might be.

The investigation on the South Korean side—we do not see a parallel investigation on the North Korean side until the very end of the film—takes place in what are regarded as neutral spaces, under the sole supervision of Sophie and the NNSC, but the very idea of neutrality is slowly eroded in the film. We first see the depositions of the three witnesses briefly in written form, bound into a thick report, then in the form of video recordings. A video camera is set up for each interrogation, and viewers see the interrogation twice at the same time, through the movie camera and through the video recording. A series of witnesses are brought in to help the investigator as well as the viewers better understand the persons implicated in the crime. The depositions of the South Korean suspect and the North Korean suspect differ, and Sophie accuses them of having written and signed false depositions. When Sophie brings in for questioning the South Korean soldier Nam (the friend Yi had introduced to his new North Korean friends) and threatens him with a polygraph test, he attempts suicide by jumping out the window.

Despite or in fact because of her presumed neutrality, Sophie takes on a more significant role as the film progresses—not merely in the investigation, but also in the actual resolution of the events that began before her arrival. As a supposed nonparticipant observer, she is allowed to determine what constitutes the truth and how to represent that truth to power. More important, however, her own story and its intersections with Korean history become more prominent as the film progresses. We learn that her father was a North

Korean general; this is the information that compromises her neutrality, leading to her dismissal from the case. But that's not all. Our understanding of Sophie (and her interpretive significance) accrue additional texture: it turns out that her father was imprisoned on Kŏje Island by the South Korean army during the Korean War. Furthermore, we discover that he was one of seventy-six prisoners who refused the opportunity to return to North Korea or go to South Korea and instead chose to leave the Korean Peninsula altogether, in his case going to Argentina, where he met and married a Swiss woman. Sophie's neutrality thus has a history, indeed a global one, and its genealogy is decidedly not neutral.

In her growing complexity, Sophie embodies the DMZ itself. She is ostensibly a figure of neutrality, a space in between antagonistic factions, whose very presence is meant to maintain the tenuous balance between conflicting interests. Echoing the formality that characterizes the behavior of the investigators stationed at Panmunjŏm, her neutrality manifests itself in the imposition of procedure, which is meant to make sense of memories—or in Nora's sense, to make history out of them—that are otherwise either imperfect, incomplete, or outright withheld. Yet Sophie is anything but neutral; or her history is merely the effect of her globalized genealogy. I do not mean that she favors one side over the other, but rather, insofar as neutrality is often opposed to history—that the neutral imperative to stay out of the conflict seems incompatible with history's dirty hands—Sophie's supposed neutrality gives way to a history that is deeply immersed in the very conflict that she was recruited to arbitrate because of her distance from the interests of its participants. By transforming a figure of neutrality into one of contingency and complicity, *J.S.A.* questions, by implication, the sense of timelessness that is often attributed to the DMZ. As we see in the film, the DMZ is a real place occupied by human beings with idiosyncratic desires, commitments, and conflicts. By insistently imagining the DMZ not as a nonplace, but one locatable in time, the film attempts to imagine it not as an interruption of history, but as its site.

The DMZ in *Yesterday*

In *Yesterday*, which is set in the year 2020, Korea has been reunified. A "Korea Border Zone" populated by Chinese, Vietnamese, Japanese, Filipinos, and Koreans, who live in an area within the zone known as the "Ghetto," has emerged at the northern edge of the country, at the Korea-China border. The film is a crime story about the investigation of a serial killer who leaves the bodies in this border region. Although the DMZ plays a part in the film, it is no longer a national border but rather a national park; the anxieties associated with the DMZ are displaced in the film onto the northern border with China and into an imagined future where that northern border is a place of outlaws, illegal immigrants, and criminals. Redevelopment plans face opposition from the residents who strike and protest, and the investigation team's search for suspects in the region during these tensions draw attention to the Ghetto as a contested site. The DMZ no longer functions as the tense politicized site that it does in *J.S.A.*, and serves instead as a memorial that is established following the film's imagined reconciliation between North and South Korea, a testament to the possibility of progress that in turn haunts the country's new site of division in the north.

Yesterday bears a crucial similarity to the other film emerging around this time set in the future positing a reunified Korea, *2009: Lost Memories*. Whereas *J.S.A.* posits a dichotomy between a relatively westernized South Korea vis-à-vis a more backward North Korea, in both of these later films, that dichotomy is discarded as issues of the regional past come to the fore, such as the return of Japan and the rise of China. The common representation of North Korea as stuck in a premodern past, which Johannes Fabian characterizes as "the denial of coevalness," ceases to be relevant—or appropriate—under the rubric of reunification and Asianization.[14] In the shift to Asianization discourse in blockbusters, South Korea not only feels inclined to grant coevalness with North Korea, but also feels pressure to achieve coevalness with its former colonizer, Japan, vis-à-vis Japan's renewed central position in the new Asia.[15] If the DMZ's geospatiality under the primacy of post–Cold War global concerns in films such as *J.S.A.* made it a key site for the staging of the troubled relationship between North and South Korea, what does the memorialization of the DMZ under an imagined reunification signal about the function of the DMZ in discourses of Asianization?

To answer, we must first remember that the blockbusters about Korean division were a pan-Asian phenomenon, with *Shiri* setting records in Japan, Hong Kong, and Taiwan. After that initial success, the South Korean film industry began to target a broad Asian audience by collaborating with local industries in China, Japan, and Hong Kong on films with similar political subject matter. This pan-Asian outlook coincided with a reemerging interest in an Asianization discourse. By the time president-elect Roh Moo-hyun started campaigning on a pro-Asia, anti-American platform in 2002, the discourse had appealed sufficiently to the South Korean public to garner their majority vote. Asia was considered a viable alternative to South Korean Marxism and discourses of globalization; Asia, in other words, became an intermediary between South Korea and the (increasingly problematic) Western World. Through the notion of Asia, South Korea could move beyond a narrow-minded nationalism and creatively refashion its place in an Asian order. The Asianization discourse also helped reframe the discussion about reunification, providing an alternative justification that would shift the terms away from its cold war origins. In engaging with the Asia discourse, blockbusters were less concerned with the position of South Korea as an American Cold War subject and increasingly interested in their position with respect to this emergent vision of Asia.[16]

The cinematic project of refashioning South Korea's place in Asia required a reconstruction of Korean history within the Asian world order, separate from the history associated with the West. This search for an alternative history manifests itself in the unconventional, nonlinear time structures that carry the plots of the blockbusters featuring a nondivided Korea, such as *Yesterday* and *2009: Lost Memories*. Set in the future, the films *Yesterday* and *2009: Lost Memories* project an imagined history (*kasang yŏksa*) into a future that contains alternative, or substitute, histories (*taech'e yŏksa*) extending back into various points in the past.

Yesterday begins amid the barrenness of the northern border, a displaced figuration of the DMZ, which is disturbed by the memory of the violent resolution of a hostage crisis that leaves several dead, including the investigator Yun Sŏk's young son, Hanbyŏl. The story of *Yesterday* then proceeds from this origin, revolving around five middle-aged male bodies that are uncovered in the border region. When another man fitting the same description is kidnapped, Yun Sŏk and the forensic analyst Kim Hŭi-su attempt to figure out the motives behind these crimes. The entire zone becomes what Takashi Fujitani calls a mnemonic site—a site of commemoration that connects the present to possible futures—but one that seems to allow for multiple meanings of that commemorated past.[17]

The killer adorns the corpses with pendants that look like DNA strands, hinting at the two Koreas' past experiments with genetic engineering and cloning, and mimicking the U.S. serial killers Richard Trenton Chase and Edmund Kemper, whose genetic makeup the forensic analyst has been mapping for years. Perhaps it is not coincidental that the killers the suspect is mimicking should have been born around the time of the Korean War, suggesting that he, too, is a product born of the events of that period. We also learn that both the investigator and analyst are plagued by migraines and memory loss, and in the climax of the film the investigators and criminals must return to the scene of the film's real crime—a ship laboratory called Luca, where a joint North and South Korean team had in the late 1990s run genetic engineering experiments on kidnapped children to create a superior generation for the post-reunification period. We learn ultimately that the killer was one of the subjects of these experiments, a boy engineered to be a militarily superior human named Goliath (Ch'oe Minsu), whose escape from the facility eventually caused the experiment to be aborted. The remaining children were then genetically mutated to erase their memories; among them, we eventually learn, were the investigator (Yun Sŏk) and the analyst (Kim Hŭi-su).

The historian Pierre Nora writes that memory differs from history in that it is "by nature multiple and yet specific; collective, plural, and yet individual. . . . Memory takes root in the concrete, in spaces, gestures, images, and objects."[18] As such, the concept of mnemonic site helps us to deconstruct national histories by reconstructing alternative histories; as Alain Delissen has suggested, if we reconstruct these alternative histories, particularly at a representational level, we can force the authoritarian and state-centered national histories "to yield . . . to the kaleidoscopic outlooks of the memory-nation."[19] Whereas the authorities in *J.S.A.* conduct a criminal investigation in order to preserve these state histories—both sides want only procedure, not results—*Yesterday* discards this reification of official history. Instead, the film foregrounds the personal involvement of the investigator and the analyst; the investigation itself provokes their own desire to remember, triggering personal memories and helping them reconstruct their own pasts. Criminal investigation gives way to memory reconstruction, an inquiry that is hidden in the recesses of the mind, yet can be prompted by an investigation of mnemonic sites, which in the film are crime scenes.

In a ghostly scene at the ship graveyard aboard Luca, the killer Goliath describes via voiceover the experiments that they were subjected to as kids. As we listen, David—the name given to Yun Sŏk when he was cloned from Goliath at the laboratory—walks through the corridors, and his memory begins to open up. We see in flashbacks (visualizations of David's memories) the children in their cells being dragged away, while we simultaneously see the remnants of the laboratory through David's eyes. Ghostly figures of David and the other children appear and disappear. When Kim Hŭi-su boards the ship, her memory is also visualized. She sees herself as a child chasing a ball down a hole, where she sees Goliath as a child. The incarceration of the children in the 1990s simulates the subsequent repression of their memory in the years since. It is only after Kim Hŭi-su and Yun Sŏk have killed Goliath and begin their escape from the bomb-rigged ship that their memories, along with the ghostly children, are set free. We see the children running down the hallway after them. Yun Sŏk momentarily shakes his wrist as if pulling someone off. Goliath's voiceover continues at this point, as if still in conversation with Yun Sŏk. The child Goliath inside the ship pulls the crank on the door shut, yet it is his adult voice asking if Yun Sŏk wants to live. When Goliath pulls the trigger on the bomb, the children reappear to push the door open, helping Yun Sŏk escape the explosion. These scenes employ what Joseph Jonghyun Jeon has called "embodied memories," in which a character in the present-day of the narrative seems to interact with the physical presence of a past version of himself.[20] *Yesterday* uses embodied memory as a way to create the effect of synchronous time: the ghost of one's former self interacts with the present self in order to create a tangible outcome. Solving the problems of the past solves the problems of the present as well. The site of the investigation is both the actual border region and the far more nebulous border of one's own memories.

The synchronous structure enables the investigators to solve both crimes at once, because they are understood as part and parcel of one another. This is possible because the crimes being investigated in the present take place in mnemonic sites, which thus evoke memories of the past. The Korean-Chinese border echoes the DMZ, which also later becomes a crime scene in the film when Goliath assassinates the remorseful doctor-turned-priest who oversaw the genetic experiments. The synchronic structure also allows the investigation of present affairs to have a double effect where the solution gives closure to memories of past injustices caused by ambitions for a better place in the Asian world order. The past in these films has not yet occurred in the viewers' real time. The audience is forced to see diegetic history (which is in the viewers' future) as separate from their own sense of history (in the past). This removal prioritizes the role of memory in the investigation and constructs continuity between diegetic time and our time that has been forgotten by those in the future, but can be remembered by seeking out the mnemonic sites that contain the history.

The fundamental issue of what constitutes the "reunified" subject is staged through the theme of cloning, an issue that would have been on the South Korean public's mind around the time of the film's release. In 1999, the

South Korean scientist Hwang Woo-suk (Hwang U-sŏk) came to the public's attention by cloning dairy cows. The questionable validity of his cloning processes and fabricated successes came to light starting in 2004, when he claimed to have successfully cloned human embryonic stem cells. He was disgraced in 2005. The investigator Yun Sŏk turns out to be David, the clone of the killer Goliath. This makes Hanbyŏl, the son who David accidentally kills and attempts to preserve through cryogenics, also a blood relation of Goliath.[21] In *Yesterday*, even more radically self-incriminating than in *J.S.A.*—which deploys the trope of brotherhood to describe the relationship between adversaries—the outcome in which David turns out to be Goliath's clone implies that to kill one's opponent is to kill yourself.[22] The synchronous nature of time in the film thus ensures a future that is inseparable from the past. The DMZ as the site of multiple crimes in multiple temporalities figures this circularity. It is both a crime scene and a memorial; and in this logic of the film, these are the same thing.

DMZ Moments

The DMZ does not ever appear in *2009: Lost Memories*—indeed, within the logic of the film, it doesn't actually exist. What becomes clear, however, is the way in which the relationship between Korea and Japan is mapped onto a template that is unmistakably borrowed from South Korean representations of its civil war with North Korea, most prominently in the overlapping tropes of brotherhood and fraternity that come into conflict with national and political allegiances. South Korean war films, like civil-war narratives in general, often center on the tragedy of brothers (or men who are as close as brothers) who must face each other on the battlefield, where their familial bond inevitably comes into conflict with national and political allegiances—a trope that *J.S.A.* explored to such great effect and that *Shiri* tweaked by turning the bond (between a man and a woman) into romantic love. Accompanying this trope is inevitably a scene of standoff in which personally intimate figures (whether the bond is fraternal or romantic) must weigh their emotional bonds against their political affiliations. Accordingly, *2009: Lost Memories* is full of guns-drawn, shot/reverse-shot standoffs, in which Sakamoto Masayuki (Jang Dong-gun), an ethnic Korean Japanese Bureau of Investigation agent, stares tensely while holding a gun on a person to whom he feels close, either by virtue of personal or ethnic connections, and thus feels conflicted about shooting. It should be noted that Sakamoto's family history contains an oblique reference, the only one in the film, to the Korean War: his father, a disgraced policeman, had been involved in a case associated with the Russian city of Vladivostok, which was the headquarters of the Soviet Union's Pacific Fleet during the war.

The film's numerous standoffs appear repeatedly, becoming a dominant trope in the film, as opposing figures point guns at each other in tense moments of pause before violent action. These are moments of suspension, in which pressure and anxiety mount, before they are resolved either by action or by withdrawal. In contemporary South Korean culture, the most visible example of this kind of tense standoff, of pause between moments of violence, is the DMZ—perhaps even more specifically, Panmunjŏm, where soldiers of opposing nations but shared ethnicity stare at each other across a line drawn in the ground. In *2009: Lost Memories*, the affective and political tensions embodied in the DMZ are disassociated from a specific locale (the DMZ), literally deterritorialized, and dispersed and recoded instead into the complex representations of conflicts between individuals in the film.

Based on an alternative history novel (*taech'e yŏksa sosŏl*) by Pok Kŏil, the film posits an "imaginary history" (*kasang yŏksa*) and the movement to "set straight the history" (*yŏksa paro ssŭgi*) of Korea in a contestation over memory.[23] The premise of *2009: Lost Memories* is that a powerful Japanese businessman has used an ancient relic discovered in 1985 to travel back in time and alter the course of history, and that the diegetic narrative of most of the film, in which Japan still rules over Korea, is the wrong course of history. The various historical trajectories of the film pivot around two actual historical junctures, which if changed would presumably lead to very different outcomes for Korea and Japan. From the Korean perspective, the assassination of Resident-General Itō Hirobumi in Harbin, Manchuria, in 1909, by the independence fighter An Jung-geun was a victory, which if reversed would signal doom for Korean liberation. From the perspective of Japan, the bombing of Hiroshima brought devastating defeat onto the nation in the Second World War. At the start of the film, we see how a Japanese businessman named Inoue has used the relic, and its historical "preknowledge," to change the events leading up to the bombing of Hiroshima, ensuring Japan's victory and supremacy in the region over Chosŏn (Korea) and larger East Asia. In the next scene, a band of Korean independence fighters attempt to seize the relic from an exhibition and restore their "stolen history" in a violent terrorist attack. Sakamoto must uncover their motivations, verify their allegations of a refracted history, and in the process grapple with his own conflicts regarding his emerging Korean subjectivity.

Beneath this elaborate chronological structure, *2009: Lost Memories* is a film about Korea's colonial relationship with Japan and, as important, is a film about the burdens of brotherhood. The two main characters love one another as if they were brothers despite the fact that one is ethnically Korean while the other is full-blooded Japanese. Both work as partners for the Japanese Bureau of Investigation in this counterfactual world in which Korean independence never happened. Saigō (Toru Nakamura), the ethnic Japanese officer, is particularly fond of Sakamoto, the ethnically Korean one, because of Sakamoto's heartfelt intervention years ago, when Saigō's relationship with the woman who would become his wife was faltering. Sakamoto wrote a letter on Saigō's behalf to the woman, convincing her that Saigō would be a worthy husband. This backstory, not surprisingly, serves as buildup to the climactic standoff in the film, which restages the classic Korean War trope of brothers fighting one another in the context of Japanese colonialism. What is unique about this particular representation is the fraternal bond between antagonists, a characteristic that is usually absent from Korean representations of colonial Japan-Korea relations, in which the Japanese figure is nearly always defined, all too simply, as the enemy.

This final standoff returns full circle to the opening scene of the film, the assassination attempt on Itō Hirobumi at Harbin Station. The presence of Saigō and Sakamoto, who have jumped through the relic's time portal and into the past, at the scene of the assassination attempt imposes the future into the past, a past that we see modified (or corrected, if we buy into the conceit of the film) before our eyes. The standoff occurs between Saigō and Sakamoto as Sakamoto aims for Inoue, who was previously sent back in time to kill An Jung-geun and prevent him from assassinating Itō Hirobumi.[24] What is startling about this ending is the way in which the logic of the DMZ and of relations between North and South Korea comes to inform the film's representation of Korea's colonial relationship to Japan. The key figure here is Saigō, Sakamoto's friend who is torn between his affection for Sakamoto and his duty to Japan. Saigō owes Sakamoto a great deal because of Sakamoto's letter to his wife, which she has never in fact shown Saigō. Saigō serves the role of the Song Kang-ho character in *J.S.A.*—the North Korean would-be brother rendered distant by real or imagined lines of political demarcation—shifting the implicit relationship between Korea and Japan. No longer sworn enemies whose entreaties must be regarded with careful suspicion, Saigō takes on the role of a long-lost brother with whom the Korean must reconcile. By mapping the experience of Japanese colonialism onto the story of the DMZ, the film demonstrates the complex mental labor involved in the construction of a sense of a unified or at least cooperative Asia at the heart of Asianization, whereby old antagonisms must be reimagined as friendships. No longer a discrete historical phenomenon, the DMZ becomes a trope through which Korea can think about repaired relationships in general.

In addition to the many standoff scenes, another metonymic invocation of the DMZ is the use of the War Memorial of Korea, in Yongsan, as a prominent filming location. In the film, this would-be memorial to the Korean War in Seoul is used in the film as Itō Hall, which, like the many other portentous places associated with the DMZ, becomes a crime scene in the film. It is also the site of the first standoff in the film, between the Japanese Bureau of Investigation (JBI) forces and the ethnic Korean independence fighters, and between Sakamoto and the leader of the independence fighters, who taunts Sakamoto in his native language. Standing in stark contrast to the hypermodern city of now-still-colonial Seoul, Itō Hall appears in the film initially as a quiet oasis of cultural preservation where Asian artifacts, seized in colonized countries over three generations of the Inoue family, are on display. Within the space of the museum, although under Japanese control, the artifacts suggest a place and culture of the precolonial past, and the exhibition acts as a guardian of cultural treasures valued for their invocation of this time past.

One element of the past, however, that does not exist in the film's version of history is, ironically, the occasion for the Yongsan war memorial, that is, the Korean War. In the counterfactual logic of the film, we must emphasize, this memorial cannot exist. If Japanese colonialism never ended, then there would have been no civil war, but of course, if we extend this logic, then there would be no Yongsan war memorial either. What does it mean to choose, as a central location for a film that imagines that the Korean War never happened, precisely the location that commemorates this war? Built in the early 1990s, the Yongsan war memorial was a complex that did not exist at all in any shape or form during the Japanese colonial period, and one whose architecture was designed to speak very specifically to the history of the war. Emphasizing a theme of "embrace," the wings of the buildings that surround the central plaza, both of which are displayed prominently in the film. That architectural embrace is doubled by the literal embrace of the *Statue of Brothers*, positioned just to the side of the central plaza, which depicts two tattered soldiers, the larger South

Korean one holding up the younger, North Korean one, who is leaning on him. Both architecture and sculpture signify a hope for future reconciliation. So although the memorial serves a distinctively patriotic function for South Korea, it does so in a way that accommodates the North Korean brother, which the South Korean brother wishes to hold once again in his arms.[25]

Against this ahistorical vision, which invokes the Korean War while denying that it ever happened, the Korean liberation group suddenly intrudes into the exhibition hall through the skylight, which resembles a camera aperture that opens and sharpens to a focused image of the scene below. The Korean liberation group shatters the museal space and the museal gaze authorized by the Japanese, and brings back the specter of the Korean War by forcing Sakamoto to confront his own feelings of ethnic fidelity. Entering through the skylight opening, the intruders violently recode the very same museum space into a violent site of remembering and of recollecting a different past denied by the reality of the film, namely a different past of a liberated Korea, by asserting their presence and resistance. However, for viewers who are familiar with the Yongsan memorial, the eruption of violence at this site is difficult to observe without thinking about the country's civil war. The Koreans' violent recoding of the museal space prior to Sakamoto's arrival enables him to reflect on his repressed Korean subjectivity and alterity, rather than on his assumed Japanese identity. Ironically, this odd transference of affective material associated with the Korean War into the context of Korea-Japan relations is already accomplished within the Yongsan memorial itself, which displays a pair of relief sculptures in the central plaza that represent Korean military opposition to Japanese aggression from the sixteenth century to the colonial period.[26] Even more ironically, we see these sculptures in the background early on in the film when the police first arrive in response to the attack at the complex.

The odd historical cross-hatching that we witness in this film stands in direct contrast to the recent movement in Korea to demolish all architectural traces of Japanese colonialism, a controversial practice subsumed under the recent effort to "settle the past," the symbolic eradication of potential sources of historical distortion. The movement to "settle history" through a search for historical truth is not limited to Japanese colonialism, but is closely related to broader associations between Japanese colonialism, Korean modernity, and the search for traces of a refracted Korean modernity removed from colonial continuity. According to the historian Ahn Byung-ook, the task has taken on three concrete forms, namely the purge of negative remnants from Japanese imperial rule, the investigation of Korean War crimes and related ideological persecution, and the prosecution of people deemed "authoritarian" who suppressed the democracy movement.[27] The "settling the past" discourse argues that the U.S. hiring of Japanese collaborators for Rhee Syngman government posts following Korea's liberation from Japan resulted in a negative perpetuation of Japanese imperial legacies. Subsequent coups and military governments furthered these suppressive injustices, blocking the "sound development" of a modern democratic Korea and resulting in a refracted modernity.

As the historian Chung Youn-tae points out, the stakes are forward looking: "The debates over the issue of 'settling the past' can be interpreted as a struggle over how to reform Korean society, manifested in a contestation over memory."[28] A critical review and elimination of past wrongdoings so that they no longer impart a negative influence or hinder the democratic development of Korean society is an important part of the "settling the past" discourse. As a joint production, the struggle to settle the past in Korea-Japan relations tackles these anxieties in a time of transition in East Asia, as both nations seek to reestablish friendlier ties. The question of how best to remove "remnants of the Japanese colonial past" (*Ilche singmin chanje ch'ŏngsan*) or "set history straight" (*yŏksa paro ssŭgi*) is a major issue, and generally envisioned as occurring through attempts "to correct and purge the wrongs of the past" and "to uncover the truths hidden or distorted in the records of the past, to disclose past injustices in history, to remember them on a societal level, and to record them in history."[29] Behind the movement is the hope that "settling the past" will bring about apology, forgiveness, and reconciliation. In contrast, *2009: Lost Memories* reconjures this past: its opening shows the reinscription of signs of Japanese colonial rule, from signs of Korean resistance to signs of Japanese victory scattered throughout the urban space, which occurs in a vision of Seoul as a colonial metropolis. For example, the statue in downtown of the Chosŏn dynasty navel hero Admiral Yi Sun-sin, who led the Koreans against Japanese invaders in the sixteenth century, is replaced by a statue of Toyotomi Hideyoshi, who led Japan's first invasions into Korea against Admiral Yi, and behind it we see the large, gray dome of the Japanese governor-general's headquarters, a building which was demolished in 1995. The introductory revisionist montage of *2009: Lost Memories* questions which memory it is that ultimately gets lost in the resurrection of alternative histories. The history of Korean national independence is lost, as is the history of any Korea-U.S. relations. Korea-U.S. relations become subsumed under Japanese colonialism as the revisionist history has the United States fighting alongside the Japanese as allies in the Second World War and ending the war by dropping atomic bombs on Berlin, not Japan. In this revision, Korea has no alignment with the United States and no role in the Cold War. History thus becomes a set of tropes that get mobilized in future relations.

Conclusion

As in *Yesterday*, the reengagement with the painful past in *2009: Lost Memories* allows for the construction of synchronous temporality in the name of historical redress, but one that ultimately allows for the reframing of history. In both cases, the history of the Korean War comes to inform Korea's emerging partnership with China and Japan, respectively, in the newly emergent discourse of Asianization. Also, the DMZ, deterritorialized and transformed into a set of related tropes, becomes a way to think about the new figurative borders that define these new relationships. The notion of DMZ, in other words, ceases to function strictly as a historical site with a specific material past, but rather increasingly functions as a comparative lens through which Korea can imagine other relationships, other borders.

It is no coincidence then that both films also foreground museums or memorials, most prominently the DMZ National Park in *Yesterday* and the Yongsan War Memorial of Korea (reimagined as the Ito Hall Cultural Center) in *2009: Lost Memories*, both of which function as what have been termed "theaters of memory."[30] Yet these spaces function less as sites of preservation than as sites of violence and often of crimes; there, actual acts of violence, involving weapons and bloodshed, only make literal the more metaphoric acts of violence that museums accomplish in their efforts to reframe history. In slightly less skeptical terms, Andreas Huyssen in *Twilight Memories* has suggested that the function of museums at a time of generational waning of memory "enables the moderns to negotiate and to articulate a relation to the past that is always also a relationship to the transitory and to death," seeing the museum thus "as a site and testing ground for reflections on temporality and subjectivity, identity, and alterity." While providing "a sense of bliss outside time, a sense of transcendence," it also opens up "a space for memory and recollection denied outside the museum's walls."[31] Huyssen's account foregrounds acts of memory in an environment in which the object of memory fades, what was earlier termed postmemory. There is a decided ambivalence to the material history of the objects in the museum, and instead the space functions as a sort of ontological echo chamber in which experiences of the past help confirm the subject's existence. Through museums, these moderns can only articulate and test their relations to the past in order to recover a mere *sense* of something greater and transcendent, and indeed a sense of themselves. Similarly, *Yesterday* and *2009: Lost Memories* use musealized spaces in a complementary relationship with the narrative of the alternative history to open up synchronous spaces for testing reflections on history and subjectivity. The DMZ in these films, in its various forms, functions as a kind of museum space, one that functions less in the geopolitical terms sketched out in *J.S.A.*, as a border between nations with a specific history, and more as a trope that helps us probe and negotiate the changing coordinates of the relationship between self and other.

The discourse of national division and reunification was a crucial factor in the formation of the Korean blockbuster, which in turn, made the film industry a viable force as part of hallyu. However, as hallyu gathered force from 1997 onward and developments enabled South Korean civilians to venture beyond the vicinity of the DMZ all the way to North Korea's Kŭmgang Mountains (which saw nearly two million South Korean tourists between 1998 and July 2008, when the Kŭmgang Mountain tourism project was halted for security reasons), the DMZ ceased to be the sole center of imagined border crossings between the two Koreas. In 2005, Cho Myŏng-nam's *The Bold Family* (*Kan k'ŭn gajok*), a comedy about a family that deceptively stages a reunification in order to receive an inheritance from their dying father, became the first South Korean film to be shot at Kŭmgang Mountains. The much publicized footage of their six-day filming experience focused on their wonderment at the wintry sights, the food, and the hospitality, and on their hopes for reunification; the actors' tourist response to the mountains contrasts with the Panmunjŏm tourist scene of *J.S.A.*, in which the tourism is more about historical observation and less about sightseeing.

Suk-young Kim argues that the DMZ has "performative qualities," "drawn from the often contentious—and therefore dramatic—interaction between the state and the border crossers as both parties deploy bodily transgression through varying strategies," and that "it is precisely the matrix of contestations between the state and the individual, emotion and constitution, that makes border crossing a highly performative event."[32] As I show in the following chapter, on tourism to Kang Je-gyu's *Taegukgi* filming locations, the prominence of hallyu discourse (specifically its insistence on circulation), along with the increased popularity of tourism, dislodges border crossings and their performative qualities from politicized borders, stages, screens, and historical tourist sites to spaces that do not have to be the DMZ or be in North Korea; monumentality and the emotions associated with real border crossing are granted to arbitrary spaces and nonhistorical objects through film, turning props and sets into what I call "transient monuments" of national division. This phenomenon severs what Kim calls DMZ's "performative qualities" from the historicized to the affective realm that is circumscribed by hallyu's commodification and mass-produced affect.

6. TRANSIENT MONUMENTS

Commemorating and Memorializing in *Taegukgi*
Korean War Film Tourism

6.1 The two brothers cry out for their mother
as they are taken to war in *Taegukgi*.

6.2 The train used in the filming of *Taegukgi* at its resting
place at Hapch'ŏn Theme Park. Photo by author.

On 10 January 2004, about a month before Kang Je-gyu's film *Taegukgi: Brotherhood of War* (2004) opened in theaters, the entire film set was transported to the coastal city of Busan.[1] The set, modeled after the city of Pyongyang (now in North Korea) and the Chongno district, a main thoroughfare in downtown Seoul, in the 1950s, was then set up again within a makeshift dome measuring approximately 3,670 square meters on the grounds of the Busan Exhibition and Convention Center (BEXCO), located in Busan's beach community, Haeundae.[2] The resulting exhibition, *Experience! Taegukgi Hwinallimyŏ* (which refers to the Korean title of the film, and translates roughly as "Experience! Flying the Taegukgi," the name of the national flag of Korea), was declared to be not only a display of the unaltered film set and contents, but also an exhibition about the Korean War. The experience it purported to offer was one of directly partaking in the production and action of a war film of unprecedented magnitude at the site (*hyŏnjanggam*), as well as in battles that actually resembled real skirmishes. In scope and in intention, it was simultaneously a grand commemoration of the Korean War and a tribute to one of the most successful films in Korean history.

The self-contained dome exhibition, complete with life-size cadavers on stretchers and in trenches and tunnels, drew deliberately from the recent popularity of virtual-reality gaming in the hopes of providing fun "edutainment" to Korean youth, for whom the Korean War has become distant.[3] Modeled on the then-growing phenomenon of film-induced tourism, in which tourism to a film site was promoted following the release of a popular film, the plan was also to give people a taste of the film before its release, putting the proverbial cart before the horse, in an effort to publicize the film. The *Experience! Taegukgi Hwinallimyŏ* exhibition stayed open for two months and drew huge crowds in its original location. It then traveled as an exhibition to Korea's larger urban centers before the film set was finally returned to its original sites, in the small town of Hapch'ŏn at the Cine Theme Park (Yŏngsang T'ema P'akŭ), and as one of many film sets that make up Buch'ŏn's Fantastic Studios for a longer, more permanent run, where the sets continued to attract visitors even several years after *Taegukgi*'s box-office success. In addition, the Taegwallyŏng Samyang Ranch, a hilly property near Pyŏngchang where some of the film's battles were filmed, also drew the interest of tourists.

But just five years after the film's release, in the summer of 2008, when I visited, *Taegukgi*'s tourist destinations were a shadow of their former selves.

Remnants of *Taegukgi* were hardly to be found at the Buch'ŏn location. Similarly, at Hapch'ŏn, the sets sat quietly with fewer and fewer visitors, drifting slowly into an amnesiac oblivion. The massive steam locomotive, too costly to be discarded, lay in a ditch off to the side of a parking lot covered in thick layers of dust, with the film's tanks and weapons crowded together into a nearby corner of the park (fig. 6.2). The film *Taegukgi*, and along with it the virtual-real experience of surviving the Korean War, had been reduced to weathered serial stills from the film, macabre decorations of the fence running the park's perimeter.

In this chapter I engage in a visual excavation of the outdoor film sets and theme parks for the film *Taegukgi* and the *Experience! Taegukgi Hwinallimyŏ* exhibition, conducted in the moments of its final deterioration and before its disposal. Although these sites arose and gained prominence from the film and the exhibition, they have since moved on to accommodate newer films and exhibitions or have fallen into ruins. Reading these sites along with the film itself, I ask a number of questions. Given that the tensions between North and South Korea remain a central, pervasive concern in South Korean culture, why did these sites wane in popularity? To what extent were these film sites conflated with Korean War sites? And what does it mean that memorial culture should "speak" at this time period specifically through such cultural forms? In short, to what extent are these film sites memorials?

The transience of the *Taegukgi* film tour sites and exhibitions stands in direct contrast to the decidedly nontransient Korean War and the prominent place national division occupies in Korean public memory. The film *Taegukgi*'s Korean War sites might be seen as "false" memorials, in that they refer to the film primarily and only indirectly to the Korean War. These sites, however, require that we divert our attention away from questions of representational authenticity and focus instead on the apparent contradiction between the sites' commemorative overlaps and transient fate. What emerges in this shift is a need to question possible changes in practices of memorialization and modes of memory-telling that have emerged in recent hallyu years. At stake in the brief and fleeting history of the *Taegukgi* film sites is the question of the transience of Korean public memory. If the fate of these temporary memorials is ultimately the garbage dump, then we must ask if the fate of Korean historical memory is similarly ignominious.

I thus explore *Taegukgi*'s tour sites as what I call "transient monuments," in their reimagination of sites of historical commemoration. This oxymoronic term reflects both the monumental scale of the Korean War film, marking crucial moments in both Korean history and Korean film history, as well as the transience of tourism as an act of consumption. In their temporal and spatial transience, these sites also reflect the passing nature of the films they monumentalize and alert us to the disposability of monuments. In using the term *monument*, I thus do not refer to a structure that exists in "static time" and in "a field of inaccessibility," marked by "distance inscribed into its function" such that approaching the monument is "always a sort of transgression of a sacral zone," as Mikhail Yampolsky has described it.[4] I invoke, instead, the Chinese art historian Wu Hung's more ambiguous notion, which is determined by subjective judgment and a "kin feeling" that links visitors to the monument in a personal way.[5] Applying Pierre Nora's notions of mnemonic sites to a study of the monuments at Tiananmen Square, Wu Hung argues for a definition of the monument, which, through the act of visitation, can overcome its impersonality and imposing quality and become instead more personally and emotionally inhabitable, thus transitioning from Nora's category of "dominant" to the other of "dominated." The monument gets reinterpreted as it becomes imbued with new subjective memories.[6] By extension, the transient monument similarly becomes a place that enables an emotional connection to the past. But in so doing, the monument also risks confusing memory with affect under the rubric of remembrance, and history becomes increasingly difficult to disambiguate from consumerism.

In the following, I provide a glimpse of the relationship between Korean War films and movie theme parks in contemporary South Korean culture, and lay out the problems that arise in situating the memory of the Korean War within places of leisure, as opposed to official commemorative observances. Then I will attempt to reassemble the dispersed 2003 BEXCO *Taegukgi* film exhibition by describing the various parts at their respective tour sites and contexts—at Buch'ŏn's Fantastic Studios, Hapch'ŏn Theme Park, and Taegwallyŏng Samyang Ranch—as a way of comprehending what happens to history in this process of textual displacement and spatial reinstitution: which aspects get restored and which get rejected. By examining these sites, as spatially displaced from visual film text to virtual-reality display to tour site, I will illustrate how, as transient monuments, these sites function as a point of transition between the real world outside the parks and the reconstructed filmic world inside, and between history as commodity and history as heritage. In the process, they enable the commemoration of alternative histories of the Korean War and national division that lie outside of the state's dominant rhetoric. It is not my purpose here to posit the value of these tour sites in celebration of *Taegukgi*, but to show that the sites' potential to offer an alternative to the state-sanctioned account and preferred modes of commemoration comes at a great cost. As history is remembered and accommodated within leisure practices formed by the giving breadths of filmic liberties, ideology is traded for affect.

Official and Intimate Memories

Taegukgi tells the tale of two brothers forced into a war that separates them, just as it divides the country. The film adheres to the standards of the war film genre, acknowledging its antecedents in Korean film history with its conventional depiction of traumatic suffering caused by national division and bipartisanship. It also appropriates the genre's themes of separation of family and sacrifice, which are often dramatized through the use of melodramatic conventions and heightened through the use of doubling. Korean War films in particular have often pushed the ideological boundaries of the times, from as early as 1965, when director Yi Man-hui's film *Seven Women Prisoners* (*7 in ŭi yŏp'oro*) dared to depict sympathy toward communist North Koreans, which violated the South's government decrees barring procommunist leanings.[7]

Such films marked turning points in how the Korean War would be remembered, and this tradition has been continued by the director of *Taegukgi*, Kang Je-gyu. In Kang's earlier groundbreaking blockbuster of national division, *Shiri*, the doubling of characters features prominently, not only as a manifestation of one nation split into two and as a figure for the incommensurability of the political situation, but also as depiction of the bind of those who wish to belong neither to the North nor to the South. In the context of Kang's earlier revisionist vision, it is no surprise that *Taegukgi* also pushes boundaries in how the Korean War is remembered. The story here is more than an account of historical memory; it is also one in which, particularly in light of the film's foray into supplementary enterprises (*puga saŏp*), memory overlaps with consumption. Indeed, *Taegukgi* is regarded as the first example of the "one source multiuse" model in Korean cinema, which integrated tourism, publishing, records, clothing, and so on into its marketing strategy.

Korea's movie theme parks have not been explored as realms for Korean War commemorative culture and collective memory-making. Because their consumption lies within Korean leisure culture, outside of the traditional realm of national politics and more formal, state-sanctioned commemorative practices like the Yongsan war memorial (which, one might add, is not without its theme-park elements), this popular form of remembering the Korean

War and the ways in which the public revisits and reimagines the war have been largely neglected. I believe that war film reenactments—and the corporeal traversal of structural replicas—offer South Koreans not only access to sites otherwise restricted to civilians due to the ongoing Korean War, but more significantly, an alternative paradigm to remembering the war away from dominant forms, and the experience of alternative histories associated with the war that have not been selected by the state to be remembered or memorialized.[8]

Movie theme parks and museums in South Korea since the late 1990s have on several occasions served in a capacity that conflates cinematic reimagination with historical reality to satisfy public curiosity and desire regarding memories about the Korean War and the national division that was the war's result. The KOFIC Namyangju Studios in Yangsuri, built in 1999, became renowned for its replica of Panmunjŏm, the heavily guarded, restricted joint security area in the demilitarized zone (DMZ) between North and South Korea. Built for Park Chan-wook's film *Joint Security Area* (*Kongtong kyŏngpi kuyŏk*, 2000), which depicts the ill-fated, clandestine friendship between North and South Korean soldiers stationed at the DMZ, the attraction drew on the symbolic reminder of the continuing national division and the memory of the student activist movement that demonstrated for reunification in the 1980s.[9] In this case, the simulacrum supplanted the original, since South Koreans are restricted from access to Panmunjŏm and from participating in Panmunjŏm tours that take tourists right up to the military demarcation line between North and South Korea and the blue Military Armistice Commission building standing over the demarcation line within the DMZ. Though South Korean civilians can enter the vicinity of the DMZ, Imjingak Pyŏnghwanuri (Imjin Pavilion Peace Park), which opened in 1972, marks the northernmost area that they can visit. The film set thus ironically becomes the primary site of memorial experience, whereas Panmunjŏm itself functions as a distant dream.

Similarly, the set for the film *Silmido*, released in 2003, was actually built on the uninhabited island of Silmido, where in April 1968 societally marginalized South Koreans sentenced to hang were covertly trained as guerillas to kill the North Korean leader Kim Il-Sung in retaliation for an attack on Chŏngwadae, the "Blue House," where South Korea's president lives. The film literally inscribed its reimagination of the events onto the site where the actual event had occurred, recognizing a classified, and therefore untold, chapter in the history of national division, and memorializing collateral sacrifices. Tourists came to the tiny island after the release of the hugely popular film to visit the sets and remember the historic event.[10] The tourism to *Taegukgi*'s sites began around the same time, in 2003, primarily in Busan, Hapch'ŏn, Taegwallyŏng Samyang Ranch, and Buch'ŏn. Visiting these sites becomes a blending of historical and film tourism. That blending raises many questions, the most important of which is: what does it mean to experience history through the mediation of film and at the intersection of tourism?

These films emphasize the possibilities for bonding across lines of political difference, as we see soldiers in shared acts of the everyday, playing hacky sack, eating chocolate pies, or swapping photographs of girlfriends. Re-creating these everyday activities, long suppressed, functions as critical commentary against a culture of militarism, as well as a vehicle for obtaining the truth and providing cinematic pleasure. We thus identify a filmic emphasis on the relationship between the everyday and Korean War–related militarism as entry into an alternative narrative of the Korean War that coexists in tension with official narratives, and we can then draw a parallel and consider the visitation of tour sites of such films as subversive commemorative acts to these alternative histories that exist in tension with the participation of official, state-sanctioned commemorative culture. On the other hand, while these narratives may offer other possibilities for remembering, such alternatives come at a great cost. History at the Korean War film tour sites is laden with the kinds of emotions that accompany historical melodrama. Part of the filmic mediation of history is to make it more affective, more felt, but at the same time this new insistence on emotion comes at the cost of other modes of historical observation. In short, history becomes increasingly proximate and affectively felt to a generation that does not remember the war, but at the cost of being decreasingly understood.

It is useful here to take a moment and look at Korea's prototype of civic commemoration, the War Memorial of Korea in Seoul. Opened to the public in 1994, this state monument and national museum is devoted to militarism, nationalism, patriotism, and the power of "manliness" in national defense. As Korea's central locus of commemoration, it aims to explain the Korean War to South Koreans, specifically within a unified history of heroic military leadership.[11] The memory and "healing" process of the Korean War and national division is here evoked through association with memories of other past wars. Sheila Miyoshi Jager argues that the memorial's builders made a conscious effort to promote, within the spaces of the memorial, particular feelings that would resonate with the Korean official culture of commemoration that "perpetuated and generated a view of the past in terms of a masculine ideal," and to emphasize memories of the war that "have also affirmed the identification of the national subject with the authority of these masculine images aimed at perpetuating the state's vision of a future reunified Korea."[12] The preferred feelings here are "restricted" to the "feeling of reverence" and "embrace": "It was within this space that *the 'petty' concerns of everyday life 'were supposed to be brushed aside* so that the visitor can confront the *extraordinary meaning of war, sacrifice, and patriotism.'* . . . It is within this inclusive space that the heroic past and the glorious present, the people and the nation, the individual and history are supposed to come together in the staged dramaturgy of national unity, reverence, and shared memory."[13] Thus, while commemoration at the memorial entails *exclusion* of the concerns of the everyday for the purposes of inclusion (of the past with the present, the people with the nation, the individual with history), the theme parks in contrast are structured *within* the everyday to *include* those people and narratives that have been excluded in the official history. Rather than the heroic, the monumental space of *Taegukgi* film locations is associated with intimate memories of individuals, namely through those of the fictive characters remembered in the past and those of the tourists who visit in the present. This emphasis precisely on the every day, dissuaded at official spaces of commemoration, is a conscious choice by *Taegukgi*'s director, not as a historical melodrama, but in order to use affect for historical purposes. The Korean war memorial symbolically imposes first and foremost a mode of historical interpretation that strongly asserts the ways in which the history of the Korean War should be remembered—that is, as heroic, masculine, and patriotic. The *Taegukgi* sites do something similar, but unlike the dominant monument or memorial, the film site is a space in which history is presented in ways that accommodate leisure rather than interrupt it. At a traditional historical monument, one is interpellated as the subject of history and experiences a momentary interruption of tourist leisure. The theme park insures and preserves an imaginary space, which stands in stark contrast to the real world. Like Walt Disney World, as an example par excellence of the theme park as a delusional utopian fantasy-state (complete with its own police and its own currency), these film theme parks present history as entirely coherent with the logic of leisure.

Buch'ŏn Fantastic Studios' Chongno:
The Transience of the Everyday

The closest *Taegukgi* site to Seoul is in Buch'ŏn at Fantastic Studios. Here, the private sphere of the home, family, and work becomes part of the Korean War film tourism experience. That emphasis embodies the directorial intention of narrating an account of "war without battle" that commemorates the every-day lives of ordinary people destroyed by the war.[14] *Taegukgi* was inspired by a documentary about the excavation of Korean War dead that aired in 2000, in which the producers had focused on the emotional impact the unearthed remains still had on those who had waited fifty years for news of their loved ones.[15] It was the material objects found in the pockets of shredded uniforms, and the knowledge of their provenance, that enabled some personal identification of the unknown soldiers and gave the surviving family members and spouses a link to specific memories amid their remembrance and mourning. *Taegukgi* intentionally rejects a grand ideological point of view in order to narrate the Korean War in terms of the loss it incurred on individuals, on people who were just trying to make the most of poverty and willingly gave sacrifices to retrieve the joy of their everyday lives. As the director, Kang, has stressed, *Taegukgi* was not to be a typical war film that turned the battlefield into a spectacular playground to stage "cheap heroism" or "ideological nihilism."[16]

The documentary of the excavation had reported some 933 remains, of which only 30 could be identified. In response to the general lack of interest in unidentified war dead that had allowed the fallen to remain in the ground for over fifty years—a stark contrast to the country's readiness to celebrate heroism—*Taegukgi* was to intervene, armed with the ability of cinematic affect, to mobilize popular interest in the Korean War with a sense of historical responsibility. It resonated with the collective unconscious of postwar generations, which held guilt around and sympathy for the unconditional sacrifices made by their parents' generation for family. The growing strife between the two brothers (as the older brother, Chin-t'ae, repeatedly risks his life at the front to receive a medal of honor so that he can earn the right to have his sickly younger brother, Chin-sŏk, discharged and returned to their mother) is removed from political ideological differences and deeply rooted in shared loyalty and nostalgia for family.

The reconstruction of Chongno Street in Seoul—that in *Taegukgi* is where we see the brothers playing and working just before the outbreak of the Korean War—ran down the center of the Buch'ŏn Fantastic Studios, creating a link between the visitor's leisure activities and the everyday as it relates to the Korean War (fig. 6.3). Historically accurate trams used to run the length of the street, about 450 meters, from the corner of the colonial period Hwashin Department Store and the Moulin Rouge Café past the Seoul YMCA all the way to Tongdaemun, the East Gate. When I visited, these trams were parked just outside Honmachi Street, which is now called Ch'ungmuro. Built in

6.3 The place Chin-t'ae and Chin-sŏk associate with happier times. Prewar Chongno, at the Buch'ŏn Fantastic Studios. Photo by author.

2001, the grounds span 39 square kilometers and include reconstructions of Myŏngdong and Ŭljiro, as well as Chongno, and feature other Seoul buildings from the 1930s to 1970, such as the Chongno Police Station, the Poshin'gak Bell, the Umigwan Movie Theater, and a re-creation of a Ch'ŏnggyech'ŏn stream that was ten meters wide and one-hundred-and-four meters long.[17] Traces of the film *Taegukgi* could be found on posters attached to the side of relevant buildings, such as the alley where Chin-t'ae had his shoe-stand, the store selling imported Italian shoes, and the noodle stand where his mother and betrothed worked. The historical site as film site was thus re-marked as a film site. The posters imply an ambiguity of recognition, and referentiality becomes here a kind of house of mirrors as the visitor conflates movie and history.

Chongno Street first appears in the film as a flashback to a day in June 1950. In the present, an aged Yi Chin-sŏk, the younger surviving brother, is just about to head to the Battle of Dumillyong excavation site, where commemoration of the unearthed is underway. He hopes to find news of his missing older brother, Chin-t'ae, who had dreamed of being a shoemaker. His memory of the Korean War thus begins not on the battlefield, but in the streets of

Chongno. As commonly seen in the war film genre, the violence of the impending war exists in tension with the residents' oblivion, which is in the flashback shattered by the arrival of military trucks announcing the onset of war—the intrusion of history within the frame of everyday life. The film thus stages a prior state of familial stability, which sets up the narrative for the gravity and violence of the war that follows; that staging, in turn, is reflected in the film's tourist destinations, whose spatial representation of the Korean War includes the everyday as part of the memory of war. Like the pair of handmade shoes that transports Chin-sŏk and the viewer to the past, the importance of objects to memory is indicated by the numerous close-ups of objects from the 1950s, still moving and functioning, not yet destroyed by the war. The first visual from the 1950s flashback is a shot of the tramcar so close that the writing on the side is illegible. Images of the ladies and students getting onto the tram zoom in on their period clothing at waist level, and a playing gramophone is shown whirring in close-up. These tight shots are further underscored by the game of hide-and-seek that the young brothers start playing, weaving in and out of the crowds along the tightly packed streets. Only after these tight shots have been established does the camera take its time to pull out into a long shot and purvey the entire length of the street. The game is, of course, a ghostly foreshadowing of the hide-and-seek they will play as they cross sides in the battle between North and South in pursuit of each other, and their playful chase through the streets inscribes the everyday with the invisible war. In their play, the brothers accidentally knock down a young friend. This same friend is later killed by their gunfire as a prisoner of war. These scenes are eventually repeated in a tearful slow-motion flashback from 1951, while Korea is still at war and the brothers have separated to fight on different sides. Toward the end of the war, after the brothers have bitterly parted ways and Chin-t'ae has defected to the North in the belief that the South has killed his brother, Chin-sŏk reads a letter addressed to his mother from Chin-t'ae that restores his fraternal bond and makes him determined to cross and retrieve his older brother. Later, right after Chin-sŏk's tearful commemoration of the deceased older brother at the excavation site in the present day, the film returns to a tight shot of the streets of Chongno just after the war. The camera pulls back, as before, only now we see the street, still devastated by the war, but in the process of recuperation, with relative peace and an everyday ordinariness restored.

The tight-shot emphasis on specific details from the past is not restricted to the film itself. A streaming black-and-white "still gallery," part of the supplementary materials on the film's DVD, show a series of props used in the making of the film, then placed on display at Buch'ŏn Fantastic Studios as part of Chongno in the 1950s (figs. 6.4–6.9). The displays were designed to pervasively and strategically integrate their own self-perceived historicity and the artifacts of historical reproduction into historical material and context as if they were real. By putting props through special antiquating technologies, the props are given the semblance of age (and thus, of value). None of these items were actually antiques from the prewar or war period; they were mere props presented as artifacts, historically accurate down to the minutest detail. They did, however, reflect the logic of transient monuments, in their careful effort to materialize the past in meticulous detail in a bunch of disposable objects. In this transformation, the objects are bestowed with a historicity that emanates from the text from which they sprung, and impart a pseudohistorical authority to the structures and space.

As in the documentary that is said to have gripped Kang, his film, too, creates an intimate link between the materiality of everyday things and the provocation of affect as a primary mode of remembering the Korean War. Not surprisingly, the *Taegukgi* sites re-created this link. It is no minor detail that the film's link between memory of the Korean War and the present is created through a pair of shoes. Chin-t'ae—a shoe shiner and aspiring shoemaker of comfortable, well-crafted shoes—has been making a pair in secret for his brother, and he hides them for Chin-sŏk to find after his death. When Chin-sŏk goes to the battlefield to commemorate him, he is wearing these shoes. As visitors walked through these sets, viewing banal objects rendered transient by knowledge of the impending war, they participated in a very particular kind of historical commemoration, which stood outside the dominant Korean War rhetoric. In spite of the assumed nontransience of the Korean War in public memory, the film exhibit relies on the transient in order to make the history and memory more proximate. Like the brothers, whose activities in play mimic their role in war, visitors wind their way through Chongno as a leisure activity, yet with an awareness of the relatively invisible war that looms.

On these recreated streets, the visitor knew that war is coming, which in turn reinforced the discrepancy between ongoing militarism in contemporary Korean everyday culture, particularly with the visibility of U.S. military in Seoul, and the proximity of the Korean War in memory. In this approach, *Taegukgi* can be aligned with other contemporary Korean visual work that manipulates media, such as photography, in order to juxtapose the memory of the Korean War with leisure practices as a way of visualizing and bringing focus to the growing abyss between continued militarism and the increasingly distant

6.4–6.9 Stills of *Taegukgi* film props placed on display at Buch'ŏn Fantastic Studios as part of Chongno in the 1950s then filmed as a streaming exhibit of historical artifacts released as supplementary material with the DVD.

proximity of war. Noh Suntag's photo series *reallyGood, murder* (2008), for example, casts into relief the continued presence of violence related to Korean War militarism in everyday life by observing families at a military war show on a weekend excursion (figs. 6.10–6.11). The playful attitudes of these families toward real signs of war are revealing of their perception of it as unreal, and of how removed they feel from a war that took place more than half a century ago. Noh exposes the consequences of such deception by using his camera to engulf the oblivious visitors at the show in dark shadows, suggesting impending death. The film and its site at Buch'ŏn similarly integrate the body into this contradictory moment at the cusp between war and leisure, film and memorial, transforming the visitors, and their emotional response, into an integral part of the transient monument.

Disposable Monuments: Hapch'ŏn Cine-Park

The most popular tourist destination that emerged from *Taegukgi* is 328 kilometers south of Seoul, in Hapch'ŏn County in south Kyŏngsang Province, an area perhaps most known for its UNESCO designated heritage site, the Buddhist Haeinsa temple that houses the wooden Tripitaka scrolls.[18] In 2003, Kang Je-gyu noticed Kaya Mountain and Hwangmae Mountain, which surround the temple, as he was looking for a site to film the battle scenes of his Korean War film. The beauty of the location, so the story goes, sent shivers down his spine.[19] Amid the spring bloom of royal azaleas and the fall scattering of wild flowers, Kang shot a bloody scene of the forty-eight-day Naktong River Battle and the excavation of the Battle of Dumillyong that frames the film. A set was built on sprawling grounds in Hapch'ŏn, modeling parts of the—now North Korean—city of Pyongyang.[20] The Cine-Park, a theme park and outdoor place of ongoing filming, is located about a ten-minute drive along a dam near the tourist district of Hweyang. At the height of its popularity, the site's wartime setting and embedded destruction were a major draw for visitors eager to participate in this "survival space," eager to experience the film and history. That it was no longer the central attraction was evidenced by the size of the Cine-Park's remaining billboards for *Taegukgi*, which paled in comparison to the much larger, billowing billboards advertising popular TV dramas being filmed there, such as *Kyongsong Scandal* (*Kyŏngsŏng sŭk'aendŭl*) in 2007 and *East of Eden* (*Eten ŭi tong tchok*) in 2008.

At the height of the park's popularity, the structures and props used for the filming of the Naktong River Battle and the excavation of the Battle of

6.10 Noh Suntag, *reallyGood, murder* #43 (2008). Courtesy of the artist.

6.11 Noh Suntag, *reallyGood, murder* #28 (2008). Courtesy of the artist.

Dumillyong were integrated into the theme park's survival experience and historical displays. Whereas the battle at Naktong River was major, the Battle of Dumillyong is relatively unknown and was brought to the public's attention through *Taegukgi*, eventually leading to plans to erect an actual memorial in Dumillyong. The objects at Hapch'ŏn thus are significant on multiple levels: they conflate the memory of a real battle with the filmic representation of that battle, complicated by the fact that many viewers and visitors didn't know if the battle had actually occurred or was concocted for *Taegukgi*. Amid this multiplicity, however, is a common vein: the monumentality of the Cine-Park is built on an intrinsic disposability; regardless of the historical verifiability of these battles, they are all memorialized by a monument without memory.

Visitors to the Cine-Park entered an enormous parking lot that reveals both its grand aspirations and former glory. Running along the perimeter of the site was a fence partially adorned with storyboards from *Taegukgi*.[21] The descriptive poster plates narrated the film's scenes, including dialogue transcripts, leading into the park's entrance from the edge of the parking lot. There were war vehicles on display just on the other side of the fence, with references near each vehicle that neatly identify the vehicle by name, use (i.e., by the North or South Korean soldiers), and the film scene in which they were used. At the height of the exhibit's popularity, the vehicles had once lined an entire *Taegukgi* wing, but by the time of my visit had been edged out into the corners of the park closer to the exit. Whereas in their initial role as part of a survival experience (in which visitors could enact being in the war) they had been placed strategically throughout the park, their eventual display along the wall and then by the parking lot resembled that of the outdoor exhibition of authentic war vehicles at the Yongsan war memorial (figs. 6.12–6.13). The exhibition of the film's vehicles differs, however, in its ability to impart to visitors a specific war experience, by situating them within particular scenes of the film.

The steam train had fared worse (figs. 6.14–6.15). For thirty days after the park's *Taegukgi* exhibits opened, the two-car steam locomotive, an exact replica of the kind of locomotive that transported young men to war, ran 13.2 km along the banks of the picturesque Sŏmjin River, which took about one hour for a round trip.[22] The floors and glass displays inside the train were at the time of my visit carpeted in a thick layer of dust. Posters on the walls depicted the scenes between the brothers, focusing mostly on images of happiness and fraternal closeness. The first display is of their school uniforms, the keepsake box with the shoes Chin-t'ae made for his younger brother, awards from school, followed by their water canister and some torpedoes, their military uniforms,

6.12 Tank from *Taegukgi* at Hapch'ŏn Cine-Park. Photo by author.

6.13 *Taegukgi* tank exhibit sign. Photo by author.

6.14 The *Taegukgi* train. Photo by author.

6.15 The interior of the *Taegukgi* train. Photo by author.

and some military personal belongings. The next train car contained several benches, and also the detritus from another part of the set, including armchairs and a print of a western painting, that had been tossed there for storage. The train thus becomes a massive container filled with a mix of film props as historical artifacts.

In the logic of the exhibit, the train stands as a monument to the scene marking the separation of the brothers from their mother and family, as it transports them to join the war. It is the site of Chin-t'ae's first act of resistance against the South Korean soldiers as he fights to pull his sickly brother from the draft, and their first act of violence against him. As their mother and family frantically search for them, the train pulls away in an extended tearful scene. The soldiers look like frightened children, not hardened fighters; the scene is hardly one of heroic volunteerism, and as these men weep longingly for their families, it is clear that sadness and fear trump ideological conviction. The film jumps immediately into close-ups of dead bodies strewn in the trenches of war at Naktong River, where the disposal and burning of corpses on the battlefield is in progress, as if associating the train with the disposability of the youths that it carried there. Chin-t'ae and Chin-sŏk's first war experience is here, not as heroes on the battlefield, but as scared children penned in a train; Chin-sŏk nearly dies from shock, as his heart falters and panic triggers an asthma attack.

With their massive size and discarded presence, the rusted tanks, jeeps, and train became a commentary on the disposability of monuments, hulking pieces of steel caught in a transition between monument and waste. These are monuments without memory. It is only in that moment of a tourist's interest (an interest which, too, is transient) that these monuments foster an affective connection to a particular historical moment. The transience of the Cine-Park's *Taegukgi* exhibit presents a stark contrast to the quality of durability, transcendence, and atemporality which Lefebvre has defined as the "irreducible foundation" of a monument as part of his critique of the failure of monumentality.[23] The ideas that a monument is imperishable and that it is a sufficient rendering of lived experience are but illusions.

The transient monument dispenses with the illusion of permanence. Everything about it is temporary. It also attends to the problem of lived experience by making the tourist's experience of the tour site a kind of double of the original historical lived experience, but in so doing it also supplants the original experience with a highly constructed affective experience, structured not only by the organization of the site itself, but also by the way in which the site extends the affects familiar to the viewers, now as tourists, of a very melodramatic film. Tourists feel that they are in history, but this kind of reenactment, by offering a point of contact between past and present, diminishes the past by connecting to a mundane present, defined in this case by the kind of consumer consumption that going to a theme park entails.

It is possible to read the disposability, the perishability, of transient monuments as an absence of will to endure as well as lack of will to push for its durability. But one can also connect the transience of these filmic and historical objects to a vision of history that is more attached to the moment, that is, one in which filmic time supplements historical time, and one that is quickly discarded after it passes. Historical lived experience becomes just another ordinary commodity. The commemoration scene in *Taegukgi*, also filmed at Hapch'ŏn, takes place in the narrative right after the scene of the Battle of Dumillyong in which the brothers fight at the front line; Chin-t'ae as a North Korean decorated soldier and Chin-sŏk as a South Korean soldier desperately trying to get his brother to defect back to the South. Chin-t'ae is unable to recognize his younger brother because he believes him to be dead. His sanity is restored as Chin-sŏk weeps, begging him to remember the time before the war and that they must go home. Chin-t'ae promises to return, but in order to get his brother to safety makes him go ahead; Chin-t'ae convinces his brother to leave by promising to personally return the fountain pen that he had given to him at the beginning of the film (figs. 6.16–6.24).

In the film, it is the discovery of the pen (replicas of which were among the most popular objects sought out by tourists) in a burned building that initially leads Chin-t'ae to believe Chin-sŏk has been killed by the South Koreans and pushes him to fight for the North; its heart-wrenching passage—from its moment of gifting at the start of the film to this moment of reconciliation and separation, and later its discovery at the excavation—can be read as a process of passing on the act of non-ideologized, affective storytelling as it changes the brothers' hands in a series of misunderstandings. The passage of time, from the Battle of Dumillyong to the excavation of the battlefield in the present, is signaled by a shot of Chin-t'ae's body crouched where he fell in battle. The crouched figure transitions into a skeleton, as the passage of time is noted by a single clanging chime. Cicadas start chirping as the camera pulls back, and Chin-sŏk is shown standing at his brother's grave. Of the items found on his brother's corpse, he picks up the fountain pen and begins to weep, imploring

6.16–6.24 (*above and opposite*) The fountain pen. *Taegukgi*.

him to return once again. His young granddaughter beside him begins to cry at the sight of his grief, as Chin-sŏk bows to the skeleton on the ground. Here the pen is far more than a commodity; it becomes an emotionally laden signifier with a significant history.

Eating History at the Samyang Mokchang Ranch

The emotional commodification of everyday objects associated with the retrieval of Korean War memory has become widespread. That commodification can even happen with something as banal as noodles. In *Taegukgi*, Chin-t'ae and Chin-sŏk's mother runs a little noodle stand in Chongno, where Chin-t'ae's girlfriend helps out. After school and in between their shifts at the shoe stand, the boys stop by to visit the two women, grabbing a bite and watching the women cook noodles over urns of boiling soup. Later in the film, just before the retreat at Yalu River, one of the boys' friends who has been captured as a POW is taken aside briefly by Chin-t'ae. They sit on a snowy ledge overlooking the valley, munching on buns, and the friend tells Chin-t'ae that he briefly saw Chin-t'ae's family. Although his brother always questions Chin-t'ae's motives, the audience is aware that Chin-t'ae's decisions are determined by his devotion to his mother, his younger brother, and his fiancée, and that it must pain him to hear about them enduring hardship. "I wish I could eat a hot bowl of your mother's noodles now," the friend says wistfully (fig. 6.25). This scene, in which Chin-t'ae first hears that his mother is ill, was shot on the mountain plateau located at the Samyang Mokchang Ranch, a nature preserve and farm in Taegwallyŏng, Kangwŏn Province (fig. 6.26). The ranch, not coincidentally, is owned by the Samyang Corporation, since 1963 Korea's foremost maker of ramen noodles. In addition to the noodle scene, other scenes shot at the ranch include the one in which the brothers and their unit are in Hyesan-jin, far up in northern Korea, in November 1950. Chin-t'ae forces POWs to fight each other to death for food, and his cruelty toward the prisoners at the makeshift camp on the plateau agitates Chin-sŏk who steps in repeatedly, despite his frailty. This makeshift camp is also where the South Koreans hear of near victory and reunification on the radio and start celebrating, only to be crushed. When Chin-t'ae hears that he has been awarded the Medal of Honor and tells his younger brother that he may now return home, Chin-sŏk refuses. The brothers here are captured in a single frame with Chin-t'ae's arm around his brother's shoulders, the frame indicating that they are still united. As they confront each other, the camera switches to shot/reverse-shots, ending

6.25 Craving a hot bowl of noodles. *Taegukgi.*

6.26 The plateau at Samyang Mokchang Ranch where the "craving noodles" scene in *Taegukgi* was filmed. Photo by author.

in a stance that fills the frame with a brother on each side separated by a gulf of mountains in the background. This use of the shot/reverse-shot to mark the point of bitter separation is commonly used to indicate national division (for instance in Kang's earlier *Shiri*), and this plateau thus becomes the site of division in *Taegukgi*. The ranch is also where the sudden mass invasion of a swelling body of endless Chinese soldiers coming over the hills (known as the *Inhejŏnsul*) was filmed, during which Chin-t'ae executes the POW from their childhood, unleashing Chin-sŏk's fury and severing their fraternal bond.

At the Samyang Mokchang Ranch, the memory of the Korean War, as told through *Taegukgi*, is integrated into a larger narrative of the nation's historical accomplishments in harnessing natural resources to better nurture ensuing generations. Within this context of responsible consumption, the entire ranch is designed to market Samyang Corporation's ramen noodles and milk to film-inspired visitors. Visitors to the ranch are taken on a guided bus tour or walk on foot up to the ranch's scenic outlook over the East Sea (a 4-km distance that takes about 80 minutes by foot), which rises up to 1,140 meters above sea level, for a tour throughout the approximately 4,900-acre property. The tour promotes some sixty ingredients, from livestock to farmed vegetables, that go from the ranch into the packages and cartons produced by the Samyang Corporation and are available at grocery stores throughout Korea. In addition to *Taegukgi*, a number of other popular films were shot at the ranch, and these films, too, become examples of creative products that spring from the ranch's fertile grounds. The tour begins and ends with ramen noodles, and images from the films are linked with images of company's packaged instant foods on signs that mark the filming location of a particular film. On the ranch, where animals and vegetables alike are commodified for quick consumption, the memory and affective experience of Korean history, too, is transitioned from retrieval into commodity. It is no surprise that visitors are often more excited about the ramen than by the historical information. Both exist in the same sphere in these parks in the service of consumer consumption. Thus, despite the fact that Samyang Mokchang Ranch, like the other *Taegukgi* sites, diminishes the illusion of monumental permanence, it exacerbates the illusion that we can easily understand historical, lived experience—ironically, by making it more rather than less accessible, and thus more amenable to commerce.

The traces of *Taegukgi* at the ranch reflect how the Korean War film gets increasingly embedded within cinematic affect over ideology. Essential to the ranch's popularity, and the abundance of affect on display, is that the tour highlights not just *Taegukgi* but the numerous other films that have also been filmed amid the ranch's dramatic vistas and across its rolling fields. Thus, in stark contrast to the emphasis on patriotism and martyrdom in a place like the war memorial, here *Taegukgi*'s war narrative becomes integrated within and accommodated by a network of melodramatic films, such as Lee Han's hugely popular *Lover's Concerto* (*Yŏnae sosŏl*, 2002), Kwak Jae-yong's *Windstruck* (*Nae yŏja ch'ingu rŭl sogaehapnida*, 2004), the drama *Autumn in My Heart* (*Kaŭl tonghwa*, 2000), and another Korean War film, Park Kwang-hyun's *Welcome to Dongmakgol* (*Welk'ŏm t'u tongmakkol*, 2005). Visitors are informed, as the bus winds to the peak of the farm, that the ranch is the largest of its kind in Asia, with a fully functioning farm, cows, petting zoo, and numerous windmills that harness the strong gusts that sweep across the plateaus for natural energy.[24] Poster plaques have been erected marking the locations where the *Taegukgi* battle scenes were shot, as if they were actual battle sites, and visitors can get off at the stops to view the panorama of the site as depicted in the film and take photographs next to the signposts. The noodle scene, at 1,100 meters over sea level, is located just below the scenic outlook onto the East Sea, next to the site of *Welcome to Dongmakgol* surrounded by towering windmills. Further down is the bike trail featured in the television drama *Autumn in My Heart*, the stretch of field from *Windstruck* where the main couple traveled before the boy died, and then the tree from *Lover's Concerto* where three friends embroiled in a love triangle rested during a rainstorm while on a trip, caught flu, and died. The battle sites of *Taegukgi* thus become part of a tour where the particulars of war become less important than broader categories of emotional strife and resolution. The tour is actually known for being a popular "date course," and many of the people who take the tour are couples, strolling from one visual text to another, taking in sites of various melodramatic tragedies. At the bottom of the hill, visitors stop by the Samyang gift shop for discounted boxes of ramen noodles and cartons of milk, and free samples of new ramen flavors (fig. 6.27).

Amid the abundance of affect on display, it is no surprise that the tour emphasizes particular moments from *Taegukgi*. The crucial fight between the brothers at Hye-san-jin, filmed at the ranch, leads to the POW's death and the final fracturing of their brotherly bond. But the narrative on the Samyang tour, however, remembers it as the site where the older brother tries to save the younger brother. Like in so many of the love stories filmed here, the ranch becomes the place of near reconciliation or togetherness in the narrative that, in retrospect, also marks the beginning of separation, by war or by death, in battle or in love.

6.27 The Samyang ramen store where the tour begins and ends. Photo by author.

Conclusion: Touring Real Pictorial Histories at BEXCO 2003

I have explored traces of *Taegukgi* in each of these tourist destinations, as textually, temporally, and geographically displaced fragments. But we also must ask: what did the *Taegukgi* experience, as a whole, feel like as a manifestation of a historical event? How does the experience of these places compare to the experience of watching the film, and to actual history? And what aspects of the Korean War get altered amid the slipperiness of memory and its fluid mobility from one iteration to the next? It would be impossible to presume that *Taegukgi* tourists visited all these sites in a particular order, so it would be foolish to think of these three places as constituting one particular narrative or historical sequence. It is possible, however, to get a glimpse of the structure that the film company imagined when shifting the film from screen to exhibition space and tour site, from the visual to the corporeal, in an attempt to breach the gulf between fiction and history.

The monumental BEXCO *Taegukgi* Exhibition Dome in Pusan, debuted in 2003, cost the equivalent of roughly US$2.5 million.[25] It contained a reproduction of the film set, the steam locomotive, twenty-five war vehicles, including armored tanks and jeeps, costumes, and some twenty thousand other items on display. (To get an idea of the scope of the exhibition, note that the War Memorial of Korea has thirteen thousand items, spread over six exhibition rooms and displays covering five thousand years of history.) Visitors experienced the exhibition by walking through several exhibition areas within the dome, which led from one to another. An armored vehicle stood guard by the entrance into the first exhibition area entitled "Experiencing the Film," a display of the filmmaking process behind *Taegukgi* that established its historical accomplishment in the context of Korean film history. Off to the left, the exhibition focused on one of the prime sets of the film, "The Streets of Chongno, Seoul, in the 1950s." Within the dome in 2003, visitors were approached by ice cream sellers and other street vendors hawking their wares, bringing to life the everyday life of Korea just before the war. The tank exhibition, which would later be displayed at the Hapch'ŏn Cine-Park, lay just beyond Chongno, clustered together as if preparing for war, marked by more giant tanks, armored vehicles, and artillery, which were promoted as having undergone strict historical accuracy checks prior to their use in the film. The exhibited 105mm weapons, grenades, and 3.5-inch recoilless rifles, for example, were said to be the same as those used during the war. In addition, through a murky tunnel, filled with dark clouds of smoke and pumped in smells, was a "Special Effects War Experience Hall" of the film's nighttime Pyongyang street-battle scenes, rigged for the full experience of gunfire, artillery, crumbling buildings, and reenactments, complete with sound and special effects. Sounds of roaring rapid gunfire resonated through the smoke, and flames crackled on the set, depicting battle on the streets of Pyongyang at night. Placards shouting communist wartime slogans against U.S. imperialism hung on buildings, and doll corpses, killed by U.S. bomb raids, lay scattered in deep trenches. Visitors then had the option of taking the steam locomotive that had transported young men to their deaths in the battlefields at the outbreak of war.

As the documentary footage of the BEXCO exhibition demonstrates, visitors were initiated into *Taegukgi*'s Korean War exhibition through an introduction to the technical workings behind the filmmaking process. This is telling of the film's position vis-à-vis its historical subject matter, and seems to reflect Allan Sekula's argument that in the viewing of historical pictures, the fragmented and disorienting condition of "imaginary temporal and geographical mobility" draws the spectator to identify with the position of the camera for some semblance of coherence.[26] The film exhibition as a point of entry clearly provides spectators with the film camera as the vehicle for coherence. The authority thus bestowed on the spectator by the technical apparatus, however, is "a kind of powerless omniscience" against which "all other forms of telling and remembering begin to fade."[27] The problem lays in the fact that, as Sekula argues, "the machine establishes its truth, not by logical argument, but by providing an *experience*," and specifically an aesthetic experience.[28] The *Taegukgi* exhibition's 1950s urban street, war experience hall, and train similarly take the spectator characteristically onward to the nostalgia, horror, and exoticism of the past, but, as in Sekula's account, aesthetic experience subsumes historical understanding.

At the exhibition, this subsuming is perhaps best emblematized by a cardboard structure of two-dimensional figures of the brothers surrounded by war-related objects, which marks the entry from film exhibition hall into the film materialized in space. A direct reference to the *Statue of Brothers*, a well-known monument at the War Memorial of Korea, these brothers on the cardboard cutout would have registered immediately for Korean visitors. The war memorial statue features a large South Korean soldier, the older brother, holding his younger, much smaller North Korean soldier brother, in an embrace, a stance which has been read as a symbolic gesture by South Korean martyrs to receive all Koreans. Strong South Korea is depicted as the "legitimate heir," "whose forgiveness of his weaker, wayward brother becomes the condition upon which North Korea is finally allowed to return to the 'arms' of the family/nation."[29]

But in contrast to the permanent 18m x 11m statue of the brothers on top of the cracked granite dome at the war memorial, BEXCO's cardboard monument of brotherhood depicted a defiant younger brother standing upright, away from his older brother. There is no "forgiving" embrace, and they look not at each other, but at the tourists entering the exhibition. In the film, the older brother crosses over to the North in blatant rejection of the South, whom he believes to have killed his younger brother, and becomes a communist soldier. The younger brother, who is actually alive, volunteers for the battlefront where he surrenders to the North to seek out his brother. Critically, the final voluntary act of both brothers is crossing. A shot of Chin-t'ae's dead body has a line of soldiers with their backs to us leaping over his corpse as his lifeless gaze peers at us. And similarly, this point of entrance, where the brothers face the visitors, who pass them and eventually turn their backs, becomes a point of crossing from aesthetic to historical, but where the historical understanding offered ahead is but a remaining pretense, soon to be subsumed by the aesthetic.

The vitality of the younger brother also points to another transformation that occurs here, in the aesthetic subsuming of historical experience. As with the

Statue of Brothers, it is the older brother who is the martyr of familial heritage, yet in his death, he refutes the image of the stronger, surviving South Korean soldier who in his persevering physical strength overpowers and upholds the weaker younger brother. Rather, it is the younger brother's effusive emotion that enables the older brother's return to sanity and a severing from the ideological hold of the North. Emotion, in other words, outlives corporeal strength. Thus the reversal disturbs familial hierarchy, establishes the effeminate younger brother as legitimate heir to South Korea's national lineage, and asserts the experience of emotion as victorious in retrieving memory and passing it on to the next generation.

This reversal of the logic of the war memorial statue indexes an important counternarrative at work in the BEXCO *Taegukgi* exhibition. The war memorial takes an ideological position, focusing on "the cruelty of communism, the great loss of civilian lives and wealth, separation of family, a refugee's life, and massacre" in wartime life, complete with dioramas depicting harsh living conditions, the impoverished market, refugee migration, and wartime underground life.[30] In contrast, the BEXCO exhibition foregrounded the film's attempt to underscore the futility of ideological differences. And rather than privilege one side over the other, the exhibition worked to depict more broadly the horrific sensorium of war as a unifying rather than dividing force. At the exhibition, and later at Hapch'ŏn Park, the "survival experience" situated in Pyongyang was supposed to give visitors a chance to experience what it was like to survive battle. The virtual-reality theme is actually very similar to that of the "Korean War Combat Experience Room" at the war memorial. Both stage special effects that trigger the senses—sight, hearing, touch, and even smell. Smoke billows from an unknown danger, the smell of gunpowder and cannons slowly gather, the sound of bullets and screams is impossible to avoid: all of these inscribe the sensation of war onto the visitors. Yet where they depart is the context of the depicted war scene. The war memorial's emphasis is on *protection*, drawing attention to the South Korean soldier's heroic efforts in defending the country and people. The exhibition and theme park's emphasis, in contrast, was on *survival*, not only of the soldiers but also of the Pyongyang civilians who were brutally murdered as a result of the Koreans fighting there. As in the film, the effects of war, such as the destruction caused by U.S. bomb raids and South Korean attacks, affect all Koreans equally, and the commonality of emotions that occurs across the characters renders ideology moot.

In comparing the BEXCO *Taegukgi* exhibition and the war memorial's Korean War exhibition, it becomes apparent that the difference in commemorative practices results in considerable discrepancies in how the Korean War is to be remembered. The BEXCO exhibition's version reflects a postmemory position in which the war is regarded as significant and even traumatic, but the affects associated with this regard reflect a generational distance from the events of the war itself. As Won Bin, the young actor playing the younger brother in *Taegukgi*, has said when asked about his thoughts on the Korean War and the difficulty of playing a role so burdened by history: "Even my previous generation [people in their thirties and forties] simply think of the Korean War as an old war in past history. As to be expected, then, we, the younger generation, feel no particular meanings regarding the Korean War. . . . Since it was a war between people of one race [*minjok*], we just assume the pain must have been that much greater."[31]

Far from resulting in a Cold War ideological nationalism, Won Bin's comment not only indicates a shifting political landscape in South Korea with respect to what was once its most vexed antagonist, but also suggest how hallyu cinema's preoccupation with repairing historical trauma with the elixir of transnational economic cooperation is accompanied by a disconcerting lack of historical specificity. While Won Bin's vague and superficial feelings about the war and North Korea authorize the cooperative optimism of the Sunshine Policy era, which coincided roughly with the period I have associated with hallyu cinema, they also seem to underwrite historical amnesia in potentially dangerous ways.

If we can bracket for a moment the great enthusiasm for the hugely popular film itself, part of the appeal of the various exhibits associated with *Taegukgi* to South Korean audiences lay in an attraction to a particular kind of tourism. During this period, under the rubric of Sunshine Policy goodwill, South Koreans were able to travel to the North, in a very limited way, for the first time since the war. Fulfilling a similar desire to see the other, once prohibited part of a divided nation, these exhibitions rendered material the touristic impulse in *Taegukgi* the film and in hallyu cinema in general. Film travel in its various modalities in this context becomes a means toward repairing historical difficulty, but at the same time, one that also seems to elide the costs of these new tenuous, hard-won virtual unifications.

CONCLUSION

K-hallyu: The Commodity Speaks in Kang Chul-woo's *Romantic
Island,* Bae Yong-joon's *A Journey in Search of Korea's Beauty,*
So Ji-sub's *Road,* and Choi Ji-woo's *if*

In contemporary Korean culture, *K-* and *hallyu* have become prefixes and suf-
fixes. The now familiar branding of *K-pop* has spawned K-drama, K-fashion,
and even K-food; hallyu has become used in such neologisms as medical-hallyu
and technology-hallyu. We recall the vision of Culture Minister Ch'oe Kwang-
shik and his call for a third wave of hallyu, which would encompass the global
marketing of Korean culture in general. Implicit in this overarching branding
trend is the way in which this *K-hallyu* complex has become synonymous with
a free trade logic in which just about any entity shipped outside of Korea—be
it person, material object, or idea—becomes understood as an export commodity and labeled with what is increasingly becoming South Korea's state-
sponsored branding terms. As I have argued in *Tourist Distractions,* hallyu cinema marks the initial thinking through and coming to consciousness of this

C.1 A K-pop star's "selfie," taken on Boracay. *Romantic Island.*

now pervasive trend. By hallyu cinema, I have referred to films emerging in the late 1990s to mid-2000s that self-reflexively register the impact of hallyu's emerging core characteristics, namely its wide distribution (as manifested in tropes of tourism) and its attempt to convert economic interests into affective terms (feeling).

Kang Chul-woo's holiday film *Romantic Island* (*Romaent'ik Aillaendŭ*, 2008) marks the fully realized appropriation of hallyu cinema into South Korea's relentless dedication to perpetuating hallyu as a soft power. If the K-hallyu phenomenon began in the 1990s as a surprise, by 2008, it had become the banner under which a highly self-conscious, orchestrated plan, designed to disseminate Korean cultural products globally, was executed with government support and guidance. Appropriately foregrounding tourism, *Romantic Island* features three couples who travel separately to the same location in the Philippines: a married couple who own a convenience store, an anal-retentive corporate heir and a single office girl who meet in Boracay while traveling, and a young convenience-store employee with, most significantly for the present discussion, a female K-pop star whom he meets on the trip. Although the couples never meet each other in the course of the story, the film interlinks their narratives through a hit-man device. Suffering from a life-threatening tumor, the husband in the pair of convenience-store owners has ordered a hit on himself so that his wife can collect life insurance, but the plan gets complicated because of the perceived similarity in appearance of the Korean men in the film to the eyes of the Filipino hit man that the convenience-store owner has hired.

Though she is part of an ensemble and though her star status remains unregistered by the other characters in the film (except for a scene in which she is recognized by other Korean tourists), the presence of the K-pop star Ka-yŏng (Eugene/Kim Yujin) signals the film's broad commitment to the connection in hallyu cinema between travel and economic prosperity. Following romantic-comedy dicta, all three couples happily sustain relationships with one another at the end of the film, despite their various challenges. More important, not only do all of the characters in the film experience emotional, spiritual, and corporeal renewal through the process of travel in the film, but they all benefit financially from the experience. The convenience store's business improves; the corporate heir learns to communicate more effectively in a business environment; the convenience-store clerk, Chŏng-hwan, gets job offers from corporations, which he turns down to become Ka-yŏng's manager; the office girl gets employed by a travel agency; and the K-pop star's career takes off. In all four cases, tourism, which serves here as a means of thinking about trans-

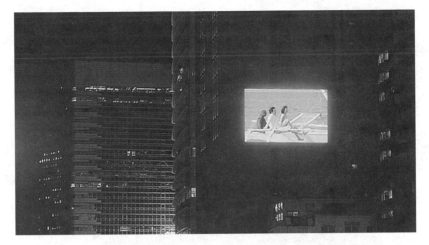

C.2 Declaring love with personal holiday photos broadcast on a jumbotron back in Seoul after the vacation. *Romantic Island*.

national circulation, is not an interruption of economically profitable activity, but rather the activity that makes profit possible.

Toward the end of the film, corporate heir Jae-hyŏk (Lee Sun-kyun) and office girl Su-jin (Lee Soo-kyung), back from their trip, go for an evening stroll through the streets of Seoul, coming to a stop on a small bridge over Ch'ŏnggyech'ŏn River. As they speak hopefully about their relationship, we see behind them in the midst of Seoul's urban landscape a slide show of their vacation photos broadcast on a jumbotron, which closes the bracketing frame of the film, which began with each couple looking at their vacation photos after the fact (fig. C.2). This use of tourist photos to frame the work of the film is reminiscent of the scene from *J.S.A.*; but whereas in *J.S.A.* the tourist's photo becomes visible to the film's audience only extradiegetically, in *Romantic Island* the photo blends seamlessly into the fabric of Seoul's urban landscape, displayed where commercials, news flashes, and nationally televised sports events would usually get shown. In *Romantic Island* travel images do not intervene or distract so much as they relay intimacy from the private realm to the public, and these publicly displayed intimate travel images embody hallyu's now expansive reach. Projected from the side of corporate buildings, the pleasures of travel appear to us inextricable from those of globalized commodity circulation. What we see in these images is not just the travel of individual actors, but the global dissemination of hallyu in general.

The photo of Ka-yŏng and Chŏng-hwan taken in Boracay is presented as if it were a selfie, but it is clear that neither of them is actually holding the camera. Instead of the camera, it is their fingers that form two corners to create a frame (fig. C.1). The bottom of their palms reach out to us as if to touch us; this materiality, here associated with hallyu products and visual images, is reminiscent of the desire for intimacy and touch associated in *Asako in Ruby Shoes* with pornography, in *April Snow* with adultery, and in *Daisy* with portraits and impressionist landscapes. In this tourist photo in *Romantic Island*, possible touch *is* the visual medium, the corporeality made feasible through travel. The intertextuality of tourism in the visual image is the kind of frame to which hallyu cinema has given form. It is one in which places that hallyu inhabits while traveling reaches out to us so that we, too, can enter those spaces and indeed those markets, which are close enough to touch.

Korean cinema's participation in international film festivals and its performance at the box office in theaters abroad has been regarded a key indicator of its global presence—sparsely in the 1960s, increasingly in the mid-1980s, and prominently in the 1990s as the socially conscious Korean New Wave filmmakers garnered the attention of foreign critics.[1] In terms of their ability to circulate in the global film circuit, many of the films discussed under the rubric of hallyu cinema in this book fall short and would not be categorized as having a global presence in these terms. But though these films did not achieve global prestige, they nevertheless articulate particularly well an emerging self-consciousness about the extent to which transnational circulation is central to K-hallyu desire. Hallyu cinema marks the point at which, after having been swept up in the wave, Korean commercial and governmental interests begin to want to generate it themselves. Thus, hallyu cinema seeks to identify and explore texts and tropes that allow for the investigation of transnational circulation and distribution networks, privileging in particular affective forms of connection as a strategy for creating unities where once political division predominated. Rather than offering an account of contemporary Korea cinema as an outcome of the global festival circuit and foreign box-office success, I have suggested that hallyu cinema must be seen as a prehistory of Korea's recent obsession with cultural export, that which I shorthand as *K-hallyu*.[2]

In chapter 1, I foregrounded the pornographic logic of the tourist imaginary in Korea and Japan's cinema of reconciliation, beginning in 1998, when Korea began phasing in Japanese popular culture under its new cultural liberalization policies, and moving to 2002, when the two countries jointly hosted the World Cup soccer tournament. Focusing on the joint film productions

Kazoku Cinema (Park Chul-soo, 1998) and *Asako in Ruby Shoes* (E J-Yong, 2000) in relation to an intercultural exchange of ethnographic exhibitions showcasing everyday life in the two countries that opened simultaneously in Seoul and Osaka in 2002, I explored the reformulation of transnational intimacy in the course of postcolonial reconciliation, now extricated from the sordid and humiliating past of sex tourism from Japan to Korea, but retaining some of its markers. Redressing a history of conflict between the two nations, the cinematic medium in these coproductions, with its emphasis on pornography, functioned as a more revealing extension of the tourist gaze, and the thematic of tourism intervened to break down geographical and visual boundaries in a move toward attempted resolution, one that found its limit, however, in its uncanny reproduction of colonial structures of exploitation.

In chapter 2, I analyzed Hur Jin-ho's *April Snow* (2002) and its popular film locations, which attracted an unprecedented number of tourists, primarily from Japan. As a highly concentrated point of attraction for tourists, the site served to demonstrate how affect spilling over from cinematic texts could potentially help to override conflicting regional politics. I focused on the relationship between the film text and tourist site, to show the formation of an intertextual and intermedial space I call *affective sites*, by which I mean an extratextual manifestation of a diegetic location that gets overwritten by the film narrative's affective dimensions, then traversed by film-inspired tourists who not only embody the characters but seek to reexperience the emotions of the narrative, its various intimacies, as inscribed into the locations of the narrative.

In chapter 3, I looked at the "making of" documentary (MOD) supplement included in the DVD release of *Musa*, the joint Korea-China martial arts film, and the possibilities of amity implicit in the film's intercultural mode of production. I suggested that the MOD, as a representation of the coproduction process between Korea and China, one of South Korea's first on-location ventures on mainland China since the Cold War, articulated the central interest of the feature film, which I read as a self-reflective narrative of the film's transnational production that functioned as a kind of MOD of emerging Korea-China relations writ large. Specifically, I argued that the anxieties of Korea-China economic relations get converted into affective terms in both the film and MOD, emerging as what I call *provisional feelings*, intensifications of affect based on mutual benefit and within the narrow scope of a particular situation and limited duration. Articulated within the context of the group travel and intercultural cooperation that characterizes both the film's narrative as well as the conditions of its production, these provisional feelings speak to the possibilities and trepidations of Korea's evolving economic relations with a China that is rapidly becoming a global power.

In chapter 4, I looked at the Sonagi Village tourist attraction in Yangp'yŏng, South Korea, which is dedicated to the Korean novelist Hwang Sun-wŏn's classic postwar novella "A Shower," and the way in which *Daisy* (2006), a collaboration between the Hong Kong director Andrew Lau and the Korean filmmaker Kwak Jae-yong, appropriates and adapts the traditional Korean trope of the *sonagi*, or sudden rain shower, for a new transnational context. The sonagi trope in Lau's hands becomes reinscribed within the context of Hong Kong neo-noir aesthetics in a film set in the Netherlands and shot with a cast of predominantly Korean actors. Based on Kwak's screenplay, cowritten with Gordon Chan and Felix Chong, the film conjoins and combines these many layers of style and sensibility into what I call *affective palimpsests*, which foreground the complex itinerancy of affective tropes that travel from one context to another, and function to build new transnational affectivities that are increasingly disarticulated from the national contexts from which they initially emerged.

In chapter 5, I focused on remembrance in the form of the imagined, filmic reconstruction of the demilitarized zone (DMZ) between North and South Korea, from the murder mystery *Joint Security Area* (Park Chan-wook, 2000) to the alternate history offered in the science fiction film *Yesterday* (Chŏng Yun-su, 2002), set in a reunified Korea in the year 2020, to the time travel film *2009 Lost Memories* (Lee Si-myung, 2002). In contrast to the stasis of the actual DMZ as historical site and truce memorial, the DMZ in filmic representations within the first hallyu wave embraced its touristic potential; though transmuted to an imagined national park and dislodged trope, it essentially retains its representation as a site foremost of attraction. These films about the DMZ, by enabling the tourist gaze on an otherwise restricted site, propelled it in its transition from the historical and material to the figurative, functioning in Korea's imagining of its relationships with China and Japan.

In chapter 6, I undertook a visual excavation of Kang Je-gyu's film about the Korean War, *Taegukgi* (2004), in relation to the film sets, theme parks, and exhibitions that drew large audiences in the wake of the film's box-office success. Looking at material traces of the film's depiction of the Korean War in their moments of dispersion, decay, and deterioration, I examined a contemporary representation of the defining event of the Korean twentieth century along with its oddly commercial brand of historicism. These film sites function as what I call *transient monuments*, which stand in direct contrast to more formal sites of commemoration. As such, they facilitate an emotional connection to the past for a generation that does not remember the Korean War, but in so doing, they risk confusing memory with affect, making history increasingly difficult to differentiate from consumerist practices.

Perhaps there is no other phenomenon that better epitomizes what I see as the core logic of hallyu cinema, if only redundantly, than the ubiquitous travel diaries and video travelogues published by hallyu stars, such as Choi Ji-woo's travel diary *if* (2005), which documents her journey to Italy, Cuba, New York, and South Africa; Bae Yong-joon's travel book, *A Journey in Search of Korea's Beauty* (2009); and So Ji-sub's photo-essay book *The Way* (2010).[3] These texts show how hallyu celebrities, who have themselves become global commodities, turn to travel and travel images as a way of identifying and coming to terms with the phenomenon they have engendered. By representing and indeed selling their own experiences of tourism, these quintessential figures of hallyu enact the quintessential economic logics of hallyu in an oddly tautological performance. Their texts self reflexively confirm hallyu's preoccupation with travel and its intimate connection to the logics of tourism, ultimately representing in the figure of the travelling hallyu star the voice of the commodity that speaks about its own status in transnational circuits of exchange. The figure of the hallyu star becomes synonymous with the ability to travel across national boundaries, a crossing accomplished as easily as that s/he manages with popular media, a characteristic which is praised appropriately as *crossover appeal*. This is evident in Choi Ji-woo's *if*, which features photographs in which she is seen interacting with African children in humanitarian efforts, as well as posing in Rome in reenactments of scenes made famous by Audrey Hepburn in *Roman Holiday*. Less personal than some of the later hallyu celebrity travel diaries, *if* is an interesting, intertextual precedent to Choi's later starring role as a hallyu star in the TV drama *Star's Lover*, which evolves around the ghostwriting of her travel diary in Japan and around her grounding herself emotionally in the process.

For the actor Bae Yong-joon, who may have had the most influence of any hallyu star in drawing people toward tourist attractions, keeping a travel diary of his trips in Korea was a process of first-person rediscovery couched in third-person terms.

I thought maybe I could uncover the hidden force that has protected me and kept me on track all these years. And I wanted to offer our beautiful, wonderful culture as a gift to all those who have cared for me. But most of all, I wanted to do it, not as Bae Yong-joon, the actor, but as an individual, lonely as ever, and in search of something that I had been longing for. I wanted to return to an earlier time, back when I first started acting, when I was still young and awkward and full of passion and earnestness for life. I wanted to start fresh. Like my family (fans) who care for me, I am just one man. . . . Lately I have become painfully aware of the fact that if that thing inside of me, that thing that enables me to long for something, were to disappear, I would be left with a soulless existence. I wanted to find that thing, in culture, in people and in my own heart.[4]

The promise of travel here is simultaneously a disavowal of himself as an actor. In the case of examples such as Angelina Jolie's travel diary, *Notes from My Travels: Visits with Refugees in Africa, Cambodia, Pakistan and Ecuador*, the attempt to erase one's star identity within the journal is part of an attempt to create a bond of commonality with readers, ironically in the form of a book that is sold as a commodity. As a global celebrity known for her humanitarian work, Jolie's hope is to inspire similar humanistic interest and work in developing nations.[5] In Bae's travel diary, the emphasis on being "like my family (fans)" and "just one man" speaks to his fear of completely losing his selfhood to the commoditized version of himself that appears on-screen. This loss of self is echoed in actor So Ji-sub's *The Way*: "I wish I were somewhere where I could go out in an easy pair of slippers without washing my face, somewhere where no one recognized me. . . . This is my face captured by the camera. Who am I?"[6] These quasi-existential musings are typical of the genre. What is ironic here, of course, is that these iconic authors seek to solve these existential crises precisely through the mode that created them. Though the implication is lost on these author-stars, the routes of travel uncannily reproduce the routes of circulation of their transnational cultural products. Unlike the therapeutic travel identified by David Martin-Jones in his analysis of Kim Dae-seung's film *Traces of Love* (*Kaŭlro*, 2006), the hallyu celebrity travel diaries by Choi, Bae, and So, in seeking the kind of therapy that Martin-Jones locates in tourism, instead reproduce the phenomenon that occasions the need for therapy in the first place.[7] So to the question "Can the global commodity speak?," not only do these texts answer yes!, but they also infer that the speech bespeaks the fact of its own circulation, one to which hallyu cinema, again and again, compulsively returns.

NOTES

Introduction

1　This discourse has roots in early twentieth-century visions of northeast Asian re-
gionalisms, by Japan, China, and even Korea, which were designed to resist Western imperialism and often to facilitate sub-imperialisms, most notoriously in the
Greater East Asia Co-Prosperity Sphere in the days of Japanese empire building.
More recently, a new cluster of conceptualizations of Asianisms have emerged,
meeting a need to provide explanation for the continuous domestic economic
growth in East Asia's four Newly Industrializing Countries (NICs)—South Korea,
Taiwan, Hong Kong, and Singapore—which were modeled after Japan, and to give
definition to an Asian identity. These discourses were subsequently destabilized in
the wake of the financial crisis that swept Asia in 1997 and 1998. In addition, the
rise of phenomena such as hallyu called into question the undifferentiated status
of postcolonial nations within the region as South Korea gained momentum as a
neo-imperialist and sub-imperialist cultural power. Most recently, questions of
Asian regionalization have been coupled with the analysis of globalization. Much
critical analysis of hallyu, as a broader category, has been based, on the one hand,
on ideas of globalization and regionalization, as articulated by Koichi Iwabuchi and
others, and, on the other, cultural nationalism, neoliberalism, and postcolonial-
ism, as illustrated most notably by Cho Hae-joang. The former underscores the
denationalization of cultural products as the dominant underlying success factor,
while the latter identifies cultural essentialism as shared across the discourses
variably rooted in national pride, national marketization, and national culture,
respectively. Following from such work has been the advancement of ideas of localization, flows, and cultural hybridity, drawing on Homi K. Bhabha's notions of
hybridity and "third space," for instance, to critique notions of homogenization and
cultural reductionism. See Iwabuchi, *Recentering Globalization*; Hae-joang Cho,
"Reading the 'Korean Wave' as a Sign of Global Shift," 148–49; and Bhabha, *The
Location of Culture*.
2　Shaviro, *Post-Cinematic Affect*, 2–10.
3　MacCannell, *The Tourist*.
4　Berlant, "Intuitionists," 845.
5　Agamben, *What Is an Apparatus?*, 36.
6　Hae-joang Cho, "Reading the 'Korean Wave' as a Sign of Global Shift."

7 This is well documented in the Korean sociologist Hae-joang Cho's 2002 semi-nal essay surveying the initial discourses that eventually emerged on the Korean Wave, which highlights "the reflexive learning process of people living in the semi-periphery of the world system" and, more specifically, the way in which news of hallyu "enabled Koreans to develop a new sense of globalization, the culture indus-try, and a newly forming Asia in a short time span." Cho refuses to reproduce any uncritical fascination, and instead focuses on how South Korea, initially surprised by the transnational regard for its cultural products, developed a sense of partici-pation in a global system through the serendipity of this experience. See Cho H., "Reading the 'Korean Wave' as a Sign of Global Shift," 148–49. (Originally pub-lished in 2002, this essay was revised and reprinted in 2005.)

8 Jeongmee Kim, "Why Does Hallyu Matter?," 47.

9 In undermining the merits of debating the origin of the concept of hallyu, John Lie in a footnote points us to Robert K. Merton's notion of the multiple origins of scientific discovery. See Lie, "What Is the K in K-pop?," 351, fn 18.

10 Hae-joang Cho, "Reading the 'Korean Wave' as a Sign of Global Shift," 148–49.

11 Soo-yeon Lee, "The Structure of the Appeal of Korean Wave Texts," 448.

12 Ibid., 448–49.

13 Ibid., 466.

14 Hae-in Shin, "Korea to Promote Third Hallyu: Minister Choe," *Korea Herald*, 24 January 2012, http://www.koreaherald.com/view.php?ud=20120124000485.

15 See Choi, *The South Korean Film Renaissance*, 23. The examples Choi offers are illuminating: *April Snow* (2005), starring Choi Ji-woo and Bae Yong-joon, presold distribution rights for $7.5 million to Japan and was one of the first films to be released simultaneously in Korea, Japan, Taiwan, Hong Kong, Singapore, and Ma-laysia. The export of Choi Ji-woo's film *Here and Forever* (*Yŏnriji*, 2006) brought in $3.5 million. Kwon Sang-woo's *Running Wild* (*Yasu*, 2006) made $4 million, and his *Almost Love* (*Ch'ŏngch'un manhwa*, 2006) made $4.5 million.

16 Korea Tourism Organization, Tourism Commercial 2003, archived online at Korea Tourism Organization, http://english.visitkorea.or.kr/enu/AK/AK_EN_1_6_1_1_5.jsp.

17 Yoon, "Shinmyoung," 107. The term *shinmyoung* has religious origins, referring to a possessed shaman performing *gut* (a Korean exorcism) in a state of spiritual and emotional ecstasy, and had been invoked in traditional folk arts as the expe-rience of "the creative process or enjoyment of art."

18 Korea Tourism Organization, Tourism Commercial 2004, archived online at Korea Tourism Organization, http://english.visitkorea.or.kr/enu/AK/AK_EN_1_6_1_1_4.jsp.

19 Hae-joang Cho, "Reading the 'Korean Wave' as a Sign of Global Shift," 169–70.

20 See Hae-joang Cho's discussion of the 2005 Samsung Economic Research Insti-tute (SERI) report *Hallyu chisokkwa kiŏbŭi hwallyongbangan* (CEO Information: Sustaining the Korean Wave and Strategies for Using the Wave for the Businesses and Companies). Released on June 1.

21 Korea Tourism Organization, Tourism Commercial 2006, archived online at Korea Tourism Organization, http://english.visitkorea.or.kr/enu/AK/AK_EN_1_6_1_1_2.jsp.

22 Appadurai, "Introduction," 57.

23 By "high-quality" film directors, Jinhee Choi is referring to those who bring remarkable style to their genre films, such as Park Chan-wook, Bong Joon-ho, and Kim Ji-woon. See Choi, *The South Korean Film Renaissance*, 144–63. Whether hallyu (the Korean Wave) is or is not indebted to the similarly termed Korean New Wave, a cinema movement marked by social consciousness in the late 1980s to the mid-1990s (by some accounts until the early 2000s), is another question altogether. For a discussion of Korean New Wave periodization, see Choi, *The South Korean Film Renaissance*, 164–67, in which she contests Kyung Hyun Kim's designation, in his book *Virtual Hallyu*, of the year 2002 as the official end of the Korean New Wave, marked by the box-office failure of the Korean New Wave director Jang Sun-woo's big-budget film *The Resurrection of the Little Match Girl*. Choi questions a presumed division between New Wave filmmaking and the film industry's demands from the mid-1990s onward, and argues for their recategorization as two, commensurable, continuous factions she refers to as the "First and Second New Wave," respectively. Jinhee Choi's more inclusive reperiodization of the Korean New Wave subcategorizes the cinema movement into two sequential periods: the "first new wave" refers to directors emerging in the late 1980s and more commonly associated with the movement, such as Jang Sun-woo, Park Kwang-su, and Lee Myung-se; the "second new wave" includes directors emerging in the latter half of the 1990s, such as Lee Chang-dong, Hong Sang-soo, Kim Ki-duk, or Im Sang-soo. See Choi, *The South Korean Film Renaissance*, 165.

24 Critics often assert that hallyu has no uniform style. Some accounts emphasize exchange between "similar" cultures. See, for example, Yoo and Lee, "'The Cultural Proximity of the Television Dramas in East-Asia Countries," 230–70; Yang, "Beyond 'Hallyu,'" 9–13. Another way of accounting for the appeal of hallyu products across cultures cites the process of rendering products culturally "odorless," through which any identifiable national markers are eradicated from consumer goods. Koichi Iwabuchi uses the term "cultural odor" to refer to an "evolved" state of a cultural product, in which "cultural features of a country of origin and images or ideas of its national, in most cases stereotyped, way of life are associated *positively* with a particular product in the consumption process" (*Recentering Globalization*, 27).

25 Appadurai, "Introduction," 13.

26 For Doobo Shim, hallyu, in the comprehensive sense including the film industry, was "an outgrowth of Korea's struggle for cultural continuity when confronted by the threat of global cultural domination" and was "indebted to the media liberalization that swept across Asia in the 1990s," providing favorable international market conditions for the export of commercially viable Korean popular culture products. Shim's account crediting the domestic media liberalization policies and

democratic reforms in the culture industry *before* hallyu provides a somewhat different perspective compared with accounts that see the shake-up and restructuring *after* the 1997 International Monetary Fund (IMF) crisis as inducing the revitalization of the film industry, enabling it to become globally viable. According to Darcy Paquet, for example, "the boom began with a crash." Several factors resulting from the IMF crisis that contributed to Korean cinema's commercial renaissance were the increased prominence of venture capital in place of receding chaebol interests; the devaluation of local currency which made imported films more expensive; and the screen quota system. See Shim, "Hybridity and the Rise of Korean Popular Culture in Asia," 28–31; and Paquet, *New Korean Cinema*, 61–63.

27 For the search for hallyu in Japan, past and present, see, for example, the newspaper column by Hong Yun-ki, a Japanese cultural historian at Hankuk University of Foreign Studies, titled "Hong Yun-ki's History Travelogue: In Search of Hallyu in Japan" (Hong Yun-ki ŭi yŏksa kihaeng ilbon sok ŭi hallyu rŭl ch'ajasŏ), published in *Segye Times* (*Segye Ilbo*) from July 2006 to January 2009. See also the travelogue on Kyushu, Asuka, and Nara published as part of the renowned *My Exploration of Korean Cultural Heritage* series by Yu Hong-jun, former director of the Cultural Heritage Administration, especially the section entitled "The Light Comes from the Korean Peninsula" ("Pich'ŭn hanbandoro put'ŏ"). Of the four main islands of Japan, Kyushu is the closest to Korea. The Asuka region, currently in Nara Prefecture in the Kansai region, and Korea's Baekje Kingdom engaged in cultural exchange. See Yu, *My Exploration of Korean Cultural Heritage, Japan Vol. 1 and Vol. 2.*

28 Levenson, *A Genealogy of Modernism*, vii.

29 Kyung Hyun Kim, *Virtual Hallyu*, xiii.

30 Ibid.

31 Ibid., 18.

32 Ibid., 5.

33 If we consider the narrative tension driving popular texts such as the popular television drama *Dream High* (*Tŭrim hai*, 2011), for example, hallyu products assert a self-reflexivity and awareness of their cultural and economic status within popular as well as intellectual discourses of aesthetics. *Dream High*, about a high school for artistically talented youth that launches forty K-pop idols annually, including one capable of winning a Grammy award in the year 2018, has a central protagonist whose narrative function is to represent the high arts (opera, Cho Sumi, Gershwin, and recognition by Juillard) and disdain for the vulgarity of K-pop. The television drama is produced by hallyu legends, the actor Bae Yong-joon and the K-pop singer JYP, and the prejudice against K-pop, here portrayed as the commercial channeling of subversive subculture, is broken down through the outright humiliation, rejection, rehabilitation, and repackaging of the embodiment of the high arts. The hybrid complexity, openness, and economic viability of hallyu aesthetics are juxtaposed with the clichéd, exclusive, and debt-

ridden circumstances of the high arts in an overt critique of arts associated with education as opposed to untapped talent and hard work.

34 Jeongmee Kim argues, "Hallyu ... is not a term that is reliant on any particular notion of artistic quality, aesthetic principle or generic content, but rather it is an evaluation of the 'exportability' of Korean products" ("Why Does Hallyu Matter?," 50).

35 Kang, "Hanryu Is the Cultural Code of East Asia," 221–22.

36 Jeongmee Kim, "Why Does Hallyu Matter?," 50.

37 Ibid., 55.

38 Lie, "What Is the K in K-pop?," 360.

39 Benjamin, *Illuminations*, 240. For explication of this notion, see Eiland, "Reception in Distraction."

40 Crary, *Suspensions of Perception*, 78.

41 North, *The Problem of Distraction*, 6.

42 Ibid., 14–15.

43 In this respect, my argument builds on a point made by Nancy Abelmann and Jung-ah Choi regarding *My Sassy Girl*: "The filmic meta-commentary serves as an effective social critique of dominant narrative of 'structures of feeling' in South Korea—of how very difficult it is to narrate against the collective and historical melodramatic grain" ("'Just Because,'" 133).

44 North, *The Problem of Distraction*, 182.

45 MacCannell, *The Tourist*, 14–15.

46 Ibid., 15.

47 Ahmed, *The Cultural Politics of Emotion*, 4, 191.

48 Ibid., 170, 191.

49 The film *Love with an Alien* is alternatively listed as *Yi guo qing yuan*, directed by Chang Gen Quan, with a release date of March 1958, for example on the IMDb site. A copy of the film *Love with an Alien* was recovered by the Korean Film Archive at the Hong Kong Film Archive in 2012. See Hyo-won Lee, "Collaboration Agreement with Shanghai Film Museum."

50 Cho et al., *Rediscovering Asian Cinema Network*, 14–23.

51 See Chong-sok Yi, *Cultural Policy White Papers*.

52 Kyung Hyun Kim, *The Remasculinization of Korean Cinema*, 52.

53 Ibid.

54 George E. Marcus, "Ethnography in/of the World System," 96. See also Falzon, "Introduction," 1–2.

55 Bruno, *Atlas of Emotion*, 16.

56 Ibid., 6.

57 Ibid.

58 Ibid., 6, 16.

59 Sangkyun Kim, *The Production and Consumption of Screen Tourism Experience*, 188. See also Hirata, "Touring 'Dramatic Korea.'"

60 Torchin, "Location, Location, Location."

61 Sangkyun Kim, *The Production and Consumption of Screen Tourism Experience*, 188–94.

62 Dorst, *The Written Suburb*, 2.

63 Ibid.

64 Ibid.

65 Ibid., 5.

66 Ibid., 3–4.

67 Ibid.

Chapter 1. Feeling Together

1 From 7–10 October 1998, the South Korean president Kim Dae-jung visited Japan. In March 1999, the Japanese prime minister Keizo Obuchi returned the visit, and gave a speech, at Korea University in Seoul, titled "Japan-Korea Relations in the New Millennium: The Creation of a New History," which emphasized three areas that should constitute the core of future Japan–South Korea cooperation, under joint leadership: "Security in Northeast Asia, the revival and prosperity of Asia, and human security." See Soeya, "A 'Normal' Middle Power," 93.

2 Ministry of Foreign Affairs of Japan, "Japan-Republic of Korea Joint Declaration: A New Japan-Republic of Korea Partnership towards the Twenty-First Century," 8 October 1998, www.mofa.go.jp/region/asia-paci/korea/joint9810.html.

3 Although a milestone in initiating Korea-Japan film, *Kazoku Cinema* was produced primarily by Korean funds as a Park Chul-soo Films production in association with Muae Productions, Youngsung Production, and Nownuri. *Asako in Ruby Shoes*, in contrast, was made later, during the first part of phase three of the liberalization program, and as such was able to benefit from larger Japanese financial participation. Korea's Koo and Film funded 60 percent of the costs, and Japan's Shochiku supplied 40 percent, a 20 percent increase in the maximum permissible in 1998. A biopic made in 1995 by the veteran Korean director Kim Su-yong, *Apocalypse of Love* (*Sarangŭi muksirok*) has also been among the films considered as the first Korea-Japan coproduction, but despite the use of a Korean workforce and locales, Korean censors deemed it "Japanese," and not sufficiently "Korean," due to the fact that it was produced by a Japanese production company and starred Japanese actors. Its release was therefore also prohibited. For reference to *Apocalypse of Love*, see Chung and Diffrient, "Interethnic Romance and Political Reconciliation in *Asako in Ruby Shoes*," 204.

4 Their ethnicity is deliberately underplayed, with the exception of some swearwords and food references.

5 Editorial, "A Year of Enmity: Japan Stands in the Way of Asian Unity," *Korea Times*, 22 November 2005.

6 The government quietly began investigating the viability of cultural liberalization between Korea and Japan in the early 1990s, through a series of quietly conducted polls and surveys. These indicated that most Koreans had already had

contact with Japanese pop culture in some form or other. On 25 February 1994, when the Ministry of Culture and Sports's presentation of the legislative proposal "Three-Stage Liberalization Policy on Japanese Popular Culture" before the National Assembly became public, a total of thirteen surveys, conducted both publicly and privately, came to light, including those orchestrated by the Korea Gallup Research Institute, Korea Research, KBS (Korea Broadcast Station), *Joong Ang Ilbo* (Central Daily), and *Segye Ilbo* (World Daily). The most comprehensive and extensive survey that played into the decision-making of the three-stage program was perhaps the Korean Gallup Survey Institute's survey commissioned by the Ministry of Culture and Sports in February 1995, three years before Phase 1 of the liberalization program. The survey revealed that a total of 90.8 percent of Koreans in Korea had already had contact with Japanese popular culture. Of these respondents, 61.5 percent said they had had "a lot," while 39.3 percent said "some," 8.6 percent replied "just a little," and a mere 0.5 percent said "not sure."

7   Ministry of Foreign Affairs of Japan, "Japan-Republic of Korea Joint Declaration: A New Japan-Republic of Korea Partnership towards the Twenty-First Century," 8 October 1998, www.mofa.go.jp/region/asia-paci/korea/joint9810.html.

8   Culture-Tourism Minister Shin Nak-kyun, cited in Choe Yong-shik, "Japanese Films to Be Allowed," *Korea Times*, 20 October 1998.

9   Chong-sok Yi, *Cultural Policy White Papers*, 431.

10   Lash and Urry, *Economies of Signs and Space*, 256.

11   Appiah, "Cosmopolitan Patriots," 91–92.

12   Dudden, *Troubled Apologies among Japan, Korea, and the United States*, 47.

13   *Asako in Ruby Shoes* is contextualized within the postcolonial most memorably in Hye Seung Chung and David Scott Diffrient's look at interethnic romance and political reconciliation in the film. See Chung and Diffrient, "Interethnic Romance and Political Reconciliation in *Asako in Ruby Shoes*."

14   Seongseop Kim and Prideaux, "A Post-colonial Analysis of Bilateral Tourism Flows."

15   Moon, "Japanese Tourists in Korea," 152.

16   Ibid., 153.

17   See Seongseop Kim and Prideaux, "A Post-colonial Analysis of Bilateral Tourism Flows," 596: "It is apparent that the strength of people-to-people flows rely on factors beyond the influence of politics. . . . The majority of tourists currently travelling between the two nations . . . have no personal experience of colonial relations. For this reason, factors other than those directly related to colonial administration and politics are now influencing decisions to travel between the two countries."

18   Kungnip Minsok Pangmulgwan, *Japan, Our Close Neighbor*, 2.

19   The loss of films from the 1930s and 1940s had constituted what So-young Kim has described as a "hollow archive" for Korean film history until the beginning of a series of discoveries (or "unearthings" [*palkul*]) of films, beginning in 1989 but primarily between 2004 and 2009. In 1989 three narrative films

from the colonial period were found in Japan's Tōhō archives: Toyoda Shirō's *Figure of Youth* (*Wakaki sugata*, 1943), Imai Tadashi's *Suicide Squad at the Watchtower* (*Bōrō no kesshitai*, 1943), and Ch'oe In-gyu's *Love and the Vow* (*Saranggwa maengsŏ/Ai to chikai*, 1945). Until 2004, these three films were the only narrative films available from this period. Sŏ Kwang-je's *Military Train* (*Kunyongyŏlch'a*, 1938) was found in the Chinese Film Archives in 2004 by the Korean Film Archive, along with An Ch'ŏl-yong's *Fisherman's Fire* (*Ŏhwa*, 1939), An Sŏ-gyŏng's *Volunteer* (*Chiwŏnbyŏng*, 1941), and Ch'oe In-gyu's *Homeless Angels* (*Chip opnŭn ch'ŏnsa*, 1941). In 2005 Yang Chu-nam's *Sweet Dream* (*Mimong*, 1936), Yi Pyŏng-il's *Spring in the Korean Peninsula* (*Pando ŭi pom*, 1941), and Pak Ki-ch'ae's *Straits of Chosun* (*Chosŏn haehyŏp*, 1943) were also found in the Chinese Film Archives. In 2006 several documentaries were found in the Gosfilmofond Archive in Russia, and Pang Han-jun's *Dear Soldier* (*Pyŏngjŏngnim*, 1944) was found in the Chinese Film Archives. Additional discoveries include An Chong-hwa's *Crossroads of Youth* (*Ch'ŏngch'un ŭi sipjaro*, 1934) in a private collection in 2007, and Hŏ Yŏng/Hinatsu Eitarō's *You and I* (*Kŭtaewa na/Kimi to boku*, 1941) in the National Film Archives of Japan. For studies on the impact of these discoveries on the archive and archiving of Korean film, see So-young Kim, "In/Visible Cinema"; Steven Chung, "Visibility, Nationality, Archive." For a discussion of the films, see the special issue of *Cross-Currents* 2, no. 1 (2013), guest-edited by Takashi Fujitani and Nayoung Aimee Kwon, especially their introduction, in which they provide an overview of the history and the stakes.

A post-screening talk on Hŏ Yŏng's film *You and I* (1941) was given by Chŏng Chong-hwan and Han Sang-ŏn on 19 May, Korean Movie Database (KMDb), www .kmdb.or.kr/vod/vod_basic.asp?nation=K&p_dataid=00166#url. *You and I* was considered lost until March 2009, when two rolls of the print (about 20 percent of the entire film) were discovered by the National Film Center in Japan. The fragments together constitute a 24-minute reel, which was screened at the National Film Center in Tokyo on 26 and 28 April 2009. A copy was purchased by the Korean Film Archive and screened on 19 and 29 May 2009. See Chonghwa Chung, "Introducing the Film and the Discovery of *Dear Soldier*," in the supplemental booklet to *The Past Unearthed, the Third Encounter* DVD Set (Seoul: Korean Film Archive, 2009), 6–7.

20 Hughes, *Freedom's Frontier*, 55.

21 See Stoler, *Carnal Knowledge and Imperial Power*.

22 Also categorized by the KMDb under the subject category of "naesŏn ilch'e" is Ch'oe In-kyu's *Children of the Sun* (*T'aeyangŭi aidŭl*, 1944), about a rural elementary schoolteacher who trains his students to volunteer for the Imperial Japanese Army; this film is part of Ch'oe In-kyu's pro-Japanese trilogy, which also includes *Love and the Vow* (*Saranggwa maengsŏ*, 1945) and *Sons of the Sky* (*Sinp'ungŭi adŭldŭl*, 1945). Under the same subject category is Okazaki Renji's *Love of Their Neighbors* (*Arŭmdaun iutsarang*, 1938), about a Korean couple who lovingly raise an orphaned Japanese child.

23 Workman, "Stepping into the Newsreel," 153.

24 Stewart, *Ordinary Affects*, 1–2.

25 *Seoul Style 2002: Life as It Is with the Lee Family*. Information available on the website of the National Museum of Ethnology in Osaka, Japan, at www.minpaku .ac.jp/english/museum/exhibition/special/200203/index.

26 MacCannell, *The Tourist*, 91.

27 The incorporation of ethnographic forms and displays in these reconciliatory films, especially through the frequent use of still frames, will perhaps evoke the "staged" field photographs of "primitive races" taken by the visual anthropologist Torii Ryuzo, or the ethnographic tableaus exhibited by Tsuboi Shogoro as part of the empire-building process in Japan. See Pai, "Capturing Visions of Japan's Prehistoric Past." There are more resemblances to be found, however, with travelogues and visual ethnographies from the colonial period, such as that exemplified by K. Kawaguchi's 1938 documentary *Tyosen (Tokyo and Peking Through Tyosen and Manchuria)*, alternatively titled *Tokyo—Peking, By Way of Choson and Manchuria (Tŏngkyŏng—Pŭkkyŏng, Chosŏnkwa Manchurŭl kŏch'yŏ)*, a travel essay mapping Japan's aspirations into Beijing via Chosŏn and Manchuria. In *Tyosen*, the travel genre is used to stage ethnographic sights with colonial interests, simultaneously showcasing Japan's territorial and transportation expansion, its conquests, and its tourist destinations. *Tŏngkyŏng—Pŭkkyŏng, Chosŏnkwa Manchurŭl kŏch'yŏ* was produced by Kawaguchi of the Ilbonyŏnghwa Sinsa in 1938 (also listed as 1939 in the KMDb), under the auspices of BTI Pictures (Tongbo Yŏnghwa Munhwa Yŏnghwabu, 東寶映畫文化映畫部).

28 Linda Williams, "Film Bodies," 4, emphasis in original.

29 Bruno, *Atlas of Emotion*, 16.

30 Urry, *The Tourist Gaze*, 145.

31 Ibid., 80–92. In Urry's notion of the tourist gaze, mass-media-influenced postmodern tourists, or what Maxine Feifer terms "post-tourists," do not mind consuming typical objects of the tourist gaze through simulated experiences such as film or TV viewing. More important, the tourist gaze defined as such is also a cultural disposition characteristic of a service class and white-collar workers, including the "new bourgeoisie" and "new petit bourgeois," who are heavily influenced by the mass media, and whose occupations involve symbolic work in which they exercise "greater freedom" to "devise ever-new cultural patterns." This cultural disposition, according to Urry, turns culture into consumption and contemporary society into spectacle (ibid., 80–82). See also Feifer, *Going Places*.

32 Foucault, *Power/Knowledge*, 155.

33 Crawshaw and Urry, "Tourism and the Photographic Eye."

34 Crary, *Techniques of the Observer*, 18.

35 Ibid., 17–19.

36 Jackson, "Converging Cultures," 194.

37 So-young Kim, "Modernity in Suspense," 307.

38 Neupert, *The End*, 102–10.

39 For an account of the capacity of the tourist imagination to address conflict, see Crouch, Jackson, and Thompson, *The Media and the Tourist Imagination*, 9–11.

40 Dudden, *Troubled Apologies among Japan, Korea, and the United States*, 47.

Chapter 2. Affective Sites

1 Keun-min Bae and Reuben Staines, "'Hallyu' Brings New Travel Trend to Korea," *Korea Times*, 23 February 2006.

2 Korean Ministry of Culture and Tourism, *2005 Cultural Policy White Papers*.

3 Ibid.

4 Keun-min Bae and Reuben Staines, "'Hallyu' Brings New Travel Trend to Korea," *Korea Times*, 23 February 2006.

5 Kangwon Provincial Government Tourism Policy Department, "Tourism Trends in 2005" ["2005 nyŏn kwan'gwangtonghyang"] (Kangwon Province: Kangwon Provincial Government Tourism Policy Department, 7 March 2006). See also the report "Kangwon Province, Number of Tourists Visiting Our Province Sees 10.2 Percent Hike in 2005" ["Kangwŏndo, 2005 nyŏn uri torŭl ch'annŭn kwan'gwanggaek 10.2 per cent chŭngga"] (Kangwon Province: Kangwon Provincial Government Tourism Policy Department, 7 March 2006).

6 Bruno, *Atlas of Emotion*.

7 For more on the relationship between tourism and media, see Rojek, "Indexing, Dragging, and the Social Construction of Tourist Sights." See also Jackson, "Converging Cultures, Converging Gazes."

8 Scholarship on film-induced tourism has attempted to negotiate the relationship between film and tourism in terms of place marketing and community tourism development, impact on destination image, authenticity and inauthenticity, and psychoanalysis. See Riley, Baker, and Van Doren, "Movie Induced Tourism"; Hyounggon Kim and Richardson, "Motion Picture Impacts on Destination Images"; Rojek, "Indexing, Dragging, and the Social Construction of Tourist Sights"; Torchin, "Location, Location, Location"; and Jackson, "Converging Cultures, Converging Gazes."

9 From actor Bae Yong-joon's website, www.byj.co.kr, 2005. English translation from "Bae Yong-joon Calls for People to Remain Rational about Tokto," *Korea Times*, 21 March 2005.

10 Sun-gŭn Kim, *Screen Tours in Search of the Emotions in Film*, preface.

11 Massumi, *Parables for the Virtual*, 28.

12 Ibid., 260, fn 3.

13 Ibid., 30.

14 Linda Williams, "Film Bodies," 4.

15 Ibid.

16 Ibid.

17 Ibid., 5.

18 Shouse, "Feeling, Emotion, Affect," para. 13.
19 So-young Kim, "Why They Had to Go on an Outing."
20 Hye-ri Kim, "Director Hur Jin-ho's *April Snow* [2]."
21 Rutherford, "Cinema and Embodied Affect," 11.
22 Linda Williams, "Film Bodies," 3; Rutherford, "Cinema and Embodied Affect," 5.
23 Brennan, *The Transmission of Affect*, 6.
24 Miller, "Korean TV Dramas and the Japan-Style Korean Wave," 18.

Chapter 3. Provisional Feelings

1 On the "martial arts craze" in South Korea in the 1960s and King Hu's influence, see Sang-joon Lee, "Martial Arts Craze in Korea." See also Zhang, *Chinese National Cinema*, 145. On King Hu and foreign film locations, see Fu, *China Forever*.
2 See Song-mi Yi, *Korean Landscape Painting*; and Song-mi Yi, *Searching for Modernity*.
3 Writing of King Hu's films, David Bordwell distinguishes between those films designed around interiors, such as the "inn films" that in the end "spill outdoors," and those built around exteriors, which unfold "across a series of breathtaking landscapes" and seascapes. In the film *Raining in the Mountains*, Bordwell observes a kind of "spatial synthesis," in which the monastery with its "honeycomb of corridors, rooftops, and passageways" is at once vast and porous but ultimately proves confining, necessarily extending into the dense, serene forests of the mountains where danger lurks. The affective dynamics here, in spite of their variations, are achieved mainly through the juxtaposition of interiors and exteriors within the film; they presume an interior that is located within a building and an exterior outside, in nature. See Bordwell, *Planet Hong Kong*, 257–58.
4 The MOD in the Korean film industry is commonly called the "Making film."
5 Xu, "Children Caught in Crossfire," 143–44.
6 Teo, "Love and Swords." According to Teo, the cost of this reconfiguration is a shift from emphasis on "delivery and expression of style," contained in carefully choreographed tableaus of action, montage, and spectacular mise-en-scène, to emphasis on plot and the interactions between the characters.
7 Xu, "Children Caught in Crossfire," 137, 145. In terms of filmic composition, the implications of this qing are less action, more human relations, character building through body movement, and more exaggerated facial expressivity.
8 Ibid., 147.
9 Ibid.
10 Ahmed, "Affective Economies."
11 Chung, "Korean Views of Korea-China Relations."
12 Woodward, "Calculating Compassion," 72.
13 Berlant, *Compassion*, 5.
14 See Jang, "The Korean Wave and Its Implications for the Korea-China Relationship," 100.

15 The reemergence in 2004 of the ongoing Koguryo history controversy, in which Chinese and South Koreans contest the historiography of the ancient Koguryo kingdom, might serve as a typical example of many of these conflicts. See Jae-ho Chung, "Korean Views of Korea-China Relations," 224–26.

16 Jang, "The Korean Wave and Its Implications for the Korea-China Relationship," 100–103. In addition, it was a relationship simultaneously of competition and mutual need; Korea faced widespread economic challenges after the 1997 financial crisis, and in China, media reforms in the late 1990s were pushing for mergers and the restructuring of small-sized and unproductive companies that had proliferated under government protection, creating a competitive environment for good programming and the acceleration of foreign cultural product imports. See ibid., 103–4. As Jang explains, "From the perspective of China's cultural industries, *hallyu* possesses elements of cooperation as well as competition. In its initial stage, its cooperative side stood out. The rapid diffusion of Korean popular culture in early years could not have been possible without Chinese TV stations and other companies actively importing Korean drama series, music, and other cultural products. *Hallyu* was not a well-planned project on the part of Korean industries. It was rather a response to the call from the Chinese market" (ibid., 104).

17 Jae-ho Chung, "China's Ascendancy and the Korean Peninsula," 154.

18 Korean Film Council (KOFIC), *A Study on the State of International Joint Production*, 89–110.

19 Jae-ho Chung, "China's Ascendancy and the Korean Peninsula."

20 See Ch'oe Wŏn-dam in Han Seung-mi et al., "Review of Korean Wave: Korean Wave Discussion" ["Hallyu hyŏnsang dasi bogi: tŭkjip jwadamhoe"], in *Image of Korea* [*Imiji obŭ koria*], ed. Media Art Center (Seoul: Yonsei University Press, 2002), 16–34, cited in Hae-joang Cho, "Reading the 'Korean Wave' as a Sign of Global Shift," 156.

21 See chapter 5, "1997–1998: Strategic Partnerships and National Rivalries," in Rozman, *Northeast Asia's Stunted Regionalism*, 205.

22 Ibid.

23 Ch'oe Wŏn-dam in Han Seung-mi et al., "Review of Korean Wave: Korean Wave Discussion" ["Hallyu hyŏnsang dasi bogi: tŭkjip jwadamhoe"], in *Image of Korea* [*Imiji obŭ koria*], ed. Media Art Center (Seoul: Yonsei University Press, 2002), 16–34, cited in Hae-joang Cho, "Reading the 'Korean Wave' as a Sign of Global Shift," 156.

24 *Chosun Ilbo*, 15 January 2003, cited in Jae-ho Chung, "Korean Views of Korea-China Relations," 154.

25 Lisa Barron, "Chinese Tourists Flood Asia," CNN.com, 6 June 2002, http://edition.cnn.com/2002/WORLD/asiapcf/east/06/06/hong.tourists/index.html.

26 Sŏ and Kim, *A Study on the Promotion of Attracting Chinese Visitors Using the Korea Fever Trend*.

27 Korean Film Council (KOFIC), *The State of Asian Joint Production and Program for Development*, 13–27.

28 Korea National Tourism Organization (KNTO), *New Hallyu Tourism Marketing.*

29 Korean Film Council (KOFIC), *A Study on International Joint Production.*

30 See Asian Film Commissions Network, an organization founded in 2004.

31 Initially, China collaborated with Korea only in finding film locations. The joint-production process eventually diversified to extend to personnel, planning, production, investment, and marketing. *Anarchist* is an example of a film made by a Korean director, with Korean actors for central roles, and some Korean staff, with the Chinese coproducers responsible for everything else, from costumes, art direction, sets, to location. Later, the film *Samgukji: Yongŭibuhwal* reversed responsibilities, with the Chinese coproducers managing the director and actors, while the Koreans took care of everything else, including investment, production and distribution. The film *Seven Swords* is an example of a multinational project involving investment by Korea, China, Hong Kong, and Japan, led by Korea's Boram Entertainment, but with Hong Kong and China in control of production. *Daisy (Teiji*, 2006), *The Promise (Wú Jí*, 2005), *A Battle of Wits (Mò Gōng*, 2006), *Red Cliff* (Korean title *Chŏkpyŏktaejŏn*, 2008, 2009), *A Good Rain Knows* (Korean title *Houshijŏl*, 2009), and *Sophie's Revenge* (Korean title *Sop'iŭi Yŏnaemaenyuŏl*, 2009) are further examples of Korea-China joint productions. See Jang, "The Korean Wave and Its Implications for the Korea-China Relationship," 106.

32 Korean Film Council (KOFIC), *A Study on the State of International Joint Production*, 105–10.

33 Ibid., 107–8.

34 2001 Pusan International Film Commission Showcase, "Report on Recent Korea-China Co-production Projects."

35 Appadurai, "Disjuncture and Difference in the Global Cultural Economy." See also Williams, *Playing the Race Card*. In these variations on the martial arts and swordplay genres, melodrama plays a crucial role in the sense described by Linda Williams, that is, "in its more general and pervasive operation as a mode of representation with a particular moralizing function operating across many genres" (ibid., 16).

36 Hight, "Making-of Documentaries on DVD," 5.

37 Arthur, "(In)Dispensable Cinema," 39.

38 Hight, "Making-of Documentaries on DVD," 5–7.

39 Ibid., 5.

40 Ibid., 13.

41 Shafransky, "Burden of Dreams." An even earlier example might be the 1908 "one-reeler" *Making Motion Pictures: A Day in the Vitagraph Studio*, which "follows the construction of a routine drama from story preparation through shooting and editing." Arthur, "(In)Dispensable Cinema, 38.

42 "*Ch'ŏnsamong* Homepage" ["*Ch'ŏnsamong* Homp'eiji"], *Cine21*, 15 February 2001, http://m.cine21.com/news/view/p/1/mag_id/387.

43 Nam, "The Secret Appeal of the DVD Supplement (3)." In its theater release, *Musa* had only been the eighth best-selling Korean film of 2001, far behind lighthearted

but highly popular fare such as *Friend, My Sassy Girl, Kick the Moon, My Wife Is a Gangster, Hi, Dharma,* and *My Boss, My Hero,* all of which had also placed in the top-ten category of all films that year to outsell the Hollywood hits *Harry Potter, Shrek, Pearl Harbor,* and *The Mummy Returns.* Koreanfilm.org, http://www.koreanfilm.org/kfilm01.html.

44 Nam, "The Secret Appeal of the DVD Supplement (3)." Although *Musa*'s MOD is not as polished, it is reminiscent of *Burden of Dreams* (1982), Les Blank's documentary on the production of Werner Herzog's epic *Fitzcarraldo* (1982) in the Amazon jungle, in its focus on filming in extreme locations and under conditions of great adversity.

45 See the insightful readings of maps in these films as well as others in Conley, *Cartographic Cinema.*

46 Ibid., 209.

47 Robert Alan Brookey and Robert Westerfelhaus describe such a relationship between primary film and supplementary material on the DVD as "layered experience," in which different aspects of the film's packaging unite to form a collective experience. Looking at the film *Fight Club,* Brookey and Westerfelhaus, citing John Fiske's concepts of "primary" and "secondary" texts, argue that though the supplementary material of MODs function like secondary texts to increase a film's profit by favoring preferred readings of the film, "they do so in a way that blurs the distinction between primary and secondary texts as they have been conceived and made use of in the past" ("Hiding Homoeroticism in Plain View," 22).

48 Hight, "Making-of Documentaries on DVD," 9. See Manovich, *The Language of New Media,* 218–33.

49 Manovich, *The Language of New Media,* 227, cited in Hight, "Making-of Documentaries on DVD," 10.

50 Bartsch, Appel, and Storch, "Predicting Emotions and Meta-Emotions at the Movie," 168.

51 Oliver, "Exploring the Paradox of the Enjoyment of Sad Films," 319.

52 *Musa* was shot in super 35mm format CinemaScope (2.35:1 CinemaScope), which is generally perceived as having more depth. The format also prioritizes mise-en-scène over camerawork and editing. See Rogers, *Cinematic Appeals,* 67.

53 Roland Barthes, "On CinemaScope," first published in *Les lettres nouvelles,* February 1954, translated by Jonathan Rosenbaum, www.jonathanrosenbaum.net/1983/01/on-cinemascope-roland-barthes/. Barthes's essay was also published in Rosenbaum, *Placing Movies.*

54 Roland Barthes, "On CinemaScope," first published in *Les lettres nouvelles,* February 1954, translated by Jonathan Rosenbaum, www.jonathanrosenbaum.net/1983/01/on-cinemascope-roland-barthes/. Barthes's essay was also published in Rosenbaum, *Placing Movies.* See also Barr, "CinemaScope."

55 See Rogers, *Cinematic Appeals,* 74: "CinemaScope's bodily address could affect the experience of narrative as well, increasing the viewer's experience of empathy—

allowing him or her to feel with rather than simply for the situation and people depicted onscreen." Writing on CinemaScope and empathy, Charles Barr has suggested that shots conveying a particular point of view—such as the nose of an airplane—can give viewer "direct insight into their sensations and through this into 'what it is like' generally for them" ("CinemaScope," 10).

56 Elley, "*Musa*," 64.

Chapter 4. Affective Palimpsests

1 Hwang, "A Shower." The IMDb lists the release date of Ko Yŏng-nam's film *The Shower* [*Sonagi*] as 13 August 1979. The Korean Film Archive's database lists the film's release date as 13 September 1979, as well as 1978. The film is commonly dated as 1978—for example, also in the KMDb—in reference to the year in which it was produced, not the year in which it was released.

2 On the debate around "national literature as class literature" and "national literature as pure literature" occurring in the occupation period 1945–1948, see Kwon, *A Study of the National Literature Movement in the Immediate Postliberation Period*. See also Park, *The Proletarian Wave*, 270; Fulton, "Pure Literature versus the Literature of Engagement."

3 On the discourse of sunsu humanism and neohumanism in the 1930s and pure literature, see chaps. 11 and 12 in Yŏngmin Kim, *A Study on the History of Modern Korean Literary Criticism*.

4 Hughes, *Freedom's Frontier*, 97; Sin, *A Study of Literary Movements in the Immediate Postliberation Period*, 151–55. In Hughes's *Freedom's Frontier* the chapters entitled "Visible and Invisible States: Liberation, Occupation, Division" and "Ambivalent Anticommunism: The Politics of Despair and the Erotics of Language" offer an especially fascinating account situating pure literature within the broader literary debates of the liberation and occupation period, as well as readings of relevant films.

5 Hwang Sun-wŏn's "Sonagi" is one of his more commonly anthologized works of short fiction, appearing in middle-school readers as part of its curriculum. Ko Yŏng-nam's film version has been described as "a cult film for Korea's 386 generation," in reference to those who were born in the 1960s, attended college in the 1980s, and were in their thirties when the term was coined in the 1990s. As the Korean Film Archive notes, "It would not be an exaggeration to say that there is virtually no Korean who does not know the story." See the entry for Ko Yŏng-nam's *Sonagi* on the Korean Film Archive's canonical list of "100 Korean Films" at www.koreafilm.org/feature/100_59.asp.

6 Howes, "Scent, Sound and Synaesthesia." See also Petho, *Cinema and Intermediality*.

7 Adapted and updated from his own 1986 film *Peking Opera Blues* (*Dāo Mǎ Dàn*), Tsui Hark's *All About Women* (*Nǚrén bú huài*, 2008), was also cowritten by Kwak Jae-yong, but this collaboration incorporates more of the female-violence

tendencies Kwak exhibited in films such as *My Sassy Girl* (*Yŏpkijŏgin kŭnyŏ*, 2001), *Windstruck* (2004), *Cyborg She* (original Japanese title *Boku no Kanojo wa Saibōgu*, 2008), and *My Mighty Princess* (*Mulim yŏdaesaeng*, 2008). See also *My Girl and I* (*Parang juŭibo*, 2005), which was written by Kwak Jae-yong and directed by Chŏn Yun-su as a remake of the Japanese film *Crying Out Love, In the Center of the World* (*Sekai no Chūshin de, Ai o Sakebu*, 2004).

8 Kwak's sensibilities originate with Hwang Sun-wŏn's story in the immediate post–Korean War period (1950–53) and with subsequent films such as Chŏng Chin-u's *Early Rain* (*Ch'ou*, 1966) and the eroticized filmic adaptation of Ko Yŏng-nam's *The Shower* (*Sonagi*, 1978), although his own popular style has come to be associated with the Korean Wave. Lau's style is identifiable with the Hong Kong neo-noir style where relentless downpour underscores the gritty world of triad crime. The sonagi trope offers an example of East Asian mainstream intercultural cinema's processes of intersensuality; possibilities for bridging national concerns through transnational efforts through nonlinguistic, haptic means; and how to read the absence of touch and de-eroticization in East Asian Cinema.

9 In Gina Marchetti's description of *Infernal Affairs*, she identifies in it the following Hong Kong New Wave elements: dramatic contrasts between facial close-ups and long shots of Hong Kong cityscapes, height, and "movements (from dynamic pans to nearly imperceptible re-framings or virtually static tableaux)," which work to "establish a rhythm that fluctuates violently throughout the film—from periods of quiet contemplation to moments of frenetic violence. This visual pace follows the twists and turns of the narrative that moves without a fixed spatial or temporal anchor" (*Andrew Lau and Alan Mak's Infernal Affairs*, 6).

10 Friedman, *Penelope's Web*, 91–95.

11 See Che-sŏ Chŏng, "Prohibited Desire and Narratives of Water." See also Chow, *Primitive Passions*, 21. In Ko's film, sequences such as the harvest and dano festival suggest a turn to the primitive as seen by Rey Chow in Chinese cinema. The exploration of sexuality in Ko's film is erotic, not pornographic, but the primitiveness of the sexuality "becomes a way to point the moral of the humanity that is consciously ethnicized and nationalized, the humanity that is 'Chinese,'" in Chow's example.

12 From the children's activity booklet "Let's Play Together at the Sonagi Village" ["Uri hamkke sonagimaŭresŏ norayo"] distributed at the Sonagi Village for the Hwang Sun-wŏn House of Literature Sonagi Village Children's Tales Research Classroom and Theater [Hwang Sun-wŏn munhakch'on sonagi maŭl tonghwa yŏngugyoshil].

13 In the sexual elision, the adaptation of Hwang's work into film is not unlike the problems faced by *Sadie Thompson*, the 1928 filmic adaptation of Somerset Maugham's "Rain," in which the story of a missionary who succumbs to a prostitute's sensuality had to be altered to make the clergyman a professional reformer instead. See Calder, "Somerset Maugham and the Cinema," 262.

14 Ch'oe, "'The Shower' and Its Theme Park."

15 Ibid.

16 Ibid., 224–25.

17 Balázs, *Early Film Theory*, 160–61.

18 Laura Marcus, *The Tenth Muse*, 348–50.

19 James Williams, *Gilles Deleuze's Philosophy of Time*, 8–9.

20 Ibid.

21 McGowan, *Out of Time*, 9–10.

22 Žižek, *Organs without Bodies*, 12.

23 James Williams, *Gilles Deleuze's Difference and Repetition*, 11.

24 Hwang, "A Shower."

25 There is a parallel here to the end of *Daisy*, where the men read the billboard signage as it shifts from a shot of its reflection in the water to the actual sign, a direct reference to the readability of signs. For further consideration on reflections, readability, and how they relate to materiality, see also the film *Sonagi* at time marker 1:01:59, where the boy is writing with a stick on the ground at night. This shot is very similar to that in *Daisy* of Chŏng-u in the town square at night.

26 Greven, "Contemporary Hollywood Masculinity and the Double-Protagonist Film"; Tony Williams, "*Face/Off.*" See also Hanke, "John Woo's Cinema of Hyperkinetic Violence."

27 MBC's television drama *Eyes of Dawn* included location shots in the Philippines and China, which was unprecedented at the time, as South Korea had yet to normalize relations with Communist China. *Eyes of Dawn* covered Korean modern history from the colonial period to the Korean War, filtering historical affect through drama. The mimicry of emotive elements of this drama in particular within the context of *Daisy* suggests a severing of the historical affect from its historical content.

28 Deleuze and Guattari, *A Thousand Plateaus*, 179.

29 Rushton, "What Can a Face Do?," 223, 225.

30 Bordwell and Thompson, *Film Art*, 219.

31 See Lewis, *Critical Readings in Impressionism and Post-Impressionism*.

32 For a discussion of impressionism in film see Schwartz, "The Impressionism of 'Elvira Madigan.'"

33 Barthes, *Image-Music-Text*, 148.

34 Kuleshov, *Kuleshov on Film*, 52.

35 Magnan-Park, "Restoring the Transnational from the Abyss of Ethnonational Film Historiography," 253.

36 Teo, "Hong Kong Cinema," 224–227.

37 Willis, "Hong Kong Cinema since 1997," 15.

38 Box Office Mojo, *Daisy*, www.boxofficemojo.com/movies/intl/?page=&wk=2006 W10&id=_fDAISY01.

1 Pak Sangho, "Director's Note: Talking about Korea Today: Making *The* DMZ" ["Kamdok such'ŏp: Han'gukchŏk sanghwangŭl kobarhanda: *Pimujang chidae* rŭl chejak yŏnch'ul hamhyŏ"], *Film Art* 6 (September 1965): 91–93, supplementary booklet included with *The* DMZ (*Pimujang chidae*) DVD, Korean Film Archive, 2010.

2 Pak Sangho wrote, "I visited Japan for a film festival and walked around Tokyo with other foreign tourists. Most of them were Europeans and they asked me to guide them around the place. I said that I was not Japanese, I was Korean. They asked me whether I was from the South or the North, and where Panmunjŏm was and whether it was a place worth visiting. I had no answers. Honestly, I had never been to Panmunjŏm. Anyhow, those foreigners seemed more interested in Panmunjŏm than in Korea itself. More likely, they thought of Panmunjŏm as a tourist site full of thrills and suspense. I was shocked, and I felt the obligation to do something; make a film of it, as a member of the nation" (ibid.).

3 Hirsch, "The Generation of Postmemory," 103.

4 As Ella Shohat and Robert Stam have noted, "Narrative models in films are not simply reflective microcosms of historical processes; they are also experiential grids or templates through which history can be written and national identity created" ("From the Imperial Family to the Transnational Imaginary," 154).

5 The South Korean film industry accounted for an unprecedented 46.7 percent of the local box-office share in 2001, causing critics of the protectionist policy to argue that it was no longer necessary. In 2002, the South Korean screen quota system still required local theaters to screen 146 days a year. In 2006, the number of days was reduced from 146 days per year to 73 days per year.

6 The term *blockbuster* from here on refers to the South Korean blockbuster, to be distinguished from the Hollywood blockbuster unless indicated otherwise, although it is still debated among film critics and scholars whether the South Korean blockbuster exhibits transformative traits or is merely imitative. Pak Kwangch'un's (Park Kwang-chun) *The Soul Guardians* (*T'oemarok*, 1998) was the first film to be marketed and promoted as a Korean blockbuster. The characteristics of the "Korean blockbuster" as defined by the newspaper *Kungmin Ilbo* on 17 July 1998: (1) huge capital investment in computer graphics and production, (2) a hybrid genre accounting for a tight narrative structure, and (3) a star-studded cast. Critics generally recognized the similarities with the Hollywood blockbuster, but point out that in comparison to other South Korean film genres, the blockbuster undeniably distinguishes itself in terms of the higher production costs, larger scale, and scope. On the South Korean blockbuster, see Berry, "'What's Big about the Big Film?'" See also So-young Kim, *The Korean Blockbuster*.

7 See Winter, *Remembering War*.

8 The difference between these forms of culture is important in Korean, as the term *taejung munhwa* can be used interchangeably to mean "popular culture" and "mass culture," but its usage to connote culture for the masses is also associated with the *minjung* movement (people's movement) to popularize politically oriented mass culture in the 1980s. In spite of the distance and distinction from the extremely nationalistic mass culture, anti-American sentiment and nationalist narratives of reunification were still disseminated through popular culture including films, escalating around the time of South Korea's 2002 presidential elections.

9 The South Korean agent played by the actor Song Kang-ho goes on to appear in *J.S.A.* as a North Korean soldier. The actor Han Suk-kyu also becomes a North Korean in *Comrade* (*Double Agent*), playing a double agent who defects to the South. The double agent in *Shiri* is played by Kim Yunjin, who later plays the forensic analyst for the Joint Asian Police in *Yesterday*.

10 See Iwabuchi, *Recentering Globalization*.

11 Delissen, "The Aesthetic Pasts of *Space* (1960–1990)."

12 Nora, "Between Memory and History."

13 Sangwon Suh and Laxmi Nakarmi, "Korea: North and South: The Movie: Historic Talks?," *Asiaweek* 26, no. 39 (6 October 2000).

14 Fabian, *Time and the Other*.

15 See Iwabuchi, *Recentering Globalization*; Funabashi, "The Asianization of Asia"; Igarashi, "From Americanization to 'Japanization' in East Asia!?"; and Wigen, "Culture, Power, and Place."

16 Some key works on the Korean Asia discourse published around this time include *Creation and Criticism* [*Ch'angjak kwa pip'yŏng 79*], special issue (spring 1993); Mun-gil Chŏng et al., *East Asia, Problems and Perspectives*; and Mun-gil Chŏng et al., *East Asia Discovered*.

17 Fujitani, "Inventing, Forgetting, Remembering."

18 Nora, "Between Memory and History," 9.

19 Delissen, "The Aesthetic Pasts of *Space* (1960–1990)," 249.

20 Jeon, "Residual Selves," 728.

21 It is also suggested that the forensic analyst, who was raised by Goliath's final victim, was in fact the daughter of the doctor-turned-priest, the mastermind behind the experiment. This turns out to be false, and it is suggested that she herself was one of the kidnapped children when we see her former child-self aiding Yun Sŏk in his escape as an adult.

22 For a reading of this brotherhood and fraternization as same-sex eroticism, see Kyung Hyun Kim, *The Remasculinization of Korean Cinema*.

23 President Park Chung Hee, a former military officer in the Japanese imperial army, stands accused of having "reentered" Japan into Korea, and of enabling and extending its oppressive structure. Presidents Chun Doo-hwan and Roh Tae-woo, who inherited the negative legacy, were tried in court for their military coups and massacres under the cause of "settling the past" in 1997. See Ahn, "The Significance of Settling the Past in Modern Korean History," 8.

24 In this elaborate configuration of aimed guns and distracted gazes between people originating from three different time frames, killing only occurs between the people from each time zone. The original confrontation between Itō Hirobumi and An Jung-geun is preserved, and Inoue, Sakamoto, and Saigō, all from the same projected future, kill each other. Thus, within the circular return of the film to the beginning, the protracted standoff between Saigō and Sakamoto actually occurs at the same time with the An Jung-geun assassination attempt but without encroaching on the event. The future exists within the frame of the past, and the standoff is as if superimposed into the past historical event distinct to the outcome of the colonial past.

25 Jager, "Monumental Histories," 405.

26 Ibid., 394.

27 Ahn, "The Significance of Settling the Past in Modern Korean History," 9.

28 Youn-tae Chung, "Refracted Modernity and the Issue of Pro-Japanese Collaborators in Korea," 19.

29 Ahn, "The Significance of Settling the Past in Modern Korean History," 8.

30 See Winter, *Remembering War*.

31 Huyssen, *Twilight Memories*, 27.

32 Suk-young Kim, DMZ *Crossing*, 13.

Chapter 6. Transient Monuments

1 *Taegukgi* is the name of the South Korean national flag. Here, I use the phoneticization used by the promoters of the film in global distribution.

2 The dome covered about one acre (1,200 pyŏng).

3 "Puga Saŏb," *Taegukgi: Special Features Part 2* (Seoul, South Korea: KD Media, 2006), DVD.

4 Yampolsky, "In the Shadow of Monuments," 104, 94. See also Yampolsky's discussion of monuments' "absolutely unique influence on the structure of time" in that they strive "in some kind of magical way to affect the course of time, either to change it or to avoid its influence" ("In the Shadow of Monuments," 95). See also Grace, "Monuments and the Face of Time."

5 Hung, "Tiananmen Square," 107.

6 Ibid.

7 The South Korean court eventually ruled in favor of the film on grounds of artistic freedom.

8 Structures of Korean postwar modernity such as Korean War public monuments and memorials functioned as social apparatuses of ideological control in the 1950s up until the late 1960s, when an alternative public-art movement began to emerge. See Mi-jŏng Kim, "Korean War Monuments in the 1960s–70s"; Mi-jŏng Kim, "Public Art of Korea in the 1960–70s"; Jung, "Medium for the Recollection of War and Changes in Discourse."

9   The history of movie theme parks and film museums in Korea has not been that long. The first film museum, the Sinyoung Film Museum, was not opened until June 1999, on Jeju Island. It is fairly conventional, with the standard hall of fame, special-effects room, an interactive animation gallery, and a film experience gallery. The state-funded Korean Film Archive's National Film Museum and Cinematheque, completed in May 2008, covers a hundred years of Korean film history divided into four periods: the Japanese colonial period (1903–1945), post–Second World War and the 1960s Golden Age (1945–1972), oppression and censorship under military rule (1972–1986), and the New Wave and Renaissance (1987–).

10 Now the only remnants of this historical pilgrimage motivated by filmic exposure, which are scattered over the 3 km (76,000 pyŏng) circumference of the island, are barbed wire, a square boxing ring made of military tent, chunks of a wooden staircase where the barracks once stood, scattered sand bags, set pieces constructed of cement, fragments of a model set of Kim Il-Sung's Palace in Pyongyang reconstructed based on satellite photographs of the actual building, and what remains of the toilet in the film. The drinking well from which the secret 684 Unit gets water in the film was the actual well used in 1968, and remains the only still-functioning "prop" of the film. Film props reconstructed to represent the actual historical event have now come to serve as traces not only for the historical event, but for both film production and consumption as well.

11 Jager, "Monumental Histories," 393.

12 Ibid., 388.

13 Ibid., 404–5, citing Lee Sung-kwan from an interview conducted by Jager, emphasis added.

14 Yŏng-jin Yi, "Reenacting the Korean War."

15 Ŭn-hyŏng Kim, "The Pain and Bondage of War."

16 Ibid. See also Yŏng-jin Yi, "Reenacting the Korean War."

17 Construction began in 2001, and the grounds measure approximately 36,696 square meters (212,000 pyŏng).

18 Hapch'ŏn lies south of Seoul, accessible by a highway, which runs along Hapch'ŏn Lake and connects to the renowned Haeinsa by a quaint road that winds through fields.

19 Kang-sŏp Pak, "*Taegukgi* Hapch'ŏn Hwangmae Mountain Filming Location: Could Those Mountains Know the Tragedy of the Opposing Brothers?" ("Taegŭkki hwinallimyŏ Hapch'ŏn hwangmaesan ch'wallyŏngjang: Ch'ongburi mattaen hyŏngjeŭi pigŭk chŏ sanŭn alkka"), *Kukmin Ilbo*, 20 February 2004, 32.

20 The set occupies approximately about 73,000 square meters (22,000 pyŏng). Pyongyang was accurately replicated down to an operating three-car, 160-passenger steam locomotive replica that cost 1.2 billion won (approximately US$1.1 million).

21 In 2006 approximately 75,000 visitors came to the Hapch'ŏn Theme Park to see the shooting of the KBS drama *Seoul 1945*, down from approximately 100,000 in 2004, and 82,000 in 2005.

22 The train ran from the old Chŏnnam Koksŏng-gun Koksŏng Station to Gajŏng Station.

23 Lefebvre, *The Production of Space*, 221.

24 http://www.samyangranch.co.kr. The ranch, built in 1972, is approximately 19.8 million square meters (6 million pyŏng).

25 This amounts to approximately 25 hundred million South Korean won.

26 Sekula, "Reading an Archive," 448.

27 Ibid.

28 Ibid., emphasis in original.

29 Jager, "Monumental Histories," 405.

30 From the War Memorial of Korea website, www.warmemo.or.kr.

31 The original interview used to be available at http://www.nkino.com/NewsnFeatures /article.asp?id=10334, now an invalid site. Excerpts of the interview with Jang Dong-gun and Won Bin, uploaded by the user named hellioss on 12 February 2004, is available on *Cine21*'s "Netizen Review" page for *Taegukgi*. http://www .cine21.com/review/nz/view/p/32345/article_no/39959.

Conclusion

1 For instance, if we consider the United States as the critical market indicator of global success, *Kazoku Cinema* (1998) showed at the Chicago Film Festival in October 1999, but was not reviewed in the press; *Asako in Ruby Shoes* (2000) was not released in the United States; the blockbuster *2009: Lost Memories* grossed $12 million in South Korea and premiered in Los Angeles in 2002, but without fanfare; *Yesterday* had no U.S. showings or release, and bombed at the South Korean box office, grossing a mere US$2 million, comparable in its poor performance (relative to its huge budget) with films like *R U Ready?* and *Resurrection of the Little Match Girl*, which failed. Though *April Snow* (2005) was shown at the Toronto Film Festival and Chicago Film Festival in 2005, it did not find U.S. distribution or get mainstream reviews in the United States. However, *April Snow*'s circulation does not reflect that it eventually grossed a total of US$21.7 million in Japan, US$2.7 million in Korea, as well as opening in France, Hong Kong, and Thailand. *Daisy* grossed US$1.3 million in China, performing highest for Korean films in China at the time, and topped the April 30 box-office list across China. Though *Daisy* did well in South Korea (US$5.8 million) and in Japan (US$2.4 million), it did poorly in Hong Kong, with a total gross of US$416,956, and in Taiwan. *Taegukgi* (2004) had a limited release in the United States, grossing US$1.1 million, compared to US$64.8 million in South Korea. However, it was also released in Austria, France, Germany, Hong Kong, Japan (US$9.7 million), Mexico, and the United Kingdom. I thank David Desser for drawing my attention to these facts and their implications.

2 In a special celebrating their tenth anniversary, the national broadcaster's international subsidiary, KBS World, aired a special three-part program dedicated to hallyu. The first part, under the title "The Great Transformation of the Korean Wave" ("Hallyu Taejŏnhwan"), establishes hallyu's affective work in helping people through trying times (such as a teenage girl struggling to raise a family after her mother abandons them), then documents how hallyu was able to spread to remote parts of the world. The program's map of hallyu's expansion (*hallyu hwaksan chido*) takes on a viral aspect, beginning with the identification of what the presenters refer to as "principal movers." The immense popularity of hallyu in the Czech Republic, for instance, is attributed to Southeast Asian foreign students, dramatized by a Filipino student with a suitcase rocking out to K-pop on his headphones against the backdrop of a public square in Prague. When he meets a Czech student, he offers him his headphones, saying he listens to any Korean music, especially K-pop. The Czech student then enthusiastically passes it on to a group of his Czech friends who join them, and they move on to meet more friends. Similarly, in photos that pop up over Brazil on a map of the world, it is suggested that hallyu spread through the Japanese community there, who were connected to K-drama sites through Japanese drama sites. In the Himalayas, hallyu is spread through K-dramas, translated into English, that are broadcast from neighboring countries. In its capacity to overcome national, racial, and religious barriers, hallyu's global reception is thus compared to the hegemonic force of Western cultures in Asia. The point of the anniversary show, we see in the second part, titled "The Hub of the Korean Wave, KBS World" ("Hallyu ŭi ttodarŭn irŭm, KBS wŏltŭ"), is to celebrate the national broadcaster's role in the global spread of hallyu. And in the third part, "The Future of the Korean Wave" ("Hallyu ŭi mirae"), the point is to prescribe what hallyu should be and what Koreans' attitudes should be. In this account, the mobility of hallyu relies on "movers," and the imperialist perception of global responsibility being fostered here to a public audience is fundamentally linked to hallyu's ability to spread (*hwaksan*), even to the most remote areas of the world. It would not be remiss to say that the wonderment of hallyu's work in remote places being presented here, especially in the preferred focus on overcoming adversity among the less fortunate and finding hope, is similar to religious proselytizing.

3 Other related examples include Korean cable channel O'live's fashion travelogues centered around women and starring the hallyu celebrity Go Ara in Japan, "Twenty Year Old's Story"; Shin Mina in France, "Shin Mina's French Diary"; Choi Kang-hee in New York City, "Six Addictions"; Han Ye-seul in Los Angeles; and Han Hye-jin in Las Vegas. The women's lifestyle channel Donga TV also aired "Kim Ji-soo's London Life" and "Kim Haneul's Travel Diary in Italy," produced by CJ E&M (Entertainment and Media) Corporation's OnStyle.

4 Yong-joon Bae, *A Journey in Search of Korea's Beauty*, 13; originally published in Korean as *Han'gugŭi arŭmdaumŭl ch'aja ttŏnan yŏhaeng* (Seoul: Sidŭpeipŏ, 2009).

Bae's travels took one year and included visits to eleven artists and investigations of thirteen different kinds of traditional Korean art.

5 Jolie, *Notes from My Travels*. See also Barron, "An Actress Compelled to Act."

6 Sŏ, *The Way*, 8, 19.

7 The director Kim Dae-seung is a protégé of the renowned director Im Kwon-taek, whom he assisted during the filming of *Sŏpyŏnje*, among others, which prominently displays Korea's landscapes. Im's touristic images of the Korean landscape ache for their loss under rapid modernization; Kim's debut film about a heterosexual couple reincarnated as two men, *Bungee Jumping of their Own* (*Pŏnjijŏmp'ŭrŭl hada*, 2001), begins and ends in New Zealand and also foregrounds travel. For David Martin-Jones's analysis of *Traces of Love*, see his essay "Time-Images in *Traces of Love*."

BIBLIOGRAPHY

Abelmann, Nancy, and Jung-ah Choi. "'Just Because': Comedy, Melodrama and Youth Violence in *Attack the Gas Station.*" In *New Korean Cinema*, ed. Chi-Yun Shin and Julian Stringer, 132–43. Edinburgh: Edinburgh University Press, 2005.

Agamben, Giorgio. *What Is an Apparatus?: And Other Essays.* Stanford: Stanford University Press, 2009.

Ahmed, Sara. "Affective Economies." *Social Text* 22, no. 2 (2004): 117–39.

———. *The Cultural Politics of Emotion.* New York: Routledge, 2004.

Ahn, Byung-ook. "The Significance of Settling the Past in Modern Korean History." *Korea Journal* 42, no. 3 (autumn 2002): 7–17.

Appadurai, Arjun. "Disjuncture and Difference in the Global Cultural Economy." *Theory, Culture and Society* 7, no. 2 (1990): 295–310.

———. "Introduction: Commodities and the Politics of Value." In *The Social Life of Things: Commodities in Cultural Perspective*, ed. Arjun Appadurai, 3–63. Cambridge: Cambridge University Press, 1986.

Appiah, Kwame Anthony. "Cosmopolitan Patriots." In *Cosmopolitics: Thinking and Feeling Beyond the Nation*, ed. Pheng Cheah and Bruce Robbins, 91–114. Minneapolis: University of Minnesota Press, 1998.

Arthur, Paul. "(In)Dispensable Cinema: Confessions of a 'Making-of' Addict." *Film Comment* 40, no. 4 (2004): 38–42.

Bae, Yong-joon. *A Journey in Search of Korea's Beauty.* Translated by Sora Kim-Russell. Seoul: Hollym, 2012.

Balázs, Béla. *Early Film Theory: Visible Man and the Spirit of Film.* Translated by Rodney Livingstone. New York: Berghahn, 2011.

Barr, Charles. "CinemaScope: Before and After." *Film Quarterly* 16, no. 4 (1963): 4–24.

Barron, Lee. "An Actress Compelled to Act: Angelina Jolie's *Notes from My Travels* as Celebrity Activist/Travel Narrative." *Postcolonial Studies* 12, no. 2 (2009): 211–28.

Barthes, Roland. *Image-Music-Text.* Translated by Stephen Heath. New York: Hill and Wang, 1977.

Bartsch, Anne, Markus Appel, and Dennis Storch. "Predicting Emotions and Meta-Emotions at the Movies: The Role of the Need for Affect in Audiences' Experience of Horror and Drama." *Communication Research* 37, no. 2 (2010): 167–90.

Benjamin, Walter. *Illuminations*. Translated by Harry Zohn. Edited by Hannah Arendt. New York: Schocken, 1969.

Berlant, Lauren. *Compassion: The Culture and Politics of an Emotion*. New York: Routledge, 2004.

———. "Intuitionists: History and the Affective Event." *American Literary History* 20, no. 4 (2008): 845–60.

Berry, Chris. " 'What's Big about the Big Film?': De-Westernizing the Blockbuster in Korea and China." In *Movie Blockbusters*, ed. Julian Stringer, 217–29. New York: Routledge, 2003.

Bhabha, Homi K. *The Location of Culture*. New York: Routledge, 1994.

Bordwell, David. *Film Art: An Introduction*. New York: McGraw-Hill, 2008.

———. *Planet Hong Kong: Popular Cinema and the Art of Entertainment*. Cambridge: Harvard University Press, 2000.

Brennan, Teresa. *The Transmission of Affect*. Ithaca: Cornell University Press, 2004.

Brookey, Robert Alan, and Robert Westerfelhaus. "Hiding Homoeroticism in Plain View: The *Fight Club* DVD as Digital Closet." *Critical Studies in Media Communication* 19, no. 1 (2002): 21–43.

Bruno, Giuliana. *Atlas of Emotion: Journeys in Art, Architecture, and Film*. New York: Verso, 2002.

Calder, Robert L. "Somerset Maugham and the Cinema." *Literature/Film Quarterly* 6, no. 3 (1978): 262–73.

Cho, Hae-joang. "Reading the 'Korean Wave' as a Sign of Global Shift." *Korea Journal* 45, no. 4 (2005): 147–82.

Cho, Young-jung, Moon-yung Huh, Yong-kwan Lee, and Dosin Park, eds. *Rediscovering Asian Cinema Network: The Decades of Co-production between Korea and Hong Kong*. Pusan: Pusan International Film Festival, 2004.

Ch'oe, Hye-sil. " 'The Shower' and Its Theme Park: A Study on the Process of Turning a Literary Work into a Theme Park" ["Sonagiwa t'emap'ak'ŭ: Munhak chakp'umŭi t'emap'ak'ŭhwa kwajŏng yŏngŭ"]. In *One Source Multi Use and Storytelling of Hwang Sun-Wŏn's Sonagi Village* [*OSMU & sŭtorit'elling*], ed. Chong-hie Kim and Hye-sil Ch'oe, 209–39. Seoul: Random House, 2006.

Choi, Jinhee. *The South Korean Film Renaissance: Local Hitmakers, Global Provocateurs*. Middletown, CT: Wesleyan University Press, 2010.

Chŏng, Che-sŏ. "Prohibited Desire and Narratives of Water: Flood Myths 'Sudden Shower' and 'Rain' " ["Kŭmjidoen yongmanggwa murŭi sŏsa: Hongsu shinhwa 'Sonagi' 'Pi' "]. *Chungguksosŏlnonch'ong*, no. 14 (August 2001): 1–16.

Chŏng, Mun-gil, et al., eds. *East Asia, Problems and Perspectives* [*Tongasia, munjewa shigak*]. Seoul: Munhak kwa chisŏngsa, 1995.

———, eds. *East Asia Discovered* [*Palgyŏn urosŏ ŭi Tongasia*]. Seoul: Munhak kwa chisŏngsa, 2000.

Chow, Rey. *Primitive Passions: Visuality, Sexuality, Ethnography, and Contemporary Chinese Cinema*. New York: Columbia University Press, 1995.

Chung, Hye Seung, and David Scott Diffrient. "Interethnic Romance and Political Reconciliation in *Asako in Ruby Shoes*." In *New Korean Cinema*, ed. Chi-Yun Shin and Julian Stringer, 193–209. New York: New York University Press, 2005.

Chung, Jae-ho. "China's Ascendancy and the Korean Peninsula: From Interest Reevaluation to Strategic Realignment?" In *Power Shift: China and Asia's New Dynamics*, ed. David L. Shambaugh, 151–69. Berkeley: University of California Press, 2006.

———. "Korean Views of Korea-China Relations: Evolving Perceptions and Upcoming Challenges." *Asian Perspective* 36, no. 2 (2012): 219–36.

Chung, Steven. "Visibility, Nationality, Archive." *Journal of Korean Studies* 16, no. 2 (2011): 193–211.

Chung, Youn-tae. "Refracted Modernity and the Issue of Pro-Japanese Collaborators in Korea." *Korea Journal* 42, no. 3 (2002): 18–59.

Conley, Tom. *Cartographic Cinema*. Minneapolis: University of Minnesota Press, 2007.

Crary, Jonathan. *Suspensions of Perception: Attention, Spectacle, and Modern Culture*. Cambridge: Massachusetts Institute of Technology Press, 1999.

———. *Techniques of the Observer: On Vision and Modernity in the Nineteenth Century*. Cambridge: Massachusetts Institute of Technology Press, 1990.

Crawshaw, Carol, and John Urry. "Tourism and the Photographic Eye." In *Touring Cultures: Transformations of Travel and Theory*, ed. Chris Rojek and John Urry, 176–96. New York: Routledge, 1997.

Crouch, David, Rhona Jackson, and Felix Thompson. *The Media and the Tourist Imagination: Converging Cultures*. New York: Routledge, 2005.

Deleuze, Gilles, and Félix Guattari. *A Thousand Plateaus: Capitalism and Schizophrenia*. Translated by Brian Massumi. Minneapolis: University of Minneapolis Press, 1987.

Delissen, Alain. "The Aesthetic Pasts of *Space* (1960–1990)." *Korean Studies* 25, no. 2 (2001): 243–60.

Dorst, John Darwin. *The Written Suburb: An American Site, An Ethnographic Dilemma*. Contemporary Ethnography Series. Philadelphia: University of Pennsylvania Press, 1989.

Dudden, Alexis. *Troubled Apologies among Japan, Korea, and the United States*. New York: Columbia University Press, 2008.

Eiland, Howard. "Reception in Distraction." *boundary 2* 30, no. 1 (2003): 51–66.

Elley, Derek. "*Musa*." *Variety*, no. 384.8 (8–14 October 2001): 64.

Fabian, Johannes. *Time and the Other: How Anthropology Makes Its Object*. New York: Columbia University Press, 1983.

Falzon, Mark-Anthony. "Introduction: Multi-sited Ethnography: Theory, Praxis and Locality in Contemporary Research." In *Multi-sited Ethnography: Theory, Praxis and Locality in Contemporary Research*, ed. Mark-Anthony Falzon, 1–23. Farnham, England: Ashgate, 2009.

Feifer, Maxine. *Going Places: The Ways of the Tourist from Imperial Rome to the Present Day*. London: Macmillan, 1985.

Foucault, Michel. *Power/Knowledge: Selected Interviews and Other Writings, 1972–1977*. Edited by Colin Gordon. New York: Pantheon, 1980.

Friedman, Susan Stanford. *Penelope's Web: Gender, Modernity, H.D.'s Fiction*. Cambridge: Cambridge University Press, 1990.

Fu, Poshek. *China Forever: The Shaw Brothers and Diasporic Cinema*. Urbana: University of Illinois Press, 2008.

Fujitani, Takashi. "Inventing, Forgetting, Remembering: Toward a Historical Ethnography of the Nation-State." In *Cultural Nationalism in East Asia: Representation and Identity*, ed. Harumi Befu, 77–106. Berkeley: Institute of East Asian Studies, University of California Press, 1993.

Fulton, Bruce. "Pure Literature versus the Literature of Engagement." In *Columbia Companion to Modern East Asian Literature*, ed. Joshua Mostow, Kirk A. Denton, and Bruce Fulton, 630–34. New York: Columbia University Press, 2003.

Funabashi, Yoichi. "The Asianization of Asia." *Foreign Affairs* 72, no. 5 (1993): 75–85.

Grace, Helen. "Monuments and the Face of Time: Distortions of Scale and Asynchrony in Postcolonial Hong Kong." *Postcolonial Studies* 10, no. 4 (2007): 467–83.

Greven, David. "Contemporary Hollywood Masculinity and the Double-Protagonist Film." *Cinema Journal* 48, no. 4 (2009): 22–43.

Guichard-Anguis, Sylvie, and Okpyo Moon. *Japanese Tourism and Travel Culture*. London: Routledge, 2009.

Hanke, Robert. "John Woo's Cinema of Hyperkinetic Violence: From *A Better Tomorrow* to *Face/Off*." *Film Criticism* 24, no. 1 (1999): 39–59.

Hight, Craig. "Making-of Documentaries on DVD: The *Lord of the Rings* Trilogy and Special Editions." *Velvet Light Trap*, no. 56 (2005): 4–17.

Hirata, Yukie. "Touring 'Dramatic Korea': Japanese Women as Viewers of Hanryu Dramas and Tourists on Hanryu Tours." In *East Asian Pop Culture: Analysing the Korean Wave*, ed. Chua Beng Huat and Koichi Iwabuchi, 143–56. TransAsia: Screen Cultures series. Hong Kong: Hong Kong University Press, 2008.

Hirsch, Marianne. "The Generation of Postmemory." *Poetics Today* 29, no. 1 (2008): 103–28.

Howes, David. "Scent, Sound and Synaesthesia: Intersensoriality and Material Culture Theory." In *Handbook of Material Culture*, ed. Christopher Tilley, Webb Keane, Susanne Kuechler-Fogden, Mike Rowlands, and Patricia Spyer, 161–72. London: Sage, 2006.

Hughes, Theodore. *Freedom's Frontier: Literature and Film in Cold War South Korea*. New York: Columbia University Press, 2012.

Huyssen, Andreas. *Twilight Memories: Marking Time in a Culture of Amnesia*. New York: Routledge, 1995.

Hwang, Sun-wŏn. "A Shower" ["Sonagi"] (1953). Translated by Brother Anthony of Taizé. http://hompi.sogang.ac.kr/anthony/Shower.htm.

Igarashi, Akio. "From Americanization to 'Japanization' in East Asia!?" *Journal of Pacific Asia* 4 (1997): 3–20.

Im, Kwon-taek, ed. *Sŏpyŏnje: Film Story* [*Sŏpyŏnje: Yŏnghwa iyagi*]. Seoul: Hanŭl, 1993.

Iwabuchi, Koichi. *Recentering Globalization: Popular Culture and Japanese Transnationalism*. Durham: Duke University Press, 2002.

Jackson, Rhona. "Converging Cultures, Converging Gazes." In *The Media and the Tourist Imagination: Converging Cultures*, ed. David Crouch, Rhona Jackson, and Felix Thompson, 183–97. New York: Routledge, 2005.

Jager, Sheila Miyoshi. "Monumental Histories: Manliness, the Military, and the War Memorial." *Public Culture* 14, no. 2 (2002): 387–410.

Jang, Soo Hyun. "The Korean Wave and Its Implications for the Korea-China Relationship." *Journal of International and Area Studies* 19, no. 2 (2012): 97–113.

Jeon, Joseph Jonghyun. "Residual Selves: Trauma and Forgetting in Park Chan-Wook's *Oldboy*." *positions* 17, no. 3 (2009): 713–40.

Jolie, Angelina. *Notes from My Travels: Visits with Refugees in Africa, Cambodia, Pakistan, and Ecuador*. New York: Pocket Books, 2003.

Jung, Ho-gi. "Medium for the Recollection of War and Changes in Discourse: A Focus on the Korean War Monuments of the Mt. Jirisan Region" ["Chŏnjaeng kiŏgŭi maegaech'ewa tamnonŭi pyŏnhwa: Chirisan'gwŏnŭi han'guk chŏnjaeng kinyŏmmŭl chungsimŭro"]. *Sahoewa yŏksa* 68 (2005): 68–100.

Kang, Jin-seok. "Hanryu Is the Cultural Code of East Asia." *Journal of International Peace* 2, no. 1 (2005): 221–28.

Kim, Hye-ri. "Director Hur Jin-ho's *April Snow* [2]: An Interview with Director Hur Jin-ho" ["Hur Jin-ho kamdogŭi *Oechul* [2]: Hŏ Jin-ho gamdok int'ŏbyu"]. *Cine21*, 8 September 2005. www.cine21.com/news/view/mag_id/28425.

Kim, Hyounggon, and Sarah L. Richardson. "Motion Picture Impacts on Destination Images." *Annals of Tourism Research* 30, no. 1 (2003): 216–37.

Kim, Jeongmee. "Why Does Hallyu Matter?: The Significance of the Korean Wave in South Korea." *Critical Studies in Television*, no. 2 (2007): 47–59.

Kim, Kyung Hyun. *The Remasculinization of Korean Cinema*. Durham: Duke University Press, 2004.

———. *Virtual Hallyu: Korean Cinema of the Global Era*. Durham: Duke University Press, 2011.

Kim, Mi-jŏng. "Korean War Monuments in the 1960s–70s: Memories of War and the Formation of Post-War Korean State Ideology" ["1950–60 nyŏndae han'guk chŏnjaeng kinyŏmmul: Chŏnjaengŭi kiŏkkwa chŏnhu han'guk gukka ch'eje inyŏmŭi hyŏngsŏng"]. *Han'guk kŭndae misulsahak*, no. 10 (2002): 273–311.

———. "Public Art of Korea in the 1960s–70s: Public Monuments in the Pak Chŏng-Hŭi Era" ["1960–70nyŏndae han'gukŭi konggong misul: Pak Chŏng-Hŭi shidae konggongginyŏmmul chungshimŭro"]. PhD diss., Hongik University, 2010.

Kim, Sangkyun. *The Production and Consumption of Screen Tourism Experience: The Case Study of Asian Audience's Responses to Hallyu and Korean TV Dramas*. Saarbrücken, Germany: Lambert Academic Publishing, 2012.

Kim, Seongseop, and Bruce Prideaux. "A Post-colonial Analysis of Bilateral Tourism Flows: The Case of Korea and Japan." *International Journal of Tourism Research* 14, no. 6 (2012): 586–600.

Kim, So-young. "In/Visible Cinema: Hollow Archive and National Cinema." In *Repatriation or the Sharing of Film Heritage: The Collection of East Asia's Lost Films and Description of the History* [*Panhwan hogŭn yŏnghwa yusan ŭi nanum: Tong Asia ŭi yusil yŏnghwa sujip kwa yŏksa kisul*], 41–66. Conference proceedings. Seoul: Korean Film Archive [Han'guk yŏngsang charyowŏn], 2008.

———, ed. *The Korean Blockbuster: Atlantis or America* [*Han'gukhyŏng bŭllokbŏsŭt'ŏ: At'ŭllant'isŭ hogŭn amerik'a*]. Seoul: Hyŏnsil munhwa, 2001.

———. "Modernity in Suspense: The Logic of Fetishism in Korean Cinema." *Traces* 1 (2001): 301–17.

———. "Why They Had to Go on an Outing" ["Kŭdŭri oech'ŭrhaeya haettŏn iyu"]. *Cine21*, 28 September 2005. www.cine21.com/news/view/mag_id/33722.

Kim, Suk-young. *DMZ Crossing: Performing Emotional Citizenship along the Korean Border*. New York: Columbia University Press, 2014.

Kim, Sun-gŭn. *Screen Tours in Search of Emotions in Film* [*Yŏnghwa sok kamdong ŭl ch'aja ttŏnanŭn sŭk'ŭrin t'uŏ*]. Seoul: Yŏksanet, 2002.

Kim, Ŭn-hyŏng. "The Pain and Bondage of War, *Taegukgi*" ["Chŏnjaengŭi kot'onggwa kulle, *Taegŭkki Hwinallimyŏ*"]. *Cine21*, 6 February 2004. www.cine21.com/news/view/mag_id/22951.

Kim, Yŏngmin. *A Study on the History of Contemporary Korean Literary Criticism* [*Han'guk hyŏndae munhak pip'yŏngsa*]. Seoul: Somyŏng ch'ulp'an, 2000.

———. *A Study on the History of Modern Korean Literary Criticism* [*Han'guk kŭndae munhak pip'yŏngsa*]. Seoul: Somyŏng ch'ulp'an, 1999.

Korea National Tourism Organization (KNTO). *New Hallyu Tourism Marketing* [*Sin hallyu kwan'gwang mak'et'ing*]. Seoul: Korea National Tourism Organization, 2003.

Korean Film Council (KOFIC). *The State of Asian Joint Production and Program for Development* [*Asia kongdong chejak hyŏnhwang kwa palchŏn pangan*]. Seoul: Korean Film Council, 2002.

———. *A Study on International Joint Production* [*Kukche kongdong chejage kwanhan yŏn'gu*]. Seoul: Korea Film Council, 2001.

———. *A Study on the State of International Joint Production* [*Kukche kongdong chejak hyŏnhwang kwanhan yŏn'gu*]. Seoul: Korea Film Council, 2001.

Korean Ministry of Culture and Tourism. *2005 Cultural Policy White Papers* [*2005 nyŏn munhwa chŏngch'aek paeksŏ*]. Seoul: Ministry of Culture and Tourism, 2006.

Kuleshov, Lev Vladimirovich. *Kuleshov on Film: Writings*. Berkeley: University of California Press, 1974.

Kungnip Minsok Pangmulgwan [National Folk Museum of Korea]. *Japan, Our Close Neighbor: Japan-Korea Joint Exhibition of Contemporary Life Culture* [*Kakkaun iut nara ilbon: Il-han kongdong kaech'oe hyŏndae saenghwal munhwajŏn*]. Seoul: Kungnip Minsok Pangmulgwan, 2001.

Kwon, Yŏngmin. *A Study of the National Literature Movement in the Immediate Postliberation Period* [*Haebang chikhu ŭi minjok munhak undong yŏngu*]. Seoul: Sŏul taehakkyo ch'ulp'anbu, 1996.

Lash, Scott, and John Urry. *Economies of Signs and Space*. Theory, Culture and Society series. London: Sage, 1994.

Lee, Hyo-won. "Collaboration Agreement with Shanghai Film Museum." *Hollywood Reporter*, 20 June 2013. http://www.hollywoodreporter.com/news/korean -film-archive-signs-collaboration-572465.

Lee, Sang-joon. "Martial Arts Craze in Korea: Cultural Translation of Martial Arts Film and Literature in the 1960s." In *East Asian Cinema and Cultural Heritage: From China, Hong Kong, Taiwan to Japan and South Korea*, ed. Kinnia Shuk-ting Yau, 173–96. New York: Palgrave Macmillan, 2011.

Lee, Soo-yeon. "The Structure of the Appeal of Korean Wave Texts." *Korea Observer* 43, no. 3 (2012): 447–69.

Lefebvre, Henri. *The Production of Space*. Translated by Donald Nicholson-Smith. Oxford: Blackwell, 1991.

Levenson, Michael H. *A Genealogy of Modernism: A Study of English Literary Doctrine 1908–1922*. Cambridge: Cambridge University Press, 1984.

Lewis, Mary Tompkins, ed. *Critical Readings in Impressionism and Post-Impressionism: An Anthology*. Berkeley: University of California Press, 2007.

Lie, John. "What Is the K in K-Pop?: South Korean Popular Music, the Culture Industry, and National Identity." *Korea Observer* 43, no. 3 (2012): 339–63.

MacCannell, Dean. *The Tourist: A New Theory of the Leisure Class*. Berkeley: University of California Press, 1999.

Magnan-Park, Aaron Han Joon. "Restoring the Transnational from the Abyss of Ethnonational Film Historiography: The Case of Chung Chang Wha." *Journal of Korean Studies* 16, no. 2 (2011): 249–83.

Manovich, Lev. *The Language of New Media*. Cambridge: Massachusetts Institute of Technology Press, 2001.

Marchetti, Gina. *Andrew Lau and Alan Mak's Infernal Affairs: The Trilogy*. Hong Kong: Hong Kong University Press, 2007.

Marcus, George E. "Ethnography in/of the World System: The Emergence of Multi-sited Ethnography." *Annual Review of Anthropology* 24, no. 1 (1995): 95–117.

Marcus, Laura. *The Tenth Muse: Writing About Cinema in the Modernist Period*. Oxford: Oxford University Press, 2007.

Martin-Jones, David. "Time-Images in *Traces of Love*: Repackaging South Korea's Traumatic National History for Tourism." In *Deleuze and Film*, ed. David Martin-Jones and William Brown, 54–70. Edinburgh: Edinburgh University Press, 2012.

Massumi, Brian. *Parables for the Virtual: Movement, Affect, Sensation*. Durham: Duke University Press, 2002.

McGowan, Todd. *Out of Time: Desire in Atemporal Cinema*. Minneapolis: University of Minnesota Press, 2011.

McKim, Kristi. *Cinema as Weather: Stylistic Screens and Atmospheric Change*. New York: Routledge, 2013.

Miller, Laura. "Korean TV Dramas and the Japan-Style Korean Wave." *Post Script* 27, no. 3 (2008): 17–24.

Moon, Okpyo. "Japanese Tourists in Korea: Colonial and Post-colonial Encounters." In *Japanese Tourism and Travel Culture*, ed. Sylvie Guichard-Anguis and Okpyo Moon, 147–71. New York: Routledge, 2011.

Nam, Tong-ch'öl. "The Secret Appeal of the DVD Supplement (3)" ["DVD söp'ülmönt'ü ŭi ŭnmirhan maeryŏk (3)"]. *Cine21*, 14 November 2002. www.cine21.com/news/view/mag_id/14971.

Neupert, Richard John. *The End: Narration and Closure in the Cinema*. Detroit: Wayne State University Press, 1995.

Nora, Pierre. "Between Memory and History: Les Lieux de Mémoire." *Representations*, no. 26 (1989): 7–24.

North, Paul. *The Problem of Distraction*. Stanford: Stanford University Press, 2012.

Oliver, Mary Beth. "Exploring the Paradox of the Enjoyment of Sad Films." *Human Communication Research* 19, no. 3 (1993): 315–42.

Pai, Hyung-il. "Capturing Visions of Japan's Prehistoric Past: Torii Ryuzo's Field Photographs of 'Primitive' Races and Lost Civilizations (1896–1915)." In *Looking Modern: East Asian Visual Culture from Treaty Ports to World War 2*, symposium volume, ed. Jennifer Purtle and Hans Bjarne Thomsen, 265–93. Chicago: Art Media Resources, 2009.

Paquet, Darcy. *New Korean Cinema: Breaking the Waves*. London: Wallflower Press, 2009.

Park, Sunyoung. *The Proletarian Wave: Literature and Leftist Culture in Colonial Korea, 1910–1945*. Cambridge: Harvard University Asia Center, 2015.

Petho, Agnes. *Cinema and Intermediality: The Passion for the In-Between*. Newcastle upon Tyne, England: Cambridge Scholars, 2011.

Qiu, Shuting. *East Asian Cinema and Cultural Heritage: From China, Hong Kong, Taiwan to Japan and South Korea*. New York: Palgrave Macmillan, 2011.

Riley, Roger, Dwayne Baker, and Carlton S. Van Doren. "Movie Induced Tourism." *Annals of Tourism Research* 25, no. 4 (1998): 919–35.

Rogers, Ariel. *Cinematic Appeals: The Experience of New Movie Technologies*. New York: Columbia University Press, 2013.

Rojek, Chris. "Indexing, Dragging, and the Social Construction of Tourist Sights." In *Touring Cultures: Transformations of Travel and Theory*, ed. Chris Rojek and John Urry, 52–74. New York: Routledge, 1997.

Rosenbaum, Jonathan. *Placing Movies: The Practice of Film Criticism*. Berkeley: University of California Press, 1995.

Rozman, Gilbert. *Northeast Asia's Stunted Regionalism: Bilateral Distrust in the Shadow of Globalization*. Cambridge: Cambridge University Press, 2004.

Rushton, Richard. "What Can a Face Do? On Deleuze and Faces." *Cultural Critique*, no. 51 (2002): 219–37.

Rutherford, Anne. "Cinema and Embodied Affect." *Senses of Cinema*, no. 25 (March 2003). http://sensesofcinema.com/2003/feature-articles/embodied _affect/.

Schwartz, Allen K. "The Impressionism of 'Elvira Madigan.'" *Cinema Journal* 8, no. 2 (1969): 25–31.

Sedgwick, Eve Kosofsky. *The Weather in Proust*. Edited by Jonathan Goldberg. Series Q. Durham: Duke University Press, 2011.

Sekula, Allan. "Reading an Archive: Photography between Labour and Capital." In *The Photography Reader*, ed. Liz Wells, 443–52. Thousand Oaks, CA: Sage, 1999.

Shafransky, Renée. "Burden of Dreams." *Cineaste* 12, no. 4 (1983): 54.

Shambaugh, David L. *Power Shift China and Asia's New Dynamics*. Berkeley: University of California Press, 2006.

Shaviro, Steven. *Post-Cinematic Affect*. Winchester: Zero, 2010.

Shim, Doobo. "Hybridity and the Rise of Korean Popular Culture in Asia." *Media, Culture and Society* 28, no. 1 (2006): 25–44.

Shin, Chi-yun, and Julian Stringer, eds. *New Korean Cinema*. New York: New York University Press, 2005.

Shohat, Ella, and Robert Stam. "From the Imperial Family to the Transnational Imaginary: Media Spectatorship in the Age of Globalization." In *Global/Local: Cultural Production and the Transnational Imaginary*, ed. Rob Wilson and Wimal Dissanayake, 154–56. Durham: Duke University Press, 1996.

Shouse, Eric. "Feeling, Emotion, Affect." *M/C Journal* 8, no. 6 (2005). http://journal .media-culture.org.au/0512/03-shouse.php.

Sin, Hyŏng-gi, *A Study of Literary Movements in the Immediate Postliberation Period* [*Haebang chikhu ŭi munhak undongnon*]. Seoul: Che 3 munhaksa, 1989.

Sŏ, Jisŏb. *The Way* [*Kil*]. Seoul: Sallim, 2010.

Sŏ, Yong-kŭn, and Hŭi-su Kim. *A Study on the Promotion of Attracting Chinese Visitors Using the Korea Fever Trend* [*Hallyurŭl hwallyonghan chungguk kwan'gwanggaek yuch'i chŭngjin pangan*]. Seoul: Korea Culture and Tourism Policy Institute, 2002.

Soeya, Yoshihide. "A 'Normal' Middle Power: Interpreting Changes in Japanese Security Policy in the 1990s and After." In *Japan as a "Normal Country"?: A Nation in Search of Its Place in the World*, ed. Yoshihide Soeya et al., 72–97. Japan and Global Society series. Toronto: University of Toronto Press, 2011.

Soeya, Yoshihide, Masayuki Tadokoro, and David A. Welch. *Japan as a "Normal Country"? A Nation in Search of Its Place in the World*. Japan and Global Society series. Toronto: University of Toronto Press, 2011.

Stewart, Kathleen. *Ordinary Affects*. Durham: Duke University Press, 2007.

Stoler, Ann Laura. *Carnal Knowledge and Imperial Power: Race and the Intimate in Colonial Rule*. Berkeley: University of California Press, 2010.

Teo, Stephen. "Hong Kong Cinema." In *The Cinema Book*, ed. Pam Cook, 224–27. London: British Film Institute, 2007.

———. "Love and Swords: The Dialectics of Martial Arts Romance: A Review of *Crouching Tiger Hidden Dragon*." *Senses of Cinema*, no. 11 (2000). http://sensesofcinema.com/2000/current-releases-11/crouching/.

Torchin, Leshu. "Location, Location, Location: The Destination of the Manhattan TV Tour." *Tourist Studies* 2, no. 3 (2002): 247–66.

Urry, John. *The Tourist Gaze: Theory, Culture and Society*. 2d edn. London: Sage, 2002.

Wigen, Kären. "Culture, Power, and Place: The New Landscapes of East Asian Regionalism." *American Historical Review* 104, no. 4 (1999): 1183–201.

Williams, James. *Gilles Deleuze's* Difference and Repetition: *A Critical Introduction and Guide*. Edinburgh: Edinburgh University Press, 2003.

———. *Gilles Deleuze's* Philosophy of Time: *A Critical Introduction and Guide*. Edinburgh: Edinburgh University Press, 2011.

Williams, Linda. "Film Bodies: Gender, Genre, and Excess." *Film Quarterly* 44, no. 4 (1991): 2–13.

———. *Playing the Race Card: Melodramas of Black and White from Uncle Tom to O.J. Simpson*. Princeton: Princeton University Press, 2001.

Williams, Tony. "*Face/Off*: Cultural and Institutional Violence within the American Dream." *Quarterly Review of Film and Video* 18, no. 1 (2001): 31–38.

Willis, Andy. "Hong Kong Cinema since 1997: Troughs and Peaks." *Film International* 7, no. 4 (2009): 6–17.

Winter, J. M. *Remembering War: The Great War between Memory and History in the Twentieth Century*. New Haven: Yale University Press, 2006.

Woodward, Kathleen. "Calculating Compassion." In *Compassion: The Culture and Politics of an Emotion*, ed. Lauren Berlant, 59–86. New York: Routledge, 2004.

Workman, Travis. "Stepping into the Newsreel: Melodrama and Mobilization in Colonial Korean Film." *Cross-Currents* 3, no. 3 (2014): 153–84.

Wu, Hung. "Tiananmen Square: A Political History of Monuments." *Representations* 35, no. 1 (1991): 84–117.

Xu, Gary G. "Children Caught in Crossfire: John Woo and a Global Affective Cinema." *China Review* 10, no. 2 (2010): 137–53.

Yampolsky, Mikhail. "In the Shadow of Monuments: Notes on Iconoclasm and Time." In *Soviet Hieroglyphics: Visual Culture in Late Twentieth-Century Russia*, ed. Nancy Condee, 93–112. Bloomington: Indiana University Press,1995.

Yang, Eun-kyung. "Beyond 'Hallyu': The Globalization of the Korean Television Industry." *Studies of Broadcasting Culture* 16, no. 1 (2004): 9–13.

Yi, Chong-sok, and Kaebarwon Han'guk Munhwa Chongch'aek. *Cultural Policy White Papers* [*Munhwa chŏngch'aek paeksŏ*]. Seoul: Ministry of Culture and Tourism [Munhwa kwan'gwangbu], 2001.

Yi, Song-mi. *Korean Landscape Painting: Continuity and Innovation through the Ages*. Seoul: Hollym, 2006.

———. *Searching for Modernity: Western Influence and True-View Landscape in Korean Painting of the Late Choson Period*. Seattle: University of Washington Press, 2014.

Yi, Yŏng-jin. "Reenacting the Korean War: The Mega Blockbuster *Taegukgi*" ["Hanguk chŏnjaengŭl chaehyŏnhanŭn chʾodaehyŏng bûllokbŏsŭtŏ *Taegŭkgi Hwinallimyŏ*"]. *Cine21*, 3 February 2004. http://www.cine21.com/news/view /mag_id/22891.

Yoo, Sae-kyung, and Kyung-sook Lee. "The Cultural Proximity of the Television Dramas in East-Asia Countries: *Wish upon a Star* of Korea, *Love Talks* of Hong Kong and *Love and Sorrow* of China." *Korean Journal of Journalism and Communication Studies* 45, no. 3 (2001): 230–70.

Yoon, Tae-il. "Shinmyoung: The Key Concept of Korean Communication Theory." *China Media Research* 6, no. 3 (2010): 107.

Yu, Hong-jun. *My Exploration of Korean Cultural Heritage, Japan Vol. 1: Kyushu* [*Naŭi munhwa yusan tapsagi, ilbon pʾyŏn 1: Pichʾŭn hanbandoro putʾŏ*]. Seoul: Chʾangbi, 2013.

———. *My Exploration of Korean Cultural Heritage, Japan Vol. 2: Asuka, Nara* [*Naŭi munhwa yusan tapsagi, ilbon pʾyŏn 2: Asŭkʾa, Nara tŭlpʾane paekchekkochʾi pʾiŏssŭmnida*]. Seoul: Chʾangbi, 2013.

Zhang, Yingjin. *Chinese National Cinema*. New York: Routledge, 2004.

Žižek, Slavoj. *Organs without Bodies: Deleuze and Consequences*. New York: Routledge, 2004.

INDEX

film props: in Buch'ŏn Fantastic Studios exhibition, 176–79; in Hapch'ŏn Theme Park exhibition, 185–88

film tourism: for *April Snow* and *One Fine Spring Day*, 73–83, 201; Buch'ŏn Fantastic Studios and, 167, 169–70, 172–79; Chinese lack of interest in, 97–99; disposable monuments at Hapch'ŏn Theme Park and, 179, 181–88; DMZ in Korean cinema and, 143–45, 165–67, 171–73; emotion as motivation for, 65–72; ephemerality of, 83, 167–68; growth of, 14–16, 62–64; Korean War in, 173–79; movie theme parks and, 169–73, 225n9; scholarship on, 214n8; Sonagi Village and, 118–20; *Taegukgi: Brotherhood of War* and, 167–96; at Taegwallyŏng Samyang Ranch, 167, 169, 172–73, 188–92

Foucault, Michel, panopticon of, 47–48

framing device: in *April Snow*, 60–64; in *Romantic Island*, 199–200; sonagi trope and, 125–27

freeze frames, false endings and, 53–55

friendship: consent and, 8; hostility and, 2–3

Fung, Allan, 21

Fujitani, Takashi, 154

Genealogy of Modernism (Levenson), 15

geopolitics: Chinese-Korea coproductions and, 93–95; DMZ in South Korean cinema and, 145–65; in "making-of" documentaries, 104–8

global affective cinema, emergence in Asia of, 92

globalization: Asian regionalization and, 205n1; cross-cultural collaboration and, 34–37; hallyu film and, 206n7; South Korean cinema and, 146–48

The Goddess of Mercy (film), 20

The Godfather (Francis Coppola's film series), 100

Golden Harvest, 20

Greater East Asia Co-Prosperity Sphere, 205n1

Guattari, Félix, 130–31; on affect, 65

hallyu ("Korean Wave" cinema), 3, 6–8; affective tourism and, 64–72, 194–96; anti-imperialist ideology and, 205n1; Chinese market for, 97–99, 139–40, 216n16; cultural hybridity in, 56–58, 207n24; DMZ images in, 144–65; emergence of, 8–16, 227n2; global presence of, 200, 225n1, 226n2; intimacy and travel in, 83–85; national division and reunification and, 164–65; social consciousness in, 207n23; statistics on profits from, 206n15; transnational collaboration on, 20–23, 195–96; travel diaries and video travelogues by celebrities in, 203–4, 227n3; travel imagery in, 22–23

Hals, Frans, 129

Han Suk-kyu, 146–47, 223n9

Hapch'ŏn Theme Park, 169, 172–73; declining visitorship at, 225n21; disposable monuments at, 179, 181–88, 193

haptic imagery: in *Daisy*, 122–27; in *The Shower* (*Sonagi*) (film), 112–20; sightseeing and, 23–27; in "Sonagi," 127–34

heart (*maŭm*): appreciation of Hur's films and, 72–83; in Korean culture, 65–72

Hedwig and the Angry Inch (John Cameron Mitchell, 2001), 101

Hepburn, Audrey, 203

Herring, Robert, 122

Hideyoshi, Toyotomi, 162

Hight, Craig, 100–103, 102

Hirsch, Marianne, 144–45

history: alternative histories in Korean blockbusters, 154–63; disposable monuments to, 185–88; experience at Samyang Ranch of, 190–92; narrative models of, 222n4; neutralization of, in Korean DMZ cinema, 148–52

Hitchcock, Alfred, 100

home theater systems, "making-of" documentaries and, 100–103

Hong Kong film industry: decline of, 96–99, 139–40; Korean collaboration with, 19–23, 99, 111, 115, 138–40, 153, 202, 217n31; neo-noir aesthetics in, 115–16, 120, 126–27, 202, 220n8; New Wave in, 116–17; post-1997 after the "handover" and, 122, 128

Hong Sang-soo, 15, 207n23

hostility, friendship and, 2–3

Hŏ Yŏng (Hinatsu Eitarō), 38

Hu, King, 89–90, 92, 215n3

Hughes, Theodore, 38